ROUTLEDGE LIBRARY EDITIONS: SECURITY AND SOCIETY

Volume 6

MERCHANTS OF DEATH

MERCHANTS OF DEATH

A Study of the International Armament Industry

H. C. ENGELBRECHT AND
F. C. HANIGHEN

LONDON AND NEW YORK

First published in 1934 by George Routledge & Sons, Ltd.

This edition first published in 2021
by Routledge
4 Park Square, Milton Park, Abingdon, Oxon OX14 4RN

and by Routledge
605 Third Avenue, New York, NY 10017

Routledge is an imprint of the Taylor & Francis Group, an informa business

Copyright © 1934 by Taylor & Francis.

All rights reserved. No part of this book may be reprinted or reproduced or utilised in any form or by any electronic, mechanical, or other means, now known or hereafter invented, including photocopying and recording, or in any information storage or retrieval system, without permission in writing from the publishers.

Trademark notice: Product or corporate names may be trademarks or registered trademarks, and are used only for identification and explanation without intent to infringe.

British Library Cataloguing in Publication Data
A catalogue record for this book is available from the British Library

ISBN: 978-0-367-56733-0 (Set)
ISBN: 978-1-00-312078-0 (Set) (ebk)
ISBN: 978-0-367-61221-4 (Volume 6) (hbk)
ISBN: 978-0-367-63282-3 (Volume 6) (pbk)
ISBN: 978-1-00-310470-4 (Volume 6) (ebk)

Publisher's Note
The publisher has gone to great lengths to ensure the quality of this reprint but points out that some imperfections in the original copies may be apparent.

Disclaimer
The publisher has made every effort to trace copyright holders and would welcome correspondence from those they have been unable to trace.

MERCHANTS OF DEATH

A STUDY OF THE INTERNATIONAL ARMAMENT INDUSTRY

BY
H. C. ENGELBRECHT
AND
F. C. HANIGHEN

ILLUSTRATED

SECOND IMPRESSION

LONDON
GEORGE ROUTLEDGE & SONS, LTD.
BROADWAY HOUSE: 68-74 CARTER LANE, E.C.4
1934

CONTENTS

CHAP.		PAGE
I	Consider the Armament Maker	1
II	Merchants in Swaddling Clothes	12
III	Du Pont—Patriot and Powder-Maker	22
IV	American Musketeers	38
V	Second-Hand Death	56
VI	Krupp—The Cannon King	69
VII	Automatic Death—The Story of Maxim's Machine Gun	85
VIII	Super-salesman of Death	95
IX	Stepmother of Parliament	108
X	Seigneur de Schneider	121
XI	The Eve of the World War—The Arms Merchants	140
XII	The World War—The War in Europe	155
XIII	The World War—Enter Old Glory	173
XIV	Plus Ça Change—	190
XV	The Menace of Disarmament	206
XVI	From Konbo to Hotchkiss	219
XVII	Status Quo	237
XVIII	The Outlook	260
	Notes and References	277
	Bibliography	289
	Index	301

ILLUSTRATIONS

                                                          FACING PAGE

GROUP I 80

    Peace-Time Consumption—Sir Basil Zaharoff—Sir Hiram Maxim—Alfred Krupp—Eugene Schneider—Krupp at Work Again—The Chimneys of Burgundy—White Smoke—Red Guns—New Tanks for Old—Polyglot Armour—Advertising—Octopus—Flying " Whale "—Aerial Draught-Board.

GROUP II 192

    Flash and Thunder—The Violet Cross—Harpies—New Style—Jolly Tars—New Style—More Work for Vickers—More Work for Bethlehem—"—and There Rained a Ghastly Dew—"—Amphibian—Heil Schneider !—The International at Work.

CHAPTER I

CONSIDER THE ARMAMENT MAKER

> To give arms to all men who offer an honest price for them without respect of persons or principles: to aristocrats and republicans, to Nihilist and Czar, to Capitalist and Socialist, to Protestant and Catholic, to burglar and policeman, to black man, white man and yellow man, to all sorts and conditions, all nationalities, all faiths, all follies, all causes, and all crimes.—Creed of UNDERSHAFT, the arms maker, in Shaw's *Major Barbara*.

> I appreciate the fact that the manufacturers of arms and ammunition are not standing very high in the estimation of the public generally.—SAMUEL S. STONE, President of Colt's Patent Fire Arms Manufacturing Co.

IN 1930, as a result of the endeavours of disarmament advocates, a treaty was signed between the United States, Great Britain and Japan. While it fell far short of disarming these powers, it did agree on a joint policy of naval limitation and so prevented for a time a costly naval building competition between these countries. President Hoover submitted the treaty to the Senate for ratification. At this point an organisation called the Navy League entered the picture. It raised strenuous objections to the treaty on the ground that it " jeopardised American security." The League failed to convince the Senate, however, and the treaty was ratified.

Presumably the Navy League was a collection of individuals who distrusted international efforts to disarm and who believed that a large navy would insure the safety of the United States and of its citizens. Some might assail these conservatives for clinging to reactionary ideas, but their point of view was a recognised patriotic policy upheld by many who had no connection with the League. But what was the Navy League and who were its backers?

Representative Claude H. Tavvener made a speech in Congress in 1916 which revealed the results of his investigations into the nature and character of the League. He cited the League's official journal to show that eighteen men and one corporation were listed as "founders." The corporation was the Midvale Steel Company from which the government had bought more than $20,000,000 worth of armour plate, to say nothing of other materials. Among the individual founders were Charles M. Schwab, president of the Bethlehem Steel Corporation, which makes armour plate and other war material; J. P. Morgan, of the United States Steel Corporation, which would profit heavily from large naval orders; Colonel R. M. Thompson, of the International Nickel Company, which dealt in nickel, that metal so necessary in making shells; and B. F. Tracy, former Secretary of the Navy, who became attorney for the Carnegie Steel Company. More than half of the founders of this energetic League were gentlemen whose business would benefit by large naval appropriations. It is evident from this that American arms makers have employed the Navy League to prevent naval disarmament.[1]

In Europe their colleagues are even more active. Hitler has now become the symbol of the return of German militarism. Even before he managed to obtain supreme power there was speculation as to his financial backers. Obviously they included German industrialists fearful of socialism, communism, and the labour unions, nationalists smarting under the "insults" of the Versailles treaty, and a host of other discontented folk. But on the list of these contributors supplying funds to the Hitler movement were the names of two capitalists—Von Arthaber and Von Duschnitz—directors of Skoda, the great armament firm of Germany's neighbour and enemy, Czechoslovakia.

Interlocking directorates are a familiar phenomenon in the United States. The real controller of industries is frequently found in the most unexpected places. In Europe the same system prevails. And so it appears that Messrs. Von Arthaber and Von Duschnitz represent a firm which is controlled by still another firm. The head of this holding company is neither German nor Czech. He is a French citizen, M. Eugene Schneider, president of the Schneider-Creusot Company, which for a century has dominated the French arms industry and which through its subsidiaries now controls most of the important arms factories in Central Europe. Some of Hitler's financial support, then, was derived from a company owned by a leading French industrialist and armament manufacturer.[2]

Arms merchants also own newspapers and mould public opinion. M. Schneider is more than just president of Creusot. He is the moving spirit of another great combine, the *Comité des Forges*. This French steel trust through one of its officers has controlling shares in the Paris newspaper *Le Temps*, the counterpart of *The New York Times*, and the *Journal des Débats*, which corresponds to the *New York Herald Tribune*. These two powerful papers constantly warn their readers of the "danger of disarmament" and of the menace of Germany. Thus M. Schneider is in a position to pull two strings, one linked to Hitler and German militarism, the other tied to the French press and French militarism.[3]

Arms merchants have long carried on a profitable business arming the potential enemies of their own country. In England to-day in Bedford Park there is a cannon captured by the British from the Germans during the World War. It bears a British trademark, for it was sold to Germany by a British firm before the war. English companies also sold mines to the Turks by which British men-of-war were sunk in the Dardanelles during the war. The examples of this international trade in arms before the war are legion, as will be shown.[4]

Nor are they lacking to-day. Recently the trial of the British engineers in Soviet Russia brought up the name of Vickers, the engineering firm which employed the accused. But Vickers has other activities besides building dams for Bolsheviks. It is the largest armament trust in Great Britain. For years relations between the Soviets and Great Britain were such that the Soviets were convinced that Britain would lead the attack of the " capitalist powers " on Russia. Yet in 1930 Vickers sold 60 of its latest and most powerful tanks to the Soviets.[5]

To-day Russia is less of a problem to England than is Germany. The rise of Hitler has reawakened much of the pre-war British suspicion of Germany. Germany was forbidden by the Treaty of Versailles to have a military air force. Yet in 1933, at a time when relations between the two countries were strained, the Germans placed an order with an English aircraft manufacturer for 60 of the most efficient fighting planes on the market, and the order would have been filled had not the British Air Ministry intervened and refused to permit the British manufacturer to supply the planes.[6]

Arms makers engineer "war scares." They excite governments and peoples to fear their neighbours and rivals, so that they may sell more armaments. This is an old practice worked often in Europe before the World War and still in use. Bribery is frequently closely associated with war scares. Both are well illustrated in the Seletzki scandal in Rumania. Bruno Seletzki (or Zelevski) was the Skoda agent in Rumania. In March, 1933, the Rumanian authorities discovered that this Czech firm had evaded taxes to the extent of 65 million lei. In searching Seletzki's files, secret military documents were found which pointed to espionage. The files were sealed and Seletzki's affairs were to undergo a thorough "airing."

A few days later the seals were found broken and many documents were missing. Seletzki was now held for trial and his files were carefully examined. The findings at that time pointed to widespread corruption of important government and army officials. Sums amounting to more than a billion lei had been distributed among the "right" officials, hundreds of thousands had been given to "charity" or spent on "entertainment," because the persons receiving these sums "will be used by us some day." The war scare of 1930 was revealed as a device to secure Rumanian armament orders, for Russia at that time was represented as ready to invade Bessarabia, and Rumania was pictured as helpless against this threat; all the hysteria vanished overnight when Skoda was given large armament orders by the Rumanian government. General Popescu, who was involved, shot himself in his study and other officials were exceedingly nervous about the revelations which might yet come. It was never revealed who Seletzki's friends in the Rumanian government had been.[7]

All these incidents took place in times of peace. Presumably arms merchants become strictly patriotic once their countries start warlike operations. Not at all! During the World War at one time there were two trials going on in France. In one, Bolo Pasha was facing charges of trying to corrupt French newspapers in the interest of the Central Powers. He was convicted and executed. In the other, a group of French industrialists were tried for selling war material to Germany through Switzerland. Although the facts were proved, these industrialists were released because they had also supplied the French armies. This is but one of a number of sensational instances of trading with the enemy during the war.[8]

Dealers in arms are scrupulously careful in keeping their accounts collected. Previous to the World War, Krupp had invented a special fuse for hand grenades. The British company, Vickers, appropriated this invention during the war and many Germans were killed by British grenades equipped with this fuse. When the war was over, Krupp sued Vickers for violation of patent rights, demanding the payment of one shilling per fuse. The total claimed by Krupp was 123,000,000 shillings. The case was settled out of court and Krupp received payment in stock of one of Vickers's subsidiaries in Spain.[9]

Reading such accounts many people are shocked. They picture a group of unscrupulous villains who are using every device to profit from human suffering and death. They conjure up a picture of a well-organised, ruthless conspiracy to wreck world peace and to promote war. Theirs is an ethical reaction easily understood. For the business of placing all our vaunted science and engineering in the service of Mars and marketing armaments by the most unrestricted methods of modern salesmanship is indeed a thoroughly antisocial occupation.

But the arms merchant does not see himself as a villain. According to his lights he is simply a business man who sells his wares in accordance with prevailing business practices. The uses to which his products are put and the results of his traffic are apparently no concern of his, no more than they are, for instance, of a motor salesman. Thus there are many naïve statements of arms makers which show their complete indifference about anything related to their industry save its financial success. One British arms manufacturer, for instance, compared his enterprise to that of a house-furnishing company which went so far as to encourage matrimony to stimulate more purchases of house furnishings. The arms maker felt that he, too, was justified in promoting his own particular brand of business.

Neither of these two points of view—the average man's accusation and the arms maker's defence—is an adequate statement of the issues involved. One may be horrified by the activities of an industry which thrives on the greatest of human curses; still, it is well to acknowledge that the arms industry did not create the war system. On the contrary, the war system created the arms industry. And our civilisation which, however reluctantly, recognises war as the final arbiter in international disputes, is also responsible for the existence of the arms maker.

Who—to be specific—has the power to declare war? All constitutions in the world (except the Spanish) vest the war-making power in the government or in the representatives of the people. They further grant the power to conscript man-power to carry on such conflicts. Why is there no ethical revolt against these constitutions? Governments also harbour and foster forces like nationalism and chauvinism, economic rivalry and exploiting capitalism, territorial imperialism and militarism. Which is the most potent for war, these elements or the arms industry? The arms industry is undeniably a menace to peace, but it is an industry to which our present civilisation clings and for which it is responsible.

It is an evidence of the superficiality of many peace advocates that they should denounce the arms industry and accept the present state of civilisation which fosters it. Governments to-day spend approximately a little under a billion pounds every year to maintain their war machines. This colossal sum is voted every year by representatives of the people. There are, of course, some protests against these enormous military outlays, and a handful of individuals carry their protest so far as to refuse to render military service and to pay taxes. But by and large it is believed that "national security" demands these huge appropriations. The root of the trouble, therefore, goes far deeper than the arms industry. It lies in the prevailing temper of peoples toward nationalism, militarism, and war, in the civilisation which forms this temper and prevents any drastic and radical change. Only when this underlying basis of the war system is altered, will war and its concomitant, the arms industry, pass out of existence.

While critics of the arms makers are thus frequently lacking in a thorough understanding of the problems involved, the apologists of the arms makers, who defend the purely commercial and non-political nature of the traffic in arms, are far from profound. The fact is that the armament maker is the right-hand man of all war and navy departments, and, as such, he is a supremely important political figure. His sales to his home government are political acts, as much as, perhaps even more so, than the transactions of a tax collector. His international traffic is an act of international politics and is so recognised in solemn international treaties. The reason this aspect has never been emphasised is that most nations are extremely anxious to continue the free and uninterrupted commerce in armaments, because they do not and cannot manufacture the arms they deem necessary for their national safety. From this the curious paradox arises that an embargo on arms is everywhere considered an act of international politics, while the international sale of arms, even in war time, is merely business.

This is the complex situation which breeds such a singular intellectual confusion. The world at present apparently wants both the war system and peace; it believes that "national safety" lies in preparedness, and it denounces the arms industry. This is not merely confused thinking, but a striking reflection of the contradictory forces at work in our social and political life. Thus it happens that so-called friends of peace frequently uphold the institution of armies and navies to preserve "national security," support "defensive wars," and advocate military training in colleges. On the other hand, arms makers sometimes make dramatic gestures for peace. Nobel, the Dynamite King, established the world's most famous peace prize; Andrew Carnegie endowed a peace foundation and wrote pamphlets on the danger of armaments; Charles Schwab declared that he would gladly scrap all his armour plants if it would bring peace to the world; and Du Pont recently informed its stockholders that it was gratified that the world was rebelling against war.

Out of this background of conflicting forces the arms maker has risen and grown powerful, until to-day he is one of the most dangerous factors in world affairs —a hindrance to peace, a promoter of war. He has reached this position not through any deliberate plotting or planning of his own, but simply as a result of the historic forces of the nineteenth century. Granting the nineteenth century with its amazing development of science and invention, its industrial and commercial evolution, its concentration of economic wealth, its close international ties, its spread and intensification of nationalism, its international political conflicts, the modern armament maker with all his evils was inevitable. If the arms industry is a cancer on the body of modern civilisation, it is not an extraneous growth; it is the result of the unhealthy condition of the body itself.

This book presents the outline of the development of this powerful industry—not its history, for that may never be fully written. Hidden in government archives are doubtless many documents which would modify or alter some of the statements made here. Others, safely protected in the files of the various arms companies—or perhaps destroyed because they were incriminating—may never reach the public. Powerful and mysterious arms salesmen like Sir Basil Zaharoff may die without ever telling the true tale of their achievements. But there are enough unguarded announcements, legislative investigations, court trials, company histories, and boasts of successful arms dealers in their own official publicity to trace the growth of this industry.

It is a long story, with its curious birth, uncertain adolescence, confident maturity, and promise of greater vitality; on the other hand, there are elements of decay and serious threats to its continued existence. It has had its great figures, its demigods, staunch adherents of its old code, pioneers of the new. It came into existence back in the Middle Ages when the arquebuse was a new and fearful weapon; it crossed the path of the great Napoleon; Thomas Jefferson had close personal relations with one of its intrepid pioneers; it was so intimately bound up with the Crimean War that a certain poem should read:

> International cannon to right of them,
> International cannon to left of them,
> International cannon in front of them
> Volley'd and thunder'd.

The Kaiser was defied by one of its heroes, " King " Krupp; the proud British empire was scared to death in 1909 by a smart little arms promoter from Leeds; and only yesterday one of its champions put over a most " patriotic " deal at Geneva. It is a past replete with extraordinary episodes, projecting an ominous shadow into the future.

CHAPTER II

MERCHANTS IN SWADDLING CLOTHES

> These in their dark Nativity the Deep
> Shall yield us, pregnant with infernal flame,
> Which into hollow Engines long and round
> Thick-rammed, at th' other bore with touch of fire
> Dilated and infuriate shall send forth
> From far with thundering noise among our foes
> Such implements of mischief as shall dash
> To pieces, and o'erwhelm whatever stands
> Adverse. . . .
>   Yet haply of thy Race
> In future days, if Malice should abound,
> Some one intent on mischief, or inspired
> With dev'lish machination might devise
> Like instrument to plague the Sons of men
> For sin, on war and mutual slaughter bent.
>   —MILTON, *Paradise Lost*, Book VI.

> Would that I had not given myself so much trouble for the love of science.—ROGER BACON.

IT all began in the "Middle Ages" with the importation of gunpowder into Europe. Kings had just learned how to employ crossbows against rebellious nobles. With small companies of accurate bowmen they were able to chase the armoured knights off the field of battle and into the shelter of baronial castles. But arrows were feeble missiles to batter in thick walls. So, funny little pipelike objects appeared. They made a terrifying noise and their own artillerymen were afraid of them, for they often back-fired. About the only mark they could hit was the broadside of a medieval château. But against these hitherto impregnable battlements they were effective. They brought a new era—an era of kings imposing obedience on robber barons and merchants plying a profitable trade in primitive cannon.

It was inevitable that the manufacturers of armour and swords should enter this business. Just as, a few years ago, livery-stable proprietors set up as garage keepers and coachmen suddenly became chauffeurs, so did the armourers of the Middle Ages adjust their tools to the making of guns and mortars. All through the Black Forest, down in Bohemia at Prague, up the Rhine at Solingen which is now the centre of cutlery manufacture, forges that had previously turned out doublets, corselets, helmets and jousting lances now produced guns. In Italy, at Brescia, Turin, Florence, Pistoia, and Milan, new arms were born from the fertile minds and agile fingers of expert craftsmen. In Spain, in Toledo and Seville, Moorish artisans shaped their famous swords—for not until the twentieth century was the sword relegated to parades and museums—and tried their skill at new weapons. But the most active centre of gun-making was in Belgium.

The country thereabouts had all the elements of nature necessary for this industry. There was plenty of iron and coal, and the rivers and roads offered excellent transportation facilities. On both sides Germany and France wasted their resources in long and costly wars, while Liége, comparatively tranquil, waxed prosperous. The Liégeois were endowed with high inventive and commercial talents and they were admirably fitted to exploit their strategic position. Black Forest forgemen might make guns for their own rulers, but Liége sold to all the western world.

But as decades went by, the sale of arms to other countries from Liége developed so fast that Charles the Bold of Burgundy issued an edict forbidding the Liégeois to manufacture arms. The burghers defied Charles and he proceeded to enforce the measure by besieging the city. His banners and bombarding cannon were successful; Liége was captured and burned, and those of its inhabitants who did not escape were slaughtered. But the arms industry has a tenacious quality undreamed of in the plans of dukes, and hardly was Charles in his grave than the plucky Liégeois were back again at their forges.

In 1576 they were responsible for a most singular transaction. In that year the Duke of Alva brought his Spanish legions to the Low Countries. He slaughtered Protestants, and Catholics too, if they displayed a tendency to act like patriotic Netherlanders. But his arms were not all made in the furnaces of Toledo or Seville. The arms makers of Liége sold him some of the guns, cannon and ammunition with which he fought their compatriots. This is the first recorded instance of the international—the anti-national—traffic in arms.[1]

Other lords besides Charles the Bold sought to curb these unscrupulous merchants. The Germans, having a vague feudal claim to the Low Countries, reminded the guilds of Liége that they were part of the duchy of Westphalia and for this reason could not legally sell arms and ammunition to the enemies of the Germans. But, like the true prototypes of Vickers and Schneider that they were, they ignored this edict. Later, when all this territory was conquered by France, they were forced to obey similar orders from French republicans and from Napoleon I. But despite this, their industry flourished. By the middle of the eighteenth century, Liége was producing about 100,000 pieces a year and was well known as one of the arms centres of Europe.

* * * * *

From the very first the arms industry had to struggle against more potent adversaries than chance rulers like Charles the Bold or the German dukes. Generals did not die in bed in olden times ; they wielded their swords gallantly in the mêlée of battle and took their chance amid the massed ranks of pikemen and cavalry. The ruling military caste of early modern times scorned these cowardly devices for killing at a distance, and guns, save for besieging purposes, were held in low esteem. Indeed, the European upper classes were very similar to the Japanese Samurai in their resistance to change. When Dutch traders came to Japan in the sixteenth century they found plenty of gunpowder but strong objections to using it in combat. According to the doctrines of the Bushido (Way of the Warrior) it was dishonourable to meet one's enemy except with cold steel face to face. The European Bushido held the arms industry back for centuries.

Only in the chase was the new method of killing considered proper. So fond did the nobles become of their first crude fowling pieces that they forbade any person not of noble birth to hunt with them. The arms makers of Liége and other cities found much profit in this early sporting goods industry—and more than profit, for as they brought in innovations and proved their worth in the field or covert, the nobles perceived the value of new inventions, and, however grudgingly, accepted them in their ordnance departments.

There were other obstacles to rapid evolution. Science was crude and slow in those heavy-footed centuries, and so it took hundreds of years to better the new instruments of war. It is indeed a far cry from the crude Liége "bombardes" to the finished product of Vickers and Schneider; and from the unwieldy arquebuse to the slim Winchester. In the case of artillery the first cannon were of ridiculously small calibre; the little pieces consisted of bands of iron held together by strips of leather. Naturally large charges of gunpowder were dangerous. Likewise small arms were really large arms, for musketeers had to rest their cumbrous arquebuses on forked rods to aim them and an assistant had to stand by with a fuse.

The problem of igniting the powder charge presented the chief difficulty to small arms inventors and merchants. From the time when Columbus discovered America up to the Napoleonic wars, progress in perfecting the lock, the trigger and the firing breech was extremely slow. Decades rolled by before the arquebuse with its portable fuse evolved into the crude match-lock in which the fuse was attached to the breech. Then a century more to develop the wheel-lock, a spring contrivance, not much better, but requiring the use of a trigger. In the seventeenth century some unknown worker hit upon the use of flint struck by steel, and so the flint-lock musket, the weapon of the soldiers of Marlborough, Frederick the Great and Washington, was invented. These flint-locks missed fire often, and when it rained the slugs of powder and ball, loosely packed in paper and rammed down the muzzle, were generally useless. And the barrels, unrifled and short in length, were incapable of accurate aim; only in masses of infantry were they at all effective. Early modern times were indeed the infancy of the arms industry.

* * * * *

In a purely commercial sense, the arms makers were awakened by the French Revolution. The execution of Louis XVI brought all Europe together in league for the extinction of the French peril. England swept the seas of French commerce; Germany was both ally and host to the embittered French *émigrés*; the Emperor of Austria, mourning his lost relative Marie Antoinette, mobilised his legions at various points— on the Rhine, in Italy, and most important of all in Flanders. Thus the arms merchants of Liége were prevented from plying their usual trade. The British blockade kept American arms shipments from arriving in French ports, and it looked as if the revolutionary government of France would have to depend on their own poorly organised arsenals. However, there was one possible channel for importations.

Would the arms makers of Germany and Austria stifle their patriotism and sell to the French enemy, and if so, would the neutral Swiss cantons let the stuff go through ? That was the problem, and the desperate Committee of Public Safety sent Citizen Tel and Citizen Chose to Geneva, to Basle, to Zurich and even to Germany and Austria, to sound out the armourers. Soon reports like the following came in to the Committee from their agents: " The landgrave of Hesse, avid for money, is ready to serve whoever will pay him the best." Cupidity triumphed, and it was the old story of the Liégeois and the Duke of Alva.

As for the neutral cantons, they were handled satisfactorily. The sellers packed their goods in the most innocent and disarming of crates so that they looked like anything but shipments of arms, and the carriers had orders to take them by certain sure and devious routes. One shipment from Germany totalled 40,000 muskets, and soon caravans of copper, that necessary metal in making shells, came all the way from Austria itself. The Swiss government assured the Emperor that they were permitting no such breach of neutrality, but the two streams flowed on—the agents equipped with fat letters of credit into Central Europe, and, in the other direction, the masked wagon-loads of arms. It was a curious parade, but as will be seen in a later and more important war, it was not to be the only one of such a nature to pass through Switzerland.

It was most effective, and while the reorganisation of domestic firearms industry was perhaps a larger factor in the supply of the French armies, yet this foreign aid from German and Austrian sources made success more certain. Valmy, Wattignies and the victories in Flanders sent the armies of the Coalition back to their bases and saved the French revolutionary government. French arsenals were now competent to equip the armies, and the French generals turned from the defensive tactics of Danton and the Committee of Public Safety to carrying the war into the enemy's camp under the Directory and Napoleon. But even the latter did not scorn aid from foreign makers of lethal weapons.[3]

* * * * *

In 1797 Robert Fulton was in Paris. He had not yet drawn the plans for his famous steamboat, but he had invented another watercraft to exploit which he formed a company. It was the first submarine, and when the Fulton Nautilus Company submitted proposals to the French government, there was much excitement in French naval circles. Old line admirals, like chivalrous knights in armour, considered the invention cowardly and unworthy of French martial honour. However, members of the Directory and scientists employed by Napoleon, who soon after seized the power from the Directory, were inclined to favour it.

Limited funds were advanced to Fulton and trials took place. The Nautilus was a crude apparatus, submerging by admitting water to the hold and rising by pumping it out, but the tests were quite successful. At one time a contract was drawn up, which curiously enough had a most patriotic clause inserted at the request of the inventor, providing that the Nautilus should not be used against the United States unless the latter used it first against France. But in the end French naval conservatism and red tape triumphed. Fulton's proposals were rejected and he went to France's adversary, England, to market his product. He found the English admirals just as conservative and contemptuous of his craft, and after discouraging negotiations he abandoned the enterprise and set sail for New York.[3]

* * * * *

Fulton's ship was hardly out of sight of Land's End when another inventor knocked on the door of English conservatism. Up in Scotland a Scots minister named Alexander Forsyth liked fowling but found his flint-lock gun a most unsatisfactory affair. On his shooting expeditions across the moors he was enraged when the powder and ball often failed to explode just after he had taken aim at a fat grouse. He had a turn for tinkering with mechanical contrivances, and he began to experiment with methods of ignition. The result was a form of the percussion cap, inserted in a pan on the breech of the gun. It was crude, but it was at least successful in withstanding the damp mists of the Scottish highlands.

Forsyth saw commercial possibilities in it and went to London to get a patent. There he met Lord Moira, head of the government ordnance works. Moira was enthusiastic about the invention, encouraged Forsyth to perfect it, and gave him a room in the Tower of London as a workshop. Preaching in a neighbouring chapel on Sundays and bent over his bench in the Tower during the week, the clergyman worked out some excellent improvements on the cap. But, alas, Moira resigned, and his successor, Lord Chatham, a believer in the *status quo* in arms, saw nothing but idle foolishness in Forsyth's work. He dismissed him and ordered him to take his "rubbish" out of the Tower.

Poor Forsyth, a victim of military obscurantism, retired with his caps and apparatus. But not before Napoleon offered him £20,000 for the invention. As in the case of Fulton, patriotism meant something to the minister. Rather than give old Bony, "the mad dog of Europe," a chance to win battles by it, he refused and retired to his kirk. Twenty years later the percussion cap was accepted by the British government, and a pension was granted Forsyth. But it came too late; the first instalment arrived the morning of his death.[4]

Thus in the case of this Scottish clergyman the various obstacles which faced arms merchants and inventors at the close of the eighteenth century were all present. They had to demonstrate the effectiveness

MERCHANTS IN SWADDLING CLOTHES 21

of their products in such inglorious ways as hunting before they could attract the notice of ordnance ministers. Then they had to overcome the rigid conservatism of the military, just as resistant to change on the score of tradition and honour in arms as a Japanese Shogun. And lastly, patriotism often restrained them from the full exploitation of their merchandise.

But by this time the industrial revolution was in full swing, capitalism was invoking new standards. Fulton and Forsyth, after all, were inventors rather than arms merchants. Would the large companies which were now growing powerful still adhere to the old code of national honour? Was patriotism strong enough to resist a new code of business?

CHAPTER III

DU PONT—PATRIOT AND POWDER-MAKER

> Take saltpetre, charcoal, and sulphur, and you can make thunder and lightning, *if you know how.*—ROGER BACON, *De Nullitate Magiae.*

ABOUT the time when Robert Fulton was cooling his heels in Napoleonic anterooms, a young man named Eleuthère Irénée Du Pont journeyed to America.[1] He was the son of a famous French radical intellectual who, like so many of his class, had long entertained a romantic love for the new republic across the Atlantic. Reports of its constitution and its founders corresponded with all the ideas of the current French writers who inspired the younger generation in France to revolt against the monarchy.

He was an intellectual, but not without an eye for commercial prospects. He saw more in America than a laboratory of political science. His father, Pierre Du Pont, had invested heavily in a Virginian land company, and his brother Victor was engaged in trade with the West Indies out of New York. Accordingly, in a rich land like America it was not long before he saw a chance to invest his own not inconsiderable patrimony.

One day he went hunting with a French veteran of Washington's army. So abundant was the shooting that he had to lay in an extra supply of powder. What he got and the price he had to pay opened his eyes. He received a very inferior grade of powder at an exceptionally high price. Now thoroughly interested, he visited powder mills, studied prices and came to the conclusion that America was a good country in which to start a powder business.

Indeed, he had some experience in this line. He had an excellent scientific education and had specialised in chemistry at Essonne. One of his father's best friends was Lavoisier, the greatest chemist of the time in France and the supervisor of gunpowder manufacture for the French government before the revolution. And Lavoisier had helped the son of his friend in his studies.

After making estimates of the cost of building a mill and purchasing supplies, Irénée returned to France to get material and financial backing. He was aided by the political situation in Europe. Napoleon was letting no opportunity pass which promised to harm his most formidable enemy, England. If young Du Pont could set going a successful powder mill in the States, England, which sold most of this product not only to America but to all the world, would be affected. Therefore the First Consul gave orders that all possible aid be given to Du Pont. So government draftsmen made plans and government arsenals manufactured machines for the new enterprise. And plentiful capital was forthcoming. The affair started under favourable auspices.

Thus in 1802 there came into being the first great American powder factory under the name of Du Pont de Nemours, Père et Fils et Cie; later Irénée, the moving spirit, changed it to his own name—E. I. Du Pont de Nemours and Company; but it was sufficiently French to attract the Francophile spirit which was prevalent in America at that time. The new company prospered from the beginning. In four years the mills turned out 600,000 pounds of powder. Irénée's calculations had proved correct. He had seen as well as Napoleon that American manufacturing could cramp English trade, and that this applied especially to powder. He had acted patriotically both for the country of his adoption and for his recent *patrie*, the enemy of England.

Also he knew the right people in America from the first. In France he and his father had been prominent in the philosophical and radical circles which prepared the way for the French Revolution. They belonged to the right wing of this group, and they barely saved their necks from the guillotine when the extremists prevailed. In the earlier days of the Revolution old Pierre was at different times both President and Secretary of the Constituent Assembly and voted against the execution of Louis XVI. Naturally after this he was out of favour with the Jacobins. Pierre retired from politics and spent his time editing the works of his master Turgot. This impeccable record as moderate radicals was a strong recommendation to the powerful group of philosophic politicians in America who sympathised with them.

Prominent among these early friends in America was Thomas Jefferson. Irénée counted on the aid of the President, and Jefferson did not fail him. The President wrote to the young powder merchant:

"It is with great pleasure I inform you that it is concluded to be for the public interest to apply to your establishment for whatever can be had from that for the use either of the naval or military department. The present is for your private information; you will know it officially by application from those departments whenever their wants may call for them. Accept my friendly salutations and assurances of esteem and respect.

"(Signed) THOMAS JEFFERSON."

In other words, Du Pont had inside influence. Orders came in as promised, and they were so satisfactorily filled that Jefferson wrote another letter to Du Pont praising the excellence of the product, which he himself had tested on a recent hunting expedition. But the orders did not come in as large quantities as expected. Perhaps it was youthful impatience, but Du Pont was not satisfied. While Jefferson had interceded in his behalf, the Secretaries of the Army and Navy had the ordering of war supplies. Although Secretary Dearborn declared that the Du Pont powder was the best, orders up to 1809 amounted to only $30,000. It seemed that Dearborn was not sufficiently impressed with the need for preparedness in peace times.

But after 1809 there was a change. British men-of-war had begun the irritating practice of "impressing" American seamen, and relations between Britain and America became embittered. War was in the offing, and in 1810 orders for powder doubled and trebled. When the War of 1812 did break out, Du Pont sold virtually all the powder the country required. Records of the company tell how the little factory at Wilmington rushed several hundred barrels of powder to Washington when that city was attacked by the British troops. Government connections, Du Pont—as well as many other war dealers—found, were very profitable.

But, like others of his craft, Du Pont also found that post-war years are the hardest. Orders declined, there were great surplus stocks, and he had spent money expanding his plant. Yet when the government wished to dispose of large quantities of damaged powder, Du Pont generously took it off their hands at a low price. On top of that there was a terrific explosion which practically destroyed the whole establishment. Patriotism, he found, was an expensive sentiment.

Yet he resolved to make his company entirely American—a difficult task in his situation, for capital was scarce in the new country. But he returned to France and found that his renown had spread to such an extent that soliciting funds was not an insuperable task. Many famous and wealthy people, among them Madame de Staël and Talleyrand, contributed to his financing. But however grateful he was, Du Pont felt that this was foreign gold, to be employed only in an emergency. He would work hard and pay it off as soon as possible.

He returned to America with new vigour. He rebuilt his plant and made it more efficient than ever. Now he sold his product to whoever wanted it—to Spain, to the West Indies and especially to the South American republics which were in ferment of revolution against Spain. It will be noticed that he was not averse, however much he sympathised with the partisans of Bolivar, to selling to both sides in these wars. This sort of transaction required credits, and he could obtain only short-term financing in America at that time. In one of his letters he complains about the strenuous rides he had to make once a week to the banking centre some sixty miles away, to take up his notes.

All the more reason then that he should be tempted to fill an order that came to him in 1833. All through 1832 the State of South Carolina had seethed with rebellious talk. Among the hot-blooded planters there were sprouting the seeds of the spirit which later produced Sumter and the Confederacy; for import duties, imposed at the suggestion of Northern manufacturers, had roused a tempest, and for the first time since the founding of the Union there was serious talk of secession.

So serious was it that among the more daring Carolina leaders there were some who laid plans for armed defence. They gave an order to one of Du Pont's agents for a shipment of 125,000 pounds of powder, and they offered, which was most unusual among Du Pont's credit-seeking clients, $24,000 in cash. Here was an excellent opportunity to clear off his foreign debts, but the integrity fostered by his radical education, together with his early love for the Union, triumphed. However much he wished to become wholly American by the erasure of his obligations, he felt that he could not achieve this independence by descending to such commercial methods. He wrote to his agent: " The destination of this powder being obvious, we think it right to decline furnishing any part of the above order. Whenever our friends in the South will want sporting powder for peaceful purposes we will be happy to serve them."

But he felt that his civic duties were not entirely satisfied by this refusal. He was now a public figure in government councils, a director of the Bank of the United States and a member of various organisations devoted to the economic welfare of the country. He hurried to Washington to see if he could assist in patching up a truce between the Northern industrialists and the fiery planters. After protracted negotiations a compromise was reached and the affair subsided. Indeed, the storm was succeeded by such a friendly calm that he could not help writing to his Southern agent in a jocular mood: "Now that the affair has ended so amiably I almost regret that we refused to supply the powder. We would be very glad to have that $24,000 in our cash, rather than that of your army."

A few years later Irénée died, after seeing his dream come true through the payment of his foreign debt and the completion of his plans for a 100 per cent. American firm. His successor, Alfred, was a little more aggressive. Vigilant for his country's defence, he observed that "our political dissensions are such that it would require the enemy at our doors to induce us to make proper preparation for defence." Such talk of "preparedness" is not unusual among arms manufacturers. Also the words "government ownership" came to plague this early war dealer, and, commenting on a Presidential message in 1837 which recommended construction of a government powder plant, he objected on the ground that it would cost the government much money without corresponding savings.

But a real test of his sincerity came in 1846—a test that was far more difficult than the one Irénée faced in 1833. Two imperialisms had clashed on the Rio Grande, and war was declared between Mexico and the United States. At the outset there was the usual slogan, "Stand by the President," raised. But James K. Polk was one of the least ingratiating persons who had ever sat in the Presidential chair. Also he was a Southerner, and it was not unnatural that Northerners should assert that the war was simply a Southern plot to bring more slave states into the Union.

James Russell Lowell began it with his jingles in the *Biglow Papers*—

> They jest want this Californy
> So's to lug the new slave-states in
> To abuse ye and to scorn ye
> And to plunder ye like sin.

Daniel Webster flung his oratory into caustic criticism of the war, and he was abetted by fanatics like Sumner. Soon, drinking of this heady fire water, Northern newspapers were fulminating against Polk and the continuance of the war. This was one of the few wars waged by the United States in which the enemy was popular. Black Tom Corwin said that American soldiers in Mexico should be welcomed by "hospitable graves," and a whole nightmare school of literature sprang up. Some papers called for European intervention. One said editorially: "If there is in the United States a heart worthy of American liberty, its impulse is to join the Mexicans." Another said: "It would be a sad and woeful joy, but a joy nevertheless, to hear that the hordes of Scott and Taylor were every man of them swept into the next world." Santa Anna, the rascally Mexican commander, became a hero in Boston and New York, and there was even a contingent of Americans who fought with the Mexican army.[3]

With this background, Du Pont, a strong Whig and anti-slavery partisan, could hardly feel much enthusiasm for the war, even if it did bring him government orders for powder. A few weeks after the declaration of war a strange order came to him from Havana for 200,000 pounds of powder. It was obviously from a Mexican source, and thus a fine opportunity was offered the powder-maker to aid "poor Mexico" and deal a blow to the slavery plot which he hated so much. But with abolitionist journals attacking the American "persecution" and prominent men everywhere urging non-co-operation and even helping the enemy, Du Pont flatly refused to fill the order.

The tempters returned a second time, more cleverly concealed. A Spaniard and a Frenchman placed an order with the Du Pont company for the same amount. They asserted that it was not destined for Mexico and went to the trouble of supplying references from two American firms. But Du Pont investigated, and came to the conclusion that it was another masked Mexican requisition. "However unjust our proceedings may be, and however shameful our invasion of Mexican territory, we cannot make powder to be used against our own country."

The gods of patriotism rewarded Du Pont after the war was over by withholding from him the usual plague of post-war depression which perennially visits arms manufacturers; for the West was expanding. In Ohio and Indiana farmers were industriously clearing away timber land, and potent charges of Du Pont powder were needed to extract the stumps. This was the first era of railway building, and powder was a necessity for railroad contractors. William Astor and his Oregon Fur Company needed powder for hunting in the Northwest. Mining was also beginning to develop.

Du Pont did not need a war, but the gods smiled and gave him one. In 1854 England, France, Turkey, and others went to war with Russia, and guns in the Crimea required powder. England had exhausted her own supply and she turned to Du Pont, while Russia also sent orders to Wilmington. Du Pont filled them both. After all, he, like other Americans of the time, felt no particular sentiment for either side in that remote struggle. From the homespun little factory on the Brandywine, shipments of the " black death " went forth to the far corners of the globe.

In these days before the Civil War, only a few rough buildings comprised the workshops, laboratory and drying-houses. Several hundred descendants of French Revolutionary soldiers served as employees, like serfs for a medieval baronial family, and the president had his office in a mere shack on the grounds, for the Du Ponts had the ingrained French spirit of conservatism. The elder Du Pont refused to employ a secretary—a far cry from the present, when secretaries to the secretary are the order of the day. Clinging to old traditions, he refused to send his product by railway, and long mule teams made deliveries even to great distances.

Du Pont, like the military traditionalists of England and Prussia of that day, turned down guncotton, which later he was forced to use. Indeed, there was not much reason why he should yield to these new things, for his natural conservatism was aided by his dominating position in the backward economic system of the time. Governments had to come to him with orders, and it was a matter of indifference to him whether he sold war material or not. Competition in the powder business was not keen. Besides, the winning of the West required so much hunting and blasting powder that he did not care whether cannon fired or not.

During the American Civil War Du Pont was again the patriot—at least the Northern patriot. Two days after the fall of Fort Sumter, when Secessionists were offering huge sums to war dealers for supplies, Du Pont wrote to his Richmond agent : " With regard to Col. Dimmock's order we would remark that since the inauguration of war at Charleston, the posture of national affairs is critical and a new state of affairs has risen. Presuming that Virginia will do her whole duty in this great emergency and will be loyal to the Union we shall prepare the powder, but with the understanding that should general expectation be disappointed, and Virginia by any misfortune assume an attitude hostile to the United States, we shall be absolved from any obligation to furnish the order." Naturally, the war brought Du Pont large orders, and he was the mainstay of the Northern government.

The Civil War had created a virtual partnership between Du Pont and the government. When the war was over this relationship was not disturbed. In close co-operation with the government Du Pont now began experiments in new powders. In 1873 he patented a new hexagonal powder, together with a machine to compress it. The government tested it and found it a success. The British heard of it and at once placed an order for 2,000 pounds of the powder. It was filled at once, possibly with the hope of securing further British orders, for Du Pont surmised that the British proposed to compare it with " an analogous powder " for which it paid an English manufacturer nine cents a pound more than the Du Pont price.

In 1889 the government made use of Du Pont in securing certain superior European gunpowders. The brown prismatic and smokeless powders of the Belgians and the Germans were reputed to be better than the American product. Under government urging Alfred Du Pont went abroad to buy the rights to manufacture these powders in America, and Eugene Du Pont went to Europe to learn the methods of manufacture.

Working hand in glove with the government became

a regular practice with Du Pont. In 1899 a smokeless powder plant was erected by the government at Indian Head, and, according to a Congressman, "the Du Pont Company assisted the officers of the United States in every possible way . . . doing everything possible to make the venture a success." A little later, Congress appropriated $167,000 to build a powder plant at Dover, N.J. According to the same Congressman, "the Du Pont Company not only gave the government officials free access to all its plants, but turned over their blueprints to them, so that when the factory was complete it represented every modern feature." [3]

A curious problem arose in 1896. Somehow there had grown up a reluctance to kill and blast with *black* or *brown* powder. Du Pont acceded to the demands of his customers by manufacturing smokeless powders in thirteen different colours. Here is a letter sent out in regard to the matter:

> "We can dye the powder almost any colour desired. We send you a box of thirteen smokeless powders—all of these are on the market and you can judge of the colours. . . . We also send you some small bottles of Du Pont powder dyed various colours. Some are very pretty. If you do not like any of them we can send others, as we have a multitude of shades."

The last decades of the nineteenth century witnessed the formation of powerful combines and trusts in American business. It was only natural that Du Pont should be transformed from a simple powder company into a gigantic combine with international ramifications. This development came as a result of the Civil War. Government orders had been so reckless that the supply of powder on the market proved a drug to the entire industry. The government sold its surplus at auction prices and the bottom fell out of the powder industry. But complaining did not help. Something must be done.

And something was done. Beginning in 1872 the Du Pont Company gradually brought "order" into the industry, and in 1907 it was not only supreme in the field, but had virtually united all powder companies in the country under its guidance, control, or ownership. It is a long story which has been told in detail by William S. Stevens in *The Powder Trust, 1872–1912*.[4]

It began with a series of price-fixing arrangements. The industry was in a state of chaos. A keg of rifle powder which ordinarily sold for $6.25 brought only $2.25. The Gunpowder Trade Association of the United States was formed in 1872 by seven of the largest companies, and immediately a minimum price was fixed for powder. Independents who would not enter the association were forced to the wall by systematic underselling. Others were brought into line by purchase of so much of their stock that they could be controlled.

The situation seemed well in hand when another threat menaced the industry. The Europeans decided to enter the American field by erecting a factory at Jamesburg, N.J. The companies concerned were chiefly the Vereinigte Köln-Rottweiler Pulverfabriken of Cologne and the Nobel Dynamite Trust Company (Ltd.) of London. This menace was met in characteristic fashion. In 1897 an agreement was signed by the two groups, the European and the American, three points of which are of interest here as an example of co-operation between armament manufacturers:

1. Neither group was to erect factories in the other's territory;

2. If any government sought bids from a foreign powder manufacturer, the foreigner was obligated to ascertain the price quoted by the home factory and he dare not underbid that price;

3. For the sale of high explosives the world was divided into four sales territories. The United States and its possessions, Central America, Colombia, and Venezuela were exclusive fields of the American powder-makers; the rest of the world (outside of the Americas) was European stamping ground. Certain areas were to be open for free competition.

With the European menace thus removed, Du Pont now sought full control of the American field. The policy pursued was one of ruthless elimination. From 1903 to 1907, one hundred competitors were bought out and sixty-four of these were immediately discontinued. This narrowed the field very considerably, leaving only such companies as were either affiliates or allies. How ruthless this process of elimination was may be seen from the description of one who was in a position to know, Hiram Maxim. He writes: "The Phoenix Company undertook to buck the Du Ponts in the powder business. They were just about as wise as the little bull who bucked a locomotive— there was no more left of the Phoenix Company than there was of the little bull." [5]

The result of this monopolistic policy may be seen in the fact that by 1905 Du Pont controlled the orders for all government ordnance powder. Having established this monopoly, Du Pont turned again to price-fixing. Hitherto prices had been quoted locally or regionally. They were one thing in the East, another in the West, still another in the South. Now, however, national prices were established from which there was no deviation.

About this time Du Pont encountered another obstacle. The Federal government had passed the Sherman anti-trust laws in 1890, and in 1907 it finally got round to taking a look into the activities of the Du Pont Company. It brought an action against the company in 1907, charging it with a violation of the Sherman Law. But the government was in a quandary. It proposed to restore conditions to what they had been before Du Pont began its monopolistic activities. Du Pont, however, had wiped out most of its competitors by purchase, so that it was impossible to restore the *status quo ante*. The government did manage to set up two great independent companies as a result of its suit.

During the World War, Du Pont supplied 40 per cent. of the powder used by the Allies, and after 1917 its orders from the United States government were enormous.[6] To-day the Du Pont Company owns and operates more than sixty plants in twenty-two states of the Union. Five research laboratories and more than eight hundred and fifty chemists and engineers have taken the place of the individual inventor. Every year it grants twenty research fellowships. It manufactures a multitude of products, including chemicals, paints, varnishes, rubber goods, cellophane, rayon, and countless others, but it is still the largest and most important powder-maker in the United States.[7] Yet it is rather significant that, according to its own figures, only 2 per cent. of its total manufactures are in military products.[8]

Locally the Du Pont Company is very powerful. It "owns" the state of Delaware; and the city of Wilmington, with its various Du Pont enterprises, hospitals, foundations, and welfare institutions, everywhere recalls the powder-maker dynasty. The three daily newspapers of Delaware are all controlled by Du Pont.[9]

This local control, like that of a great feudal lord over his fief, has by and large satisfied the Du Ponts. They have never sought prominence in national politics, though members of the family have—almost by accident—become United States Senators. Their relationship with the government has always been very close, and this has been due just as much to the government as to the Du Ponts. In their early period the demand for hunting and blasting powder was so active, and later their enterprises were so diversified, that they did not need wars to insure prosperity. But whenever the government required its aid, in peace and in war, the company was ready to co-operate—usually with neat profits for itself.

Du Pont could afford to cling to his ideals; he could indulge in the sometimes expensive sentiment of patriotism, so well was he entrenched. But there were other merchants, less secure and less scrupulous.

CHAPTER IV

AMERICAN MUSKETEERS

The Yankees beat all creation. There seems to be no limit to what they are able to do.—LORD WOLSELEY to Hiram Maxim.

AMERICA made excellent gunpowder. It also produced superior small arms. The end of the Civil War gave a tremendous impetus to the sales campaign of American arms manufacturers. The bottom had more than fallen out of their domestic market. With large plant, personnel, and stocks on their hands, the arms manufacturers had to seek foreign outlets. Moreover, the second-hand merchants were pressing them in the smaller countries, and they found it necessary to seek out the ordnance departments of the Great Powers. But the most potent cause for expansion was that the world was ready to buy American small arms.

A trio of American manufacturers had emerged whose products were now world famous—Colt, Winchester, and Remington. As early as 1851, at the London World's Fair, American rifles were a sensation, and they received medals. The British sent commissions to the United States to study factory methods, and they were gladly and proudly shown through various arsenals. This hospitality had its reward in immediate and large orders. Between 1855 and 1870 the following governments bought American machinery for the manufacture of rifles and pistols: England, Russia,

Prussia, Spain, Turkey, Sweden, Denmark, and Egypt, to mention the most important. Others followed in subsequent years—namely, Japan, Argentina, Chile, Peru, and Mexico.

So important did this branch of American industry become that the United States government issued a special *Report on the Manufacture of Fire-arms and Ammunition*, prepared by Charles H. Fitch, giving detailed descriptions with drawings of American machinery for the manufacture of small arms.[1] The *Report* records that there were then thirty-eight establishments in the United States making small arms and five establishments manufacturing ammunition for these.

There was a reason for this. Back in the early years of the century, Eli Whitney, the inventor of the cotton gin, turned his attention to rifles. He told Jefferson that he could make rifles so much alike that any part of one would fit another. Army officers ridiculed the idea, but Whitney went ahead and set up a shop which demonstrated the practical value of interchangeable parts. Whitney's muskets were used in the War of 1812 and scored a great victory for this kind of manufacture. Whitney's principle was adopted by all of modern industry and made possible the era of mass production.[2]

Samuel Colt was one of the first to develop Whitney's ideas.[3] He was enchanted by the idea of the arms merchants' business from his early youth. He had been absorbed by the story of Fulton's attempt to sell a submarine and torpedo to the French and English governments, and he had an aptitude for inventing. He perfected a torpedo which amazed President Tyler, but it did not impress the military traditionalists of the War Department, who took no steps to aid in its development. Indeed, some of Colt's early struggles bear a certain resemblance to Fulton's.

However, it was not a torpedo upon which he based his hopes. It was the first revolver of modern times. There were many four-barrelled pistols made before the nineteenth century, but they had all been handicapped by unsatisfactory firing devices and general clumsiness of construction. But at the time Colt began tinkering with pistols, the percussion cap was in use. Colt took out a patent on his first revolver in 1835. He established a factory in Paterson, N.J., capitalised at $250,000, and submitted his product to the War Department.

Trial was made before a committee of officers, who reported unanimously that they were "entirely unsuited to general purposes of the service." But Colt would not be discouraged by the obtuseness of these conservatives. He made further improvements in the weapon and took it himself to Florida, where the United States was waging a form of Guerilla warfare with the Seminole Indians. There he interested many army officers, who reported favourably on it, but not strongly enough to make the War Department reverse its decision.

Colt's company failed in 1842, a victim of military conservatism, but meanwhile, unknown to the executives, the revolver was making a great success in Texas. Fighting conditions there required some improvement on the slow-firing muskets in use at that time. It was horseback fighting with stealthy Indians and Mexicans who could use the lariat, and a weapon was needed which could be fired rapidly from the saddle. Colonel Walker and other dare-devils who made up the famous Texas Rangers found the new revolver a priceless and indispensable arm in this sort of warfare. Indeed, the history of the conquest of the great plains was largely the history of the Colt revolver. These weapons in the early 'forties sold for as much as $200 apiece, which must have given the bankrupt Colt ample cause for thought when he recollected that he had offered them to the War Department for $25.

The Mexican War brought a reversal of Colt's misfortune. General Zachary Taylor found that his scouts who were Texas Rangers were invaluable, and that one of the reasons was their use of the revolver. Accordingly, he sent imperious demands to the War Department for large orders of Colts. The War Department gave Colt an order for 1,000 revolvers at a price of $24,000, and the inventor immediately started another factory in Connecticut to fill the order. It is said that he had great difficulty in obtaining in the East a sample revolver to serve as a model for his workmen, so much in demand were they in the South-west. From this time on Colt's fortune was made.

He adopted Whitney's system of accurate manufacture, by machinery, of revolvers and carbines; and all his products were neatly and uniformly made. The great virtue of his process was that parts were interchangeable—a virtue that hand-made pistols and rifles lacked. Soon he had a fine business, sending shipments of triggers, sights, barrels, mainsprings, etc., to all parts of the country where revolver users wished to repair their weapons. That this was a revolutionary procedure, virtually unknown in Europe, may be noted in the minutes of the British commission to investigate the conditions of small arms manufacture. Colt, who had established a factory in London, made a great impression on his English interlocutors by his positive opinions on the superiority of his process of manufacture. The following is testimony to the condition of the small arms situation in Europe at that time:

INVESTIGATOR: Do you consider that you make your pistols better by machinery than by hand labour?
COL. COLT: Most certainly.
INVESTIGATOR: And cheaper, also?
COL. COLT: Much cheaper.

Colt became immensely wealthy, and a large part of his business came from abroad. He sold to the Czar of Russia, particularly, and his products were in use during the Crimean War, on both sides. His home in Connecticut, well named *Armsmear*, was filled with jewelled snuff-boxes, diamonds, testimonial plates and other gifts from such monarchs and leaders as the Czar of Russia, the Sultan of Turkey, the King of Siam, Garibaldi, and Louis Kossuth.

* * * * *

The Winchester rifle also benefitted by American efficiency processes. It was much in demand, and Winchester was noted particularly for his far-travelling and aggressive salesmen. The Winchester repeating rifle, a new marvel in the 'sixties, became so famous that the Arab tribes of Africa later demanded Winchesters even from their second-hand dealers. When Winchesters were not available in sufficient numbers, the merchants of used guns at times forged the Winchester label on the gun and thus satisfied their customers.

The Winchester can tell of other triumphs. In the 1860's Mexico became the stage of French imperialist ambitions. Napoleon III placed Maximilian and his devoted queen Carlotta on the Mexican throne, but the Mexicans resented the foreign invasion and refused to recognise their new monarch.

Among the leaders of the rebellion was Don Benito Juarez, former President of Mexico. Juarez had heard of the wonderful repeating rifles of Winchester and immediately placed an order for these new products of Yankee ingenuity. The Winchester Repeating Arms Company was ready enough to fill the order, but it wanted to be sure of its money before making delivery.[4]

"Colonel" Tom Addis, world salesman extraordinary, took a shipment of 1,000 rifles and 500,000 rounds of ammunition to Brownsville, Texas, right on the Mexican border. For two months he waited here before Juarez gave orders that the munitions be brought to Monterey. Addis journeyed the 240 miles by ox-cart train, placed his cases in a storeroom and covered them with the American flag. For more than four months Juarez tried to get these arms, promising to pay later; but Addis insisted on cash. Meanwhile Maximilian heard of the Winchesters at Monterey and made frantic efforts to get them for himself. Addis notified the Juarez forces that unless he received payment at once the arms would be sold to Maximilian. Almost immediately keg after keg of loose silver coin arrived and the arms were delivered to Juarez.

Another great problem remained for the doughty Addis: the delivery of his kegs of silver to his company. He loaded his coin into an old stage-coach and headed north for the American border. Hardly out of Monterey he halted the stage-coach, bound his Mexican driver and threw him into the back seat with a noose around his neck. Then he turned out of the highway, where he suspected an ambush, and dashed back to the United States over an old abandoned road. Nine months after leaving the Winchester factory with the munitions, Addis landed his kegs of silver in safety at Brownsville. These Winchesters were one of the factors in the overthrow of Maximilian in Mexico.

The comment of Darlington, who tells this story, is also interesting:

"This is more than a tale of adventure incurred in the line of duty. It gives some hint of how hardy missionaries of industry were, even so shortly after the Civil War, spreading the gospel of American business into the foreign field."

* * * * *

In 1816 Eliphalet Remington, a young American frontier lad, begged his father to buy him a rifle. All the other boys had them and he wanted one too. Hunting was good in the neighbouring woods and Eliphalet had ambitions. Remington senior refused his son's request, and that refusal was to make history.

Young Eliphalet went and made his own gun, took it to a neighbouring town to have it rifled, and discovered that he had an excellent hunting implement. The neighbours discovered this fact also, and before the lad realised it he had become one of the first arms manufacturers in the United States. In this simple and inauspicious manner one of America's outstanding contributions to the armoury of Mars had its beginning.

In 1828 young Remington's business compelled him to move to larger quarters, and when the Mexican War came, he was able to take over a government order for rifles. The Civil War increased the demands for Remington rifles to such an extent that the company was obliged to work day and night. Overwork resulted in the death of the owner.[5]

The company went right on. When the war orders stopped it was virtually ruined. The armament maker's point of view is rather graphically presented by a paragraph heading in the Remington official history which reads: " Peace and Disaster." But if peace meant disaster to the company, it also taught it an important lesson. A company that manufactured more rifles than it could sell to hunters, or to its own government, must seek foreign business.

The moral was so obvious that its implications were grasped at once. One brother was now sent abroad as sales agent and he stayed on the job constantly. Remington rifles were excellent, and orders began to pour in. In 1867 the United States Navy ordered 12,000 and Spain 85,000. In 1868 Sweden took 30,000 and Egypt 50,000. Business was certainly picking up. In the following years there was no let-up. Among the rifles delivered were the following: 145,000 to France; 21,000 to New York State; 10,000 to Porto Rico; 89,000 to Cuba; 130,000 to Spain; 55,000 to Egypt; 50,000 to Mexico; and 12,000 to Chile.

Now and then misfortune dogged the company's steps. Thus Prussia was ready to place an order for 20,000 rifles. The Prussian king himself came out to the rifle range to try out the rifle. He placed the stock against his shoulder, sighted, pressed the trigger—and nothing happened. He threw the rifle away in disgust and cancelled the order. Examination showed that the cartridge was defective.

Another upset occurred in Turkey. Prospects were

good for fitting out the entire Turkish army with Remingtons—a matter of 400,000 rifles. In Turkey, as in many other countries, army orders were placed only after the proper persons had been "seen." In crude vernacular this is called "graft"; the Turks called it "royalties," and the amount of "royalties" demanded by the officials was enormous. Remington refused the order.

This Turkish story was repeated several times elsewhere. Huge orders would be in the offing and the contracts almost signed, when strong intimations were made that the necessary "royalties" must be paid first. Always Remington refused and foreign orders dropped away rapidly. At the same time foreign countries were beginning to build their own rifle factories, equipped with American machinery, and foreign business declined still further. Faced with the dilemma of curtailing his output or diversifying his manufactures, Remington adopted the latter course. Typewriters, sewing machines, and farm implements were added to the list of Remington manufactures and prosperity returned.

Another significant fact in the history of the company was its consolidation with the Union Metallic Cartridge Company. One factory in Ilion, N.Y., producing rifles and pistols and another in Bridgeport, Connecticut, producing cartridges was an excellent business arrangement. The cartridge factory supplied ammunition to those who bought rifles, while typewriters, sewing machines, and farm implements created a substantial basis for peace-time activity.

But the more the sales curve dropped, the more vigorously the Remington salesmen pushed their fight for orders—even in the most remote places. Business scouts reported that orders might be had in China. There was always some fighting in that country. They had heard strange stories about the Chinese and their peculiar prejudices and customs. Perhaps the Chinese would not like an agent with Western clothes —many Chinese hated the " foreign devils." Well, that was easy. One agent put on Chinese clothes, made his way to Peking and gained the ear of Li Hung Chang, who ordered rifles for the Chinese army. Thereupon a catalogue was issued in the Chinese language and more orders were secured.

In fact, the Chinese were more progressive than the French. When the Remington-Lee repeaters appeared on the market the Chinese were among the first to buy them. Shortly afterwards they met the French in battle, and Chinese progressiveness defeated French conservatism. At the Battle of Lang Son in the 'eighties the French with their Kropatchek guns were three times repulsed by the Chinese armed with Remington-Lees. The American-made guns could be recharged in a few seconds, while those of the French took much longer. The latter were at the mercy of the foe when their magazines were empty.

During the Russo-Turkish War (1879) both belligerents placed their orders with the Remington company. The Turkish order of 210,000,000 rounds of ammunition was the largest order placed in the United States up to that time. The rest of this tale must be told by the official historian : " Then Russia and Turkey decided to fight. Both patronised the Bridgeport factory, and the strange situation developed of one plant daily grinding out thousands of cartridges for the combatants to fire against each other in deadly battle. Both nations had their inspectors at the works.

The officers treated each other with formal courtesy while they inspected millions of the little messengers of death which were to fill the air of South-eastern Europe with noise and destruction."

At the same time business prospects appeared in Cuba. The island was in revolt against the cruelties of the Spanish masters. The revolutionists knew good rifles and ammunition, hence they bought from Remington. But there was danger that the Spaniards would have to be content with inferior products. They tried to buy from Remington, but Remington was busy with Russian orders. Would the Russians stand in the way of the Spaniards and insist on having their orders filled first? Would they permit so unfair a war to be waged in which one side was equipped with Remington rifles and ammunition while the other was not? The Russians found a way out. General Gorloff rejected a large order of cartridges. There was nothing wrong with the cartridges, but a secret understanding existed that Spain would be enabled to buy them. Thus was prevented what threatened to be a wholly unfair conflict. Every reasonable person will agree with the comment of the Remington chronicler: " It was well that Spain secured this shipment, since the (Cuban) Insurrectionists had not neglected to provide themselves with Remington rifles and UMC ammunition."

Remington was not unknown in South America—the continent of wars and revolutions. Sometimes the Latin republics fought one another, at other times they were busy with one of their meaningless insurrections in which the Outs tried to become the Ins. Sometimes foreign war and internal revolt would occur simultaneously. In one case there was the curious situation of two nations, Colombia and Venezuela, at war with each other, while a separate insurrection was proceeding in each country ; all four of the warring bodies fired UMC bullets from Remington rifles.

But Remington's biggest exploits came during the Franco-Prussian War.[6] The French were in dire need of arms and munitions of all kinds. Among others, they appointed Remington as their American agent, and promised him first 5 per cent. and then 2·5 per cent. commission on all purchases. Remington set to work at once. He needed arms that were ready for immediate shipment, and he decided that the U.S. government was the best place to get them. It was only a few years after the Civil War and Congress had passed legislation authorising the sale of all " damaged " arms. This was Remington's opportunity.

Remington did not act in his own name. He appointed as his agent one Thomas Richardson, who carried on the negotiations with the government officials. The U.S. Army had a considerable number of Springfield breechloaders manufactured in 1866. Richardson determined to get these. Oddly enough, the responsible ordnance officials were ready at once to sell the rifles. About 37,000 of them were called in from all parts of the nation. They were taken away from the soldiers and sent to the New York armoury. After some minor repairs they were ready for shipment to France.

But Remington also wanted ammunition with these guns. He haggled with the officials and made his purchase of the rifles depend upon an adequate supply of cartridges. Now the army had only 3,000,000 cartridges at hand, which was not nearly enough. How would he get the rest ? The ordnance officials obligingly gave orders to the government arsenal at Frankford to manufacture additional cartridges. In the end, Remington received from the government 17,000,000 cartridges, most of which were specially manufactured for this order. *The United States government itself was thus manufacturing and selling munitions to one of the belligerents in a war—a bad breach of neutrality.* International law had always recognised the right of private firms in neutral countries to sell munitions of war to any and all belligerents, subject of course to the laws of contraband and to the danger of confiscation if caught. But for a neutral *government* to do this was an unneutral act.

Remington, elated over this first success, continued his work. He went to the navy officials and he made them an offer. The navy had nine Gatling guns in good condition. Suppose now that it were possible to secure nine new Gatling guns in six months without the least charge, would the navy relinquish these nine immediately to Remington? The navy agreed. Remington took the Gatling guns and sent them to France. Colt, famous manufacturer of pistols and machine guns, was given an order for nine of the latest Gatling guns to be delivered in six months. In addition, the government demanded a guarantee deposit of $14,000 until the new guns were delivered. Remington made the deposit and the Gatling guns went from the navy arsenals to France.

Still Remington was not satisfied. The officials had been accommodating, commissions had been good, and he believed he might make more purchases from the government. At that time the navy was manufacturing 10,000 rifles in the Springfield armoury. The guns were not quite complete. Suddenly an agent of Remington appeared at the navy offices and reported that the new guns were " defective." An inspector immediately proceeded to the armoury and reported that Remington was right. But the guns were not really " defective." They were incomplete. As " defective " arms, these new navy rifles were subject to sale according to the provisions of Congress. Remington at once bid for them and they were allotted to him. The rifles were then completed and France received another shipment of 10,000 rifles.

News of these proceedings could not be kept secret. The Germans heard of it, but they did nothing. The war was in their favour, and Bismarck remarked, jokingly, that it was not very difficult to collect these American arms on the Loire. The German-Americans protested, and finally a Senate committee was appointed to examine into the matter. On the committee was Carl Schurz. Since Schurz was a German-American and since he produced all the important witnesses which revealed the real facts in the case, he was practically accused of treason, and it was charged that German spies had furnished him the information. The committee report justified the actions of the ordnance officials and the matter seemed ended.

Then Carl Schurz arose in the Senate, and in one of his most famous speeches he tore the entire Committee Report to pieces. A lame attempt of the committee majority to reply fell flat, and Schurz succeeded in telling all the facts and branding them as unneutral acts against a friendly country. Schurz's speech is still remembered, and was recalled by a member of Congress as recently as 1928.

These energetic feats of salesmanship reached a climax during the siege of Paris. The Germans, now on the threshold of complete victory, had drawn their iron cordon around the French capital, and the French defence was badly disorganised; in particular they needed guns and ammunition, not only to withstand the siege, but also to arm the various troops which were still operating in the provinces. It should be no surprise, then, to learn that Remington had a salesman on the spot. Mr. W. W. Reynolds, their agent, was in the beleaguered city.

Certainly the right place and the right time, for he secured a large order from the desperate government. But how could he get through the German lines to place it? Gambetta, fiery leader of the new government, had secured a balloon in which he planned to escape and to rouse the spirits of the people in the rest of the country. Reynolds secured another balloon, and the two men passed safely over the German lines. Reynolds placed the order with his company.

Colt, Winchester, and Remington illustrate the importance of the Industrial Revolution in the arms industry. The machine-made rifle and pistol with their interchangeable parts were bound to take the place of the best products of skilled artisans turning out hand-made weapons. All nations who could afford the new death machine, with its technical perfection, equipped their armies with these inventions of American ingenuity.

But they were expensive, and not all war departments found their budgets adequate to permit them to be up-to-date. After a time, this difficulty was also solved. Constant improvements made for a high obsolescence rate and the discarded arms of the wealthier powers could find their way to the less favoured nations. The organisation and exploitation of this special traffic was left to a separate branch of the arms merchants.

NOTE

About 1880 the United States government was ready to follow the lead of other powers and to construct armour-plated battleships. There were at this time no armour-plate plants in the country, but the steel men understood the trend of the times, and the Bethlehem Steel Co. sent a representative to Europe to study in particular the armour-plate factories and gun forges in England and France. Shortly after this an opportunity was granted to Bethlehem Steel to acquire the licenses of Whitworth and Schneider " for the exclusive use in this country of their processes for making armour plate and guns." Washington was consulted in the matter, and when its reply was favourable these patents were acquired. That was the beginning of the armour-plate industry in the United States. Bethlehem was soon joined by Carnegie and later by Midvale Steel and Ordnance—the Big Three of the armour-plate ring.[7]

In 1886 the navy advertised for bids on domestic armour plate and gun steel. In 1887 Bethlehem was ready for work and took over the first government orders. Two years later, a new process, the so-called Harveyised steel, was introduced. In 1894 Krupp produced his famous armour plate, and tests before the ordnance engineers of the European admiralties showed a 20 to 30 per cent. superiority over Harveyised steel. Bethlehem and Carnegie secured the exclusive American rights for this new steel, paying heavy license fees and $45 to $50 a ton as royalty. American experts were at once dispatched to Krupp's factories at Essen in order to study the new process.

With all the facilities at hand for manufacturing armour plate, Bethlehem and Carnegie at once sought foreign markets. Bethlehem issued its catalogues in three languages, English, French and Spanish, advertising its guns,

54   MERCHANTS OF DEATH

munitions, and armour plate. Such formidable foreign names as Compagnie des Aciéries de Bethlehem and Compañía de Acero de Bethlehem are merely the Bethlehem Steel Company decked out in its French and Spanish finery.

And orders did come in from abroad. Both Bethlehem and Carnegie were so proud of their Russian orders that they displayed pictures of armour plate made for Russian battleships in Pennsylvania from Krupp patents.[8] Bethlehem also records in its 1916 catalogue of *Mobile Artillery Material*, that " the Bethlehem Steel Company has furnished ordnance material for practically every country of the world. Among the most recent purchasers may be mentioned the United States, Russia, Greece, Italy, England, France, Argentina, Chile, Cuba, and Guatemala."[9]

Against this background, the story of Carnegie's defective armour plates will be readily understood.[10] In September, 1893, James H. Smith, a Pittsburgh attorney, presented proof to the Navy Department that the government was being defrauded by Carnegie, Phipps Co. in the manufacture of armour plate. Following a peculiar government custom, the Secretary of the Navy agreed to pay the informants 25 per cent. of all that the government might recover from Carnegie.

A rigid examination was now held in the Carnegie shops and systematic deception was revealed in the making of armour plate. It would seem that the process of armour plate making is not always attended by success. Frequently a fault or defect shows in the steel which makes it useless for armour plate. Hence government inspectors are always present, weeding out the obviously defective steel and selecting one plate from each group for special ballistic tests.

At the Carnegie shops these test plates were taken and, without the knowledge of the government inspectors, re-annealed and re-tempered at night to make them better and tougher. The reports on the length of time each plate had been heated and annealed were deliberately falsified, and the government received a certain amount of inferior armour plate at regular prices. This whole fraudulent procedure, it was charged, was carried on under the direction of Superintendents (Smiling Charlie) Schwab, Corey, and Cline.

After extensive investigation, the government committee sustained all the charges, and recommended that penalties be assessed at 15 per cent. of the cost of the armour plate delivered, which would have amounted to a fine of $288,000. Chairman Frick of the Carnegie company was heard by the Navy Department and he admitted most of the charges. Meanwhile not a word about the entire " scandal " appeared in the press.

On December 20, 1893, Carnegie visited the White House and had a long conference with President Cleveland. He told newspaper men that he had discussed the tariff with the President. Three weeks later, on January 10, 1894, the President addressed a letter to the Secretary of the Navy in which he reviewed the entire case. He held that the company was guilty of " irregularities " and that the government was entitled to damages, but he believed that the fine imposed was too severe and that 10 per cent. was sufficient. Accordingly the Carnegie, Phipps Co. paid a fine of $140,484.94.

The President's view of the matter was not shared by many naval officers or by the investigating committee. The story finally reached the newspapers, and Congress took up the matter. A blistering Congressional report condemned Carnegie. To this day the feeling persists. Cleveland has his champions who point out that the Congressional committee was motivated by political considerations, and that the workmen themselves, due to a bonus system, acted largely on their own inspiration. Others see in this incident merely another instance of profiteering on the part of the arms manufacturers.

CHAPTER V

SECOND-HAND DEATH

> "War," says Machiavel, "ought to be the only study of a prince," and by a prince he means every sort of state, however constituted. "He ought," says this great political doctor, "to consider peace only as a breathing time, which gives him leisure to contrive, and furnishes ability to execute military plans."—BURKE, *A Vindication of Natural Society*.

THE market for second-hand rifles is apparently better than that for second-hand motor-cars. In fact, the used rifle has a distinct advantage over the used car: it lasts much longer. Hence there is a constant call and a persistent use for old rifles.

Rifles are retained, even if they are out-of-date, so long as they fire accurately. In 1903 George C. Maynard of the National Museum wrote: "Many thousands of the old Army muzzle loading muskets with the 36-inch long barrels are in constant use by hunters throughout the country, and while they bear no comparison with the newest and most improved rifles, they still do effective work. Many a countryman who would never dare (nor afford) to use a smokeless powder magazine rifle clings to his old army musket, carries his powder in a bottle and his shot tied up in a rag, and when he goes hunting his family are seldom disappointed in anticipation of rabbit pie for dinner. In one Maryland county within twenty miles of the Nation's capital there are no less than 1,000 single-barrel muzzle loading guns in service."[1]

SECOND-HAND DEATH

There are a great many uses for old guns besides hunting. Every great war brings back into service rifles and guns formerly discarded, some for actual fighting, others for drill purposes.

Nor is that all. The "backward" countries are always an astonishingly good market for old and obsolete firearms. The Arab tribes in Arabia and Africa, for instance, still frequently use weapons that seem like museum pieces, although the enterprising arms merchants are now beginning to supply them with machine guns, much to the dismay of the mother countries. Instances of this sort of traffic are not at all rare. The north-west frontier of India, for instance, showed much disturbing restlessness before the World War and caused the British great concern. The reason for this was the fact that British, French, and Belgian traders were selling old rifles and good ammunition to these tribes. The British shipped through Muscat, while the French operated through Jibutil. Over 200,000 rifles were thus supplied to the natives. The British finally put a stop to the traffic, but the accumulation of war material went right on, possibly in anticipation of smuggling expeditions. In 1911 about 200,000 rifles and 3,000,000 rounds of ammunition were stored by these international traders, waiting for an opportunity to sell them in this *hinterland*.[2]

An excellent illustration of the importance and use of second-hand firearms is furnished by the American Civil War. The Northern armies were in dire need of rifles and ammunition. Manufacturers worked day and night, but they were unable to keep up with the mounting demand of the Union armies. At the outbreak of the war, especially, the dearth of rifles was so alarming that a search began for old weapons which were still usable or which could be made serviceable in much shorter time than was required for the manufacture of new arms. Somebody thought of European stocks. Surely in Europe there must be thousands of rifles lying around idle which might be remodelled and put into service. A lively trade in discarded European rifles developed, and every rifle, no matter how defective or out-dated, was bought, hurriedly repaired, and sold to the government—frequently at outrageous prices.

Many of these rifles, of course, were perfectly usable and gave good service to the soldiers. However, wartime conditions then as always produced dishonest dealers in used weapons, and there were widespread scandals. Congressional investigations uncovered some very flagrant cases of this traffic and exposed a morass of profiteering. Lincoln was so moved by the conclusions of the investigating committees that he declared that these greedy business men " ought to have their devilish heads shot off."

At the very outset of the war Philip S. Justice, a rifle manufacturer, fell foul of the ordnance inspectors. He obtained a contract to supply 4,000 rifles. He charged the government $20 apiece. The rifles were found to be so dangerous to the soldiers using them that the government declined to pay the price. In fact, Philadelphia got a very bad name with the soldiers as a centre for the production of defective rifles. Colonel Thomas D. Doubleday made a survey of the situation and found deplorable conditions. The rifles had every appearance of having been old condemned muskets or so-called new rifles made from parts of old and condemned pieces. Many of them burst, so that the men became afraid to fire them; in others hammers broke off; sights came off even with the gentlest handling, etc. The barrels were found to be very light, sometimes not one-twentieth of an inch thick, and the stocks were made of green wood which shrank, so that bands and trimmings became loose. The bayonets were often of such frail composition that they bent like lead, and many of them broke off during bayonet drill. Some of the rifle barrels were rough inside from imperfect boring and burst during target practice.[3]

So flagrant and widespread were these abuses that there was much talk about the necessity of government arsenals to insure good arms. One expert estimated that the arms, ordnance and munitions of war bought by the government from private contractors and foreign armouries since the beginning of the war cost, over and above the positive expenses of their manufacture, ten times as much as would establish and put into operation the arsenals and foundries which the government could build itself. Muskets which the contractors sold, on the average, for about $22 apiece could have been made in national workshops for one-half that price.

One of the Congressional investigators, Representative Wallace, summarised his findings: "When we look at the manner in which our army and government have been defrauded by peculators, we must shrink from the idea of trusting to private contractors to furnish the necessary means for our national defence. Dependence upon private contractors for arms and munitions of war is too precarious and uncertain in all respects, as well as too costly, upon which to rest such an important and vital interest of the nation."[4]

Among the profiteering arms merchants of the Civil War was John Pierpont Morgan. Morgan was in his middle twenties when the war broke out, but he did not enlist or shoulder a gun during the entire conflict. He had heard of the great lack of rifles in the army and he decided to do his share in bringing relief.[5]

A few years previously the army had condemned as obsolete and dangerous some rifles then in use, known as Hall's carbines. These rifles were ordered to be sold by auction, and they were disposed of at prices ranging between $1 and $2, probably as curios. In 1861 there still remained 5,000 of these condemned arms. Suddenly on May 28, 1861, one Arthur M. Eastman appeared and offered $3 apiece for them. This high price should have made the officials suspicious, but apparently it did not. Behind Eastman was a certain Simon Stevens who was furnishing the cash for the transaction, but the real backer of the enterprise was J. P. Morgan.

After the condemned guns had been contracted for, Stevens sent a wire to General Frémont at St. Louis informing him that he had 5,000 new carbines in perfect condition. Did Frémont want them? Immediately an order (amounting to a contract) arrived from Frémont urging that the rifles be sent at once. They were bought from the government and Morgan paid $3.50 apiece for them, a total of $17,486. These condemned carbines were now moved out of the government arsenal and sent to Frémont, and the bill presented was $22 apiece—that is, $109,912, a profit of $92,426.

When Frémont's soldiers tried to fire these "new carbines in perfect condition," they shot off their own thumbs. Great indignation was roused by this transaction when it became known, and the government refused to pay Morgan's bill. Morgan promptly sued

SECOND-HAND DEATH

the government, and his claim was referred to a special commission which was examining disputed claims and settling them.

This commission, curiously enough, did not reject the Morgan claim entirely and denounce him for his unscrupulous dealings. It allowed half of the claim, and proposed to pay $13.31 a carbine, that is, $66,550.00 for the lot. This would have netted Morgan a profit of $49,000. But Morgan was not satisfied. He had a "contract" from Frémont and he was determined to collect in full.

Accordingly he sued, in Stevens' name, in the Court of Claims—and the court promptly awarded him the full sum, because "a contract is sacred"—a decision that was the opening wedge for hundreds of other "dead-horse claims" which Congress had tried to block. Of this affair Marcellus Hartley, who himself had brought over from Europe huge quantities of discarded arms and had sold them to the government at exorbitant prices, declared: "I think the worst thing this government has been swindled upon has been those confounded Hall's carbines; they have been elevated in price to $22.50, I think."

These curious dealings, however, must not obscure the importance of the second-hand rifle in the Civil War. Another indication of the extent of this traffic in a later period may be found in a notation from the *Army and Navy Journal* which records that, for the year 1906, $1,000,000 was paid into the United States Treasury from the sale of obsolete and condemned government stores.

The largest of these used-arms dealers is probably Francis Bannerman & Sons of New York City. This extraordinary company got its start in 1865 after the

Civil War, when it bought at auction sales large quantities of military goods. Its New York office at 501 Broadway is the finest military museum in New York City. Up the Hudson near West Point it owns an island on which stands its arsenal, built like an old Scottish castle. It furnishes antiques to museums and collectors and costumes to theatrical groups, but it also solicits business from all war departments. It publishes a fascinating catalogue entitled *War Weapons, Antique and Modern—Cannon, Muskets, Rifles, Saddles, Uniforms, Cartridges*. This book of 364 pages with 5,000 illustrations sells at 50 cents a copy (de luxe edition, $3) and more than 25,000 copies are sold every year. It is from this catalogue, 1933 edition, that the following materials are taken.

The Bannerman salesroom " contains the most wonderful collection of ancient and modern military goods ever shown. Nothing to equal it in the world. Our goods are found on every sea, in every land round the world." [6]

The history and activities of the company are very interesting :

> " During the sixty years in which we have been in this work, our business has grown so that the U.S. Government now depends upon us to purchase at their sales the large quantities of obsolete and discarded goods. . . . We purchased 90 per cent. of the guns, ammunition, and other military goods captured in the Spanish War . . . We have agents in foreign countries who buy and sell military goods for us. . . .
>
> " Our reputation is known to all as the *Largest Dealers in the World in Military Goods*. Round the world travellers tell us that there is no other establishment in the world where is carried such a large and assorted stock as ours. Even in great London buyers would have to visit at least six different places in order to purchase

the variety of goods that could be obtained in greater assortment, and in larger quantities, in our store. . . .

"In our salesroom we have on view upwards of 1,000 different kinds of guns, from the early match-lock up to the present-day automatic. . . . We have on exhibition over a *Thousand Different Kinds of Pistols*, from the earliest hand cannon, fired with a fuse, up to the latest selfloading automatic. . . . In cannon we have a large and complete stock, from the ancient iron barrel, encased in a wood log, up to the present-day semi-automatic rifled cannon for battleships. . . .

"On short notice we can deliver promptly from our stock 100 high power rapid-fire guns at bargain prices."

Who buys from this arms merchant's mail order house?

"Our customers include many of the South and Central American governments. Some of the Mauser rifles [7] purchased after the War of 1898 were delivered to European and Asiatic governments. For years we have supplied the Dominican and Haytian governments. Our largest customers are governments who, having limited financial resources, must necessarily purchase army guns and supplies at low prices, and who are not averse to adopting a good serviceable gun which has been cast aside by a richer and stronger government.

"We purchase large quantities of arms, which we hold in our island storehouse, for times of emergency, when arms are in demand, when even obsolete serviceable guns are purchased by first-class governments, as in 1861, when Lincoln sent agents to Europe to buy up all the guns available to arm the volunteers, and also to keep them from the Southern Confederacy. . . . Cuba depended on us to furnish, on short notice, millions of cartridges and other military supplies." [8]

But not everybody can buy at Bannerman and Sons. "*No firearms are ever sold in our store to any minor. We will not sell weapons to anyone who we think would endanger the public safety.*"

Specific and detailed instances of sales are also recorded. Thus for instance:

> "Recently a shipping firm in Europe gave us an order to convert a large ocean passenger steamship into a warship for a South American government. In one week the peaceful passenger ship sailed, altered by us into a man-of-war, fully armed and equipped: a record for quickness that could scarcely be beaten to-day in any up-to-date government establishment." [9]

Another great achievement is reported from the Russo-Japanese War:

> "During the Russian-Japanese War we personally submitted samples to the Japanese War Department in Tokyo of 10,000 McClellan army saddles, 100,000 army rifles, 100,000 knapsacks, 100,000 haversacks, 100,000 sets of equipments, 150,000 gun slings, 20,000,000 cartridges, together with a shipload of assorted military goods." [10]

The *Army and Navy Journal* [11] hints at another Bannerman business success. It reports that the Panama revolutionists were equipped with "thousands of rifles suspiciously like the Mausers captured from the Spanish forces in Cuba." Since the President of the United States had "encouraged" the revolution from Colombia,[12] it was charged that the United States government had sold these guns to the Panamanians. The Secretary of War explained the matter. Of the 21,154 rifles and carbines captured in Cuba and Porto Rico, 20,220 were sold at auction, 18,200 of these to Bannerman. "What he did with the weapons the Government has no means of knowing, but the insinuation that it knew they were to be used in the revolt in Panama is both ludicrous and contemptible." [13] The inference seems clear, however, that Bannerman did sell them to the Panamanians.

That this arms merchant should advocate preparedness is easy to understand. The way he does it is rather unique. " The peace of the world is preserved to-day by the use of weapons. ' Oh dear,' said a reverend friend whom we met in boys' church club work, ' what a horrid business you are in; dealing in weapons of war.' We answered his remark by asking him if he would tell us how many swords were reported in the company of the twelve Apostles. . . . He saw the point and answered: ' Two, and Peter used one of them with good effect.' Two swords in a company of twelve makes rather a good percentage in favour of weapons. . . ."

To this is then added the pious comment: " St. John's vision of Satan bound and the one thousand years of peace are not yet in sight. We believe the millennium will come, and have for years been preparing by collecting weapons now known as Bannerman's Military Museum, but which we hope some day will be known as ' The Museum of Lost Arts,' when law and order will be preserved without the aid of weapons. As a sincere Christian life is the surest individual safeguard against wrongdoing, so we believe that when the nations and their rulers, who now profess to be Christians, shall live up to their prayer of ' Our Father,' there will be no more violations of His commandment ' Love thy neighbour.' Then war shall be done away and *Peace Shall Reign on Earth*." [14]

This religious argument recurs several times. Quite obviously Bannerman and Sons is devoutly Christian. Take this comment, for instance: " The statement has been made that there never has been, is not, and never will be a ' Christian soldier.' What of Oliver Cromwell, of ' Chinese Gordon,' of Sir Henry Havelock, of Captain Phillip, of our own Navy, and a host of other God-fearing men, who did not and do not think it inconsistent with their duty to their Maker to take service in the ranks of their countries' fighting machines ? " [15] An argument hardly new and scarcely original. The following comment, however, is a bit puzzling: " The Good Book says that in the millennium days swords shall be turned into plowshares and spears into pruning hooks. We are helping to hasten along the glad time by *selling cannon balls to heal the sick.*" [16]

In glancing through this fascinating catalogue one's eye is caught by interesting items which can be appreciated only by personal examination of the volume. A short list is here appended with the purpose of whetting the appetite of the curious:

> Chaplains' uniforms together with " a fine new black felt hat with leather sweat band "; [17]
>
> A bullet machine " casting upwards of 100,000 bullets a day. A good opportunity for War Department to obtain at bargain prices "; [18]
>
> The model of a primitive machine gun from 1718 with the legend:
>> Defending King George, your Country and Lawes Is Defending Your Selves and Protestant Cause; [19]
>
> Famous Colt Gatling guns with 8,000,000 rounds of ball cartridges. " Great bargain prices to any Government War Department desiring to equip their army with a first-class outfit "; [20]
>
> An " illustration showing short barrel gun mounted on camel's back for use in desert countries by Arabian Governments "; [21]
>
> German army field cannons with canister shot, 2,400 rounds, each weighing $8\frac{1}{4}$ pounds. " The entire outfit is stored at our Island Arsenal, all packed, the cannons in boxes, the carriages and limbers taken apart and wrapped in burlap bagging ready for immediate delivery

to National War Departments at bargain prices. Five minutes' time for telephoning to our Island and delivery will begin — no red tape delay with our quick deliveries "; [22]

12-pounder Hotchkiss mountain gun on carriage with limber. " These fine guns and outfits should be particularly desirable to South American Government War Departments or to any government for service in mountainous countries." [23]

Surely, if anyone is going shopping for bargains in rifles, cannon and ammunition, or if some " backward " country wants the best and largest selection of second-hand arms, Bannerman and Sons is the place to visit.

The catalogue also contains some unusual historical lore. One incident relates to the Civil War. Christopher M. Spencer, inventor of the Spencer Carbine, after much difficulty in getting his product before officials, finally got a hearing from Lincoln himself. An amusing incident occurred typical of both arms merchant and the famous rail-splitter. Spencer set up a target against a tree, fired a few shots at it and then handed the gun to the President, who took aim and got results less satisfactory than did the inventor. He handed the gun back to the inventor with the remark: " When I was your age I could do better." But Spencer had won the President, and he left with an order for all the carbines he could furnish.

Spencer at once proceeded to organise a company of which James G. Blaine was a stockholder. Blaine was then Congressman from Maine; later he was to be Senator from the same state, Secretary of State in two cabinets, and even Presidential nominee of his party. Blaine was " our most prominent political leader between Lincoln and Roosevelt " and an idol of the peace movement. As stockholder in the Spencer

Arms Company he was apparently not very comfortable, since he inscribed on the letters which he wrote to the secretary of the company a note reading : " Burn these letters." This little-known side of Blaine's life harmonises rather well with his other shady dealings in western railways and land schemes, for which even his own partisans bitterly denounced him.[24]

The other incident which finds a place here deals with the Spanish-American War. The Catalogue records : " When the Spanish war broke out, international law prevented open sale of arms by European manufacturers to the United States.[25] To get round the law, a large steamship was loaded with boxes of cannon, ammunition, etc., the boxes being covered with coal. When the steamer was within a short distance of the American coast, the crew abandoned the ship. Singularly it was an American warship that discovered the abandoned ship and towed her to the Navy Yard." [26]

The traffic in second-hand arms is profitable. In times of peace the smaller countries can be depended on as regular customers, and in times of war even the great powers make use of old serviceable arms, at least for drill purposes. In times of peace, however, the great powers insist on the best and most modern armaments and they demand these from their arms manufacturers. This governmental drive for constantly more destructive death machines did much to develop the armament industry. This fact becomes ever more evident as the story of the European arms manufacturers unfolds.

CHAPTER VI

KRUPP—THE CANNON KING

> Alfred Krupp's life was Longfellow's noblest poem, *lived* —not written—and of him can it surely be said that he has, in dying, left behind him " footprints on the sands of time " that will comfort many a " shipwrecked brother " yet unborn.—Captain O. E. MICHAELIS, U.S. Army.

THE War of 1870 between Prussia and France was a triumph for Krupp cannon. It was more; it was a successful climax to over a score of years of effort on the part of the greatest German arms maker. Krupp had to struggle against military conservatism. In Prussia he faced a century-old military caste beside which the American War College, which did so much to discourage Colt, was relatively progressive. He had to perfect his products—a lesser task since he had all the ingrained German mechanical talent and dogged persistence. And lastly he had to solve in his own way the problem of markets, which had caused little difficulty to Du Pont. In doing this he forged more than steel cannon barrels—he introduced a new code of arms dealing.

The Krupp family through four generations possessed all the qualities that make for success. It was familiar with the psychology of business and sales and adapted this knowledge to the peculiar problems of the armament trade. It was scientific and inventive and developed many new processes invaluable in its field. It was thoroughly convinced of its patriotism and took occasion repeatedly to impress this fact upon the authorities. It believed in religion and advocated prayer as an element of industrial success. It was "paternal" to all its workers, provided many opportunities for recreation and various welfare measures for its employees, and hated all Socialists venomously. In a political campaign it issued a powerful appeal to all its workers to avoid this vicious doctrine and its agitators, and it suffered great paternal disappointment when the workers elected Socialists in spite of this.

Krupp had many friends, admirers and defenders; it also had many enemies, critics and detractors.[1] The official historian of the company is Wilhelm Berdrow. His two-volume biography of Alfred Krupp and his collection of Krupp letters are important materials; but they are also very disappointing, for Berdrow was apparently not permitted to publish the most significant letters of Krupp, which must be derived from other sources. Furthermore, his work carries only to 1887, precisely the point when the connection between Krupp and the German government grew closest and when the full international activity of the armament makers began to unfold.

The Krupp company had its modest beginnings in the early nineteenth century. When Friedrich Krupp died in 1826, his steel works were left to ten-year-old Alfred. Before Alfred Krupp died in 1887, the name Krupp was famous throughout the world. Alfred began this accomplishment in a most conservative way. He devoted himself at first only to the manufacture of materials useful in peace—machines, railroad trucks, etc. Through incessant experimentation he had perfected a crucible steel which was tough and durable. In 1842 he finally managed to produce a cannon of crucible steel, and he was now on the road to success in the armament industry.

Progress, however, was still exasperatingly slow. The military refused to be budged from their conservative ideas. Not until 1849 did the Prussian Artillery Testing Committee agree to test his gun, and even then no orders were forthcoming. But Krupp was doggedly persistent. He exhibited his gun at all industrial exhibitions, together with his other crucible steel products. He went to London in 1851 and received the award of the highest distinction. He exhibited at Munich in 1854 and in Paris in 1855. He presented his gun to the Prussian king, Frederick William IV, in spite of the open opposition of military circles. Results were completely lacking.

Finally in 1856 there was a rift in the clouds. The khedive of Egypt, Said Pasha, decided that the Krupp cannon were all that their manufacturer claimed for them and he placed the first substantial order for the guns. This was immediately followed by a French order for 300 cannon, but the order was cancelled due to lack of funds. The French were later to regret this lack of funds and indifference to Krupp products.

The tide was now definitely turning. An indication of this was given when the Prussian Regent, Prince William, visited the Krupp factories. The Prince had heard of Krupp and of his persistent efforts to have his gun adopted by Prussia; also of the scorn with which the military spoke of Krupp guns. Alfred Krupp now revealed his first flash of genius as a salesman. He had just installed a 30-ton hammer, named by his men "Fritz." Like all hammers of this kind, "Fritz" was versatile with an able man in charge.

So Krupp decided to show off "Fritz." Would His Majesty like to see "Fritz" do his tricks? Yes? Very well. Would His Majesty be gracious enough to let his humble servant have his watch for a minute? Thanks a thousand times, Gracious Majesty. Now if His August Majesty will watch closely, he will see one of the marvels of modern science. We will put the watch on the "anvil." Now—see that hammer descend with lightning speed and with terrific force? Look out for that watch! But already the hammer has stopped. Just the fraction of an inch above the royal watch it has come to rest. Such is the perfection of modern science.

The Prince smiles. He is pleased as a child with a clever mechanical toy. No doubt the hammer can do other tricks. Of course, of course, Your Highness. Now, for instance, we will take a nut and place it below the hammer. Down comes the hammer, just far enough to crack the nut but not to crush it to formless pulp. Wonderful! Astounding! A man who had machines of this kind and who could operate them thus expertly was interesting, to say the least.[2] Perhaps the military were just stubborn old conservatives to stand by their old bronze cannon. Back to Berlin went Prince William with a feeling of admiration in his heart. The beginnings of a valuable friendship were thus laid. In the same year Krupp received his first order for cannon from Prussia.

The tide had turned now, as statistics show. From 1853 to 1861 the Krupp plants at Essen grew from $2\frac{1}{2}$ to $13\frac{1}{2}$ acres; by 1873 they had expanded to 86 acres and in 1914 they covered 250 acres. As to workers employed, they rose from a mere handful to the population of a good-sized city. In 1849, as he was vainly seeking to market his cannon, he had 107 employees. By 1860 this number had increased to 1,057. By 1914 he had 80,000. These figures cover only the Essen plant, for long the centre of the world's cannon technique and manufacture. Krupp's other enterprises employed many more workers.

The 1860's were highly important for Krupp, because they demonstrated beyond a doubt the practical value of his crucible steel cannon as instruments of war. Krupp's wrestling at this time with the problem of patriotism is also highly interesting. For years Krupp had been insisting on his patriotism. This argument, he evidently believed, would move the indifferent Prussians to do business with him. Before large orders were received from abroad, he placed the needs of Prussia ahead of all other countries. In 1859 he pointed out that certain Prussian guns were not very well known abroad, because their construction was a state secret. " If Prussia is equipped and the design is known, if we cannot prevent it, then other states may follow, and if we then accept similar orders for other states, it should be in the first place for friends and allies of Prussia." [3]

In 1860 he wrote that he considered the supply of guns to the Royal Prussian Army " less as a piece of business than as a matter of honour." At the same time there are already strong indications that his strict interpretation of patriotism was not good business. He had made application for the renewal of one of his patents and the Minister of Commerce delayed granting the request. Krupp wrote to his friend, Prince Regent William, pointing out what his patriotism was costing him. Other governments had given him " dazzling promises and assurances of protection " if he would establish branches in their countries, but hitherto he had resisted these temptations.

> "Without outside promptings, I have of my own initiative, in the interest of our country, left such expedients up to the present untouched, and in spite of the higher prices which could indubitably be realised, I have refused to supply any crucible steel guns to foreign countries when I believed I could serve my native land thereby." [4]

The Prince Regent took the hint and ordered the renewal of the patent, " in recognition of the patriotic sentiments which Commercial Counsellor Alfred Krupp of Essen has frequently displayed, particularly in declining foreign orders offered to him for guns, orders which promised him substantial profit."

Krupp had now learned the technique. When he wanted something from the government, he must speak of his patriotism and include a veiled threat that he might sell his guns to other nations. To Von Roon he wrote about one of his patents:

> " In such circumstances it is possible for me to continue the practice, which I have hitherto adopted voluntarily, of declining orders for guns, which might possibly some day be turned against Prussia, and to renounce the advantages of such orders, as well as the profit from the sale of this new mechanism in the same quarters." [5]

In 1863 Russian orders arrived. Krupp was also asked to co-operate in the work of design, and for years the best of the Czar's ordnance designers were in and out of his workshops and his house. The Danish War (1864) and the beginnings of the navy of the North German Confederation helped to keep the ball rolling. Krupp's name acquired an international reputation, and that reacted on his native land. It was another case of a prophet having no honour in his own country until his foreign disciples singled him out.

Slowly the years went by. Foreign orders were increasing. Less and less is heard from Krupp on the subject of patriotism. In 1866, when the Austrian war was almost a certainty, the Minister of War, Von Roon, appealed to Krupp not to sell guns to Austria : " I venture to ask whether you are willing, out of patriotic regard to present political conditions, to undertake not to supply any guns to Austria without the consent of the King's Government." [6]

The rôles were now reversed. No more was Krupp appealing to the government's patriotism to get orders ; the government was appealing to him to be patriotic and not to sell guns to an almost certain enemy. To be sure, Krupp had already sold cannon to Austria's allies, the South German states, so the damage was done. Von Roon was referring to another order which Austria had recently placed. Krupp's reply to Von Roon shows the change which had occurred. He assured the Minister that the work on the new order had not yet begun, hence there was no reason for anxiety. At the same time, he was obviously put out by this government " interference " and this little lecture on patriotism, and he told it to the Minister in unmistakable terms : " Of political conditions I know very little ; I go on working quietly, and if I cannot do that without disturbing the harmony between love of my country and honourable conduct, I shall give up the work entirely, sell my works, and shall be a rich and independent man."

But this was too good an opportunity to let pass

without again calling attention to the shameful neglect which he had experienced at the hand of Prussia. He continues: "I may remind Your Excellency that I accepted the order from Austria at a time when the relationships between the two countries were of the most friendly nature, and with all the more thankfulness just then, since the Prussian navy disapproved of my crucible steel as gun material, and the leading expert was working for the introduction of bronze instead of crucible steel." From this time onward, with profitable foreign business available in increasing volume, Krupp had no further trouble with "patriotism."

In 1866, in the Austro-Prussian War, came the first test of Krupp's cannon in war. To be sure, Austria's allies also were equipped with Krupp's guns, but even so the test was not conclusive. The Prussians won decisive victories and the war was over in seven weeks, but the Prussian artillery had been handled so badly that it was impossible to say what rôle Krupp's cannon had played in the Austrian *débâcle*.

Krupp was still eagerly looking for markets and the French looked to him like promising customers. Had not Napoleon III decorated him on the occasion of the Paris World's Fair? Did not this French emperor know good guns when he saw them? Krupp decided that France was a good prospect. Twice he sent letters to Napoleon III accompanied by a catalogue. Twice he was rebuffed. Here is one of the letters:

April 29, 1868.

SIR:

Encouraged by the interest which Your Majesty has shown to a simple industrialist and the fortunate results of his efforts and of his great sacrifices, I dare to approach you again with the humble prayer to accept the enclosed catalogue which represents a collection of illustrations of the various objects manufactured in my factories. I dare to hope that the four last pages above all will attract the attention of Your Majesty for a moment. You will find there the crucible cannons which I have manufactured for various great powers of Europe. These will, I hope, persuade Your Majesty to pardon my audacity.

With the deepest respect and the greatest admiration, I am,

Your Majesty's most humble and devoted servant

KRUPP.

The reply to this was:

The Emperor has received with great interest the catalogue which you have sent and he has ordered me to thank you for communicating with him and to tell you that he earnestly hopes for the success and expansion of your industrial enterprises which are destined to render great services to humanity.[7]

Shortly before the outbreak of the Franco-Prussian War, Krupp achieved another triumph. Hitherto British guns had been supreme. Now in 1868 Krupp arranged for competitive trials between his cannon and the Woolwich guns of the British. The test took place at the Tegel Proving Grounds near Berlin. The British, at this time, were living on their reputation and had fallen a bit behind in artillery construction. They still adhered to muzzle loaders, while Krupp had definitely gone over to breechloaders. All of this was conclusively proved by the tests. The British were, of course, slow to admit this, but the Belgian, Nicaise, proclaimed Krupp's guns superior to those of the British, and both Belgium and Russia adopted them.

In 1870 the long-anticipated Franco-Prussian War finally broke over Europe. It was an important occasion for Krupp. Again his cannon were to be tested by war. This time there could be no doubt as to their effectiveness and superiority. Fortunately for Krupp, the French had not bought his much advertised artillery and hence it was a clean-cut issue between Krupp and non-Krupp guns. The Germans marched into France taking their Krupp guns along. It was marvellous. One of those Krupp cannon would be aimed at the enemy positions, and in no time at all opposition had died. The Krupp cannon fired accurately, their aim was precise, they stood up under the hardest usage. Everybody was agreed that Krupp cannon had won the war.

If Napoleon III had any doubts as to the soundness of this analysis, he was soon convinced of his error. Passing through Belgium on his departure from France, the Belgian and French military men discussed the late war with him and pointed out to him regretfully and reproachfully that the Krupp guns had done the work. Now Belgium had been smart and had placed its orders with Krupp, but Napoleon III had resisted Krupp's salesmanship. Thus the war had been lost.

Other achievements for Krupp followed closely. His agents were everywhere, taking advantage of every political friction, bribing their way, using ambassadors and diplomatic officials to secure them an open door. One student of Krupp's history says: " The court of the Cannon King was tacitly counted among the European courts. A motley picture of international representatives of almost every civilised state met in order to have forged cannon with which to do battle each with the other." [8]

There was hardly a war or a frontier skirmish in which Krupp guns did not enter.

> "When Servian and Bulgarian, Turk and Greek do battle with each other, Krupp guns deal death and destruction to both sides. When European powers undertake frontier defence, their fortresses bristle with Krupp guns. Even when travelling in Africa, sailing up the Nile, or in Asia among the almond-eyed subjects of the Flowery Kingdom, Krupp guns bear grim witness to the progress of civilisation." [9]

Sometimes these sales were attended by curious circumstances. The guns sold to China were later turned on the Germans in the Boxer Rebellion. Spain ordered huge Krupp guns, ostensibly for the purpose of turning them secretly against the British at Gibraltar, but they were so large that they could not be concealed and they served to heighten the British suspicions of Germany. Andorra, the tiny republic in the Pyrenees, bought a gun from Krupp which it could not fire without sending the projectile beyond its frontiers.

In the 1890's a new development occurred at Krupp's. The great navies were about to make their appearance. Krupp could not, of course, foresee that one of the super-dreadnoughts would cost more money than most university endowments, but he understood that there would be profitable business. In anticipation of this, he had experimented with armour plate for warships.

Steel-armoured vessels were already in use by the French in the Crimean War, but these "iron-clads" were not sea-going. They were merely wooden vessels plated with iron. This armour plate covering for wooden vessels was increased to the point where some plates were 24 inches thick. Further development along this line was impossible, because the limit of floating power had been reached. Then steel ships were introduced. At first a French process prevailed. Then Harveyised plate came in, that is, steel mixed with nickel for hardening.

At this point Krupp began his experiments. By 1893 he had evolved armour plate of such excellence that there could be no doubt as to its superiority over all other. Tests were made in which all other armour plate was shattered to pieces, but Krupp's plate was not even cracked. Having demonstrated this to all the world, Krupp at once announced the conditions under which his armour plate was for sale. Any country might buy it from him, or it might manufacture it in its own factories—on payment of a heavy licence fee and of a royalty of about £9 per ton. No great power in the world was in a position to refuse Krupp's terms. Krupp's armour plate was the best, and all navies had to have it. One after the other the naval powers built with Krupp armour plate, so that in 1914 the navies of Great Britain, France, Italy, Japan, Germany, and the United States were built of Kruppised steel.

From this beginning Krupp expanded into shipbuilding. In 1896 he acquired the Germania shipyards in plenty of time for the naval bill of 1900. Of course, this shipyard took orders also from other countries and many a foreign warship was built here by Krupp.

The German government then grew interested in submarines. By this time, Krupp and the government were almost partners. The company was reorganised

PEACE-TIME CONSUMPTION
The United States contributes to the £924,657,534 yearly business of armament manufacturers

[*Copyright Acme*

SIR BASIL ZAHAROFF
Super-Salesman of Death

SIR HIRAM MAXIM
Inventor of Automatic Death

ALFRED KRUPP
The King That Was

EUGENE SCHNEIDER
The King That Is

KRUPP AT WORK AGAIN [Copyright German Tourist Information Office
The Krupp plant at Essen

THE CHIMNEYS OF BURGUNDY [Copyright Ewing Galloway
Schneider munition works at Le Creusot, France

WHITE SMOKE
U.S. Troops in Mock Chemical Warfare
[Copyright *Acme*

RED GUNS
Soviet Motorised Machine-Gun Battery
[Copyright "*Wide World*"

NEW TANKS FOR OLD [*Copyright Acme*

This new tank, leaping 35 feet, renders obsolete present defences—and provides more orders at the factory. It travels 120 miles an hour, and can be transported by air

POLYGLOT ARMOUR
Manufactured by an American firm from German parents for the Russian Navy

Left: ADVERTISING
British Vickers advertises the "World Famous Vickers-Carden-Loyd Tank" in German *Militar Wochenblatt*

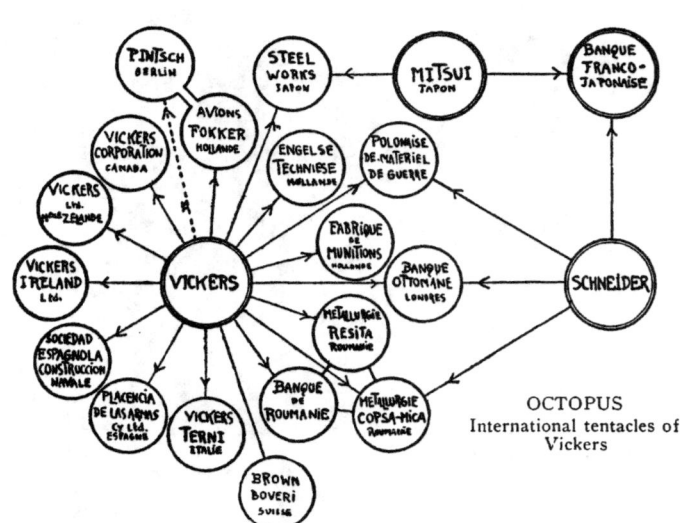

OCTOPUS
International tentacles of Vickers

FLYING "WHALE"

New army "Mystery" bomber with revolving glass turret for gunners. Carries 2,000 pounds of bombs at 200 miles an hour

[Copyright Acme

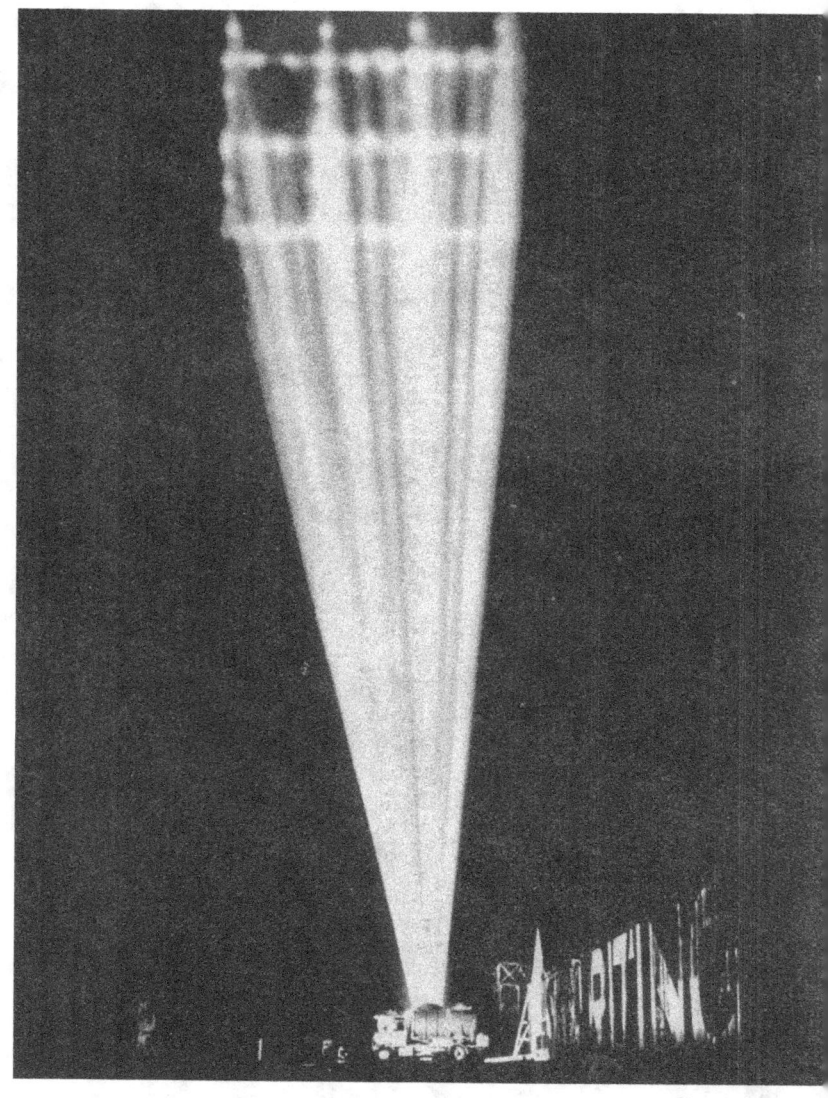

AERIAL DRAUGHT-BOARD

[*Copyright Acme*

New British anti-aircraft searchlight, most powerful so far invented, catches enemy craft in a hollow grid, and instantly determines height, speed, and direction

in 1903 and Emperor William II became one of its largest shareholders. Government loans were always available for Krupp. Special yearly grants were made for experiments. Hence when submarines began to interest the German navy, it is not surprising that Krupp in 1906 was granted some £200,000 for submarine experiments. The hold which the German armament manufacturers, and especially Krupp, had on the German government may be seen from the fact that for ten years before the World War the German authorities bought virtually no armaments abroad but had all their orders filled at home. In this, Germany was unique among all nations of the world.

Through the aid of the government Krupp also acquired a huge new proving ground at Meppen. This was a ten-mile range on which even the largest guns could be tested. It would be the height of naïveté to imagine that Krupp guarded this proving ground with great care against the intrusion of foreigners. Quite the contrary! Krupp was eager to have all nations witness his technical triumphs in artillery, and the test of some new weapon or death-device was generally the occasion for the assembling of brigadier-generals, admirals, and ordnance experts from all countries, so that the new device might receive the fullest publicity and be sold to all who wanted it.[10]

After the disastrous defeat by the Japanese in 1904–05, the Russians set to work in earnest to reconstruct their military machine. Elaborate plans were drawn for a modern army with the best and most up-to-date equipment, an efficient navy, and modern arms factories. There was an almost indecent rush by the armament manufacturers of the entire world to secure orders in this rehabilitation scheme. The arms merchants of England, France, Belgium, Germany, Austria, and the United States all gladly enlisted in this task. When the World War broke out in 1914 this reconstruction work was not yet fully completed, but the allied and rival forces of the arms international achieved marvels in the time available. Krupp took a prominent part in re-arming Russia, not only in the construction of artillery factories but also in the building of the Baltic fleet. And this in spite of the fact that Russia was a fast friend and close ally of France, Germany's "hereditary enemy."

No modern business methods were unknown to Krupp. The power of the press was understood and appreciated. Krupp owned or controlled three great newspapers, the *Rheinisch-Westphaelische Zeitung*, the Berlin *Taegliche Rundschau*, and the *Neueste Nachrichten*. It was a simple matter to rouse public opinion to a patriotic frenzy at any time by war scares or by giving prominent space to the armament activities of other countries, especially during the feverish years before the War.

Krupp also remained in close touch with the War and Navy Departments of Germany. Officers of all ranks, especially the high officials of the army and the admiralty, were on his pay rolls and could be counted on to favour Krupp when contracts were let by the government.

Even then Krupp was taking no chances. One of his men, Brandt, was an army ex-officer with many friends in the War Office. It was this man's business to keep closely in touch with his old comrades and to discover in advance what orders were to be placed, what the specifications would be, and what his competitors had bid. In this business, money frequently changed hands between Brandt and his old comrades-in-arms. When this "scandal" was aired in the Reichstag, it was shown that on the financial side there had been merely petty bribes, tips; the secret information of the War Office had been made available to Krupp's agent largely because he was an old friend and a former soldier.

In 1912 the statistics of Krupp's business showed that he had manufactured 53,000 cannon since his advent as arms maker. Of these, 26,000 had been sold to Germany and 27,000 to 52 foreign countries.

Krupp's story reveals definitely the problem of the modern armament manufacturer. Inventiveness produced a superior product and the development in technology made possible the mass production of arms. Immediately the problem of markets arose and tied to that were the further problems of patriotism and business methods. After some hesitation, Krupp decided that a strict interpretation of patriotism was injurious to business and he embarked on a programme of world-wide sales. Moreover, Germany needed Krupp just as much as Krupp needed German orders and this co-operation developed into a virtual partnership. At the same time the German government was encouraging and establishing an alien kingdom in the heart of Germany, a power which it could not control, yet could not do without. It was a situation which was becoming common—ominously common—in the Western world.

From this story Krupp emerges as typically merchant and typically German. He was efficient, persevering, industrious, capable of perfecting inventions, and logical to the extent of following his business through to its ultimate markets wherever they were. But there is little colour, little audacity in his make-up, and none of the Yankee propensity for extracting novel death-dealing "gadgets" from his pedlar's pack. It was reserved for an American to exploit in an ingenious way the now productive field of European and Asiatic armament customers.

CHAPTER VII

AUTOMATIC DEATH—THE STORY OF MAXIM'S MACHINE GUN

Maxim, it is all right and highly commendable for a man to be very patriotic and do all he can for his country, but you are one of the directors of an English company. We are neutral; we cannot take sides.—A fellow director to Hiram Maxim.

WHEN Hiram Maxim, world famous as the inventor of a wholesale killing machine, turned his inventive genius to perfecting a medical inhaler, he was told " that he had ruined his reputation absolutely " and a scientific friend deplored that he should descend to " prostituting his talents on quack nostrums." This caused the Yankee from Maine to philosophise : " From the foregoing it will be seen that it is a very creditable thing to invent a killing machine, and nothing less than a disgrace to invent an apparatus to prevent human suffering." Curiously enough, Maxim's life seems to show that he accepted his ironic reflection as literally true, and he spent far more time on his " killing machine " than on anything else.

There are three Maxims whose names loom large in the history of guns and ammunition : Hiram, the inventor of the Maxim machine gun ; his brother Hudson, the inventor of smokeless cannon powder ; and Hiram's son, Hiram Percy, the inventor of the Maxim Silencer.[1] The greatest of these was Hiram.

Hiram Maxim's autobiography, *My Life*, is one of the liveliest and most revealing self-histories ever written. For sheer gusto, for pride in achievement, and as a record of human activity, it recalls Benvenuto Cellini. It is, to a great extent, the history of the invention and sale of the Maxim machine gun.

Maxim was an incorrigible inventor and a vivid personality. He loved nothing better than to sit over some intricate problem of mechanics with compass and rule, and invariably he emerged with a solution. His inventions run into scores, ranging all the way from improvements in the curling iron, riveting machines, and locomotive headlights, to fire extinguishers, gas and electric lights, flying machines, machine guns and cartridges. He was proud of his physical prowess and was adept in the use of his fists and in wrestling. He moved at ease among kings and shahs, generals and admirals, ordnance experts and mechanics. He dealt freely with English and Germans, Russians and Chinese. He was pugnaciously agnostic and wrote himself down as a Protestant in religion, " because I protest against the whole thing." If he was proud of one achievement above all others, it was his invention of the machine gun.

Machine guns existed before Maxim. There were the Gardner gun, the Gatling gun, and the Nordenfeldt gun, among others. All of these operated on the principle of a turning crank. The gunner revolved a handle and hundreds of shots could be fired in a minute. But there was one drawback. These guns jammed very readily. A gunner who saw the enemy approaching might easily grow nervous and turn the handle too rapidly. Then the machine jammed through over-rapid feeding and the gunners were helpless. This happened often enough to cause a lively distrust of all machine guns.

Hiram Maxim applied himself to this problem in 1883, and in 1884 he patented a gun based on an entirely different principle. He used the recoil of the gun to move the cartridge belt and was thus able to produce a machine which fired 666 shots a minute. There was no handle to turn, hence no nervous gunner could jam it. As a mechanical invention it was a stroke of genius, as a slaughtering machine it was unspeakably effective. Very shortly Maxim became allied with Vickers, and his gun was part of the Vickers' armoury on sale to the rest of the world.

Maxim was an American who had adopted British citizenship. He had invented his machine gun in England. The English were first to see it. Many distinguished visitors appeared at the demonstrations, especially royalty and the nobility. Lord Wolseley was greatly impressed. The officials of the War Office came to inspect and stayed to praise. The Prince of Wales was given an opportunity to operate the gun and the photographers had a busy day taking pictures. England had been conquered.

Maxim's next thought was of America. He wrote to all the principal gun and pistol manufacturers in the United States, informing them that the automatic system, as invented by him, would soon be applied to all small arms. He further advised them to use this system, which had been patented in the States. But the American manufacturers in this instance belied their reputation for progressive methods. Maxim did not receive a single favourable reply; indeed some of the correspondents ridiculed the invention.[2] Apart from this sad experience there were no further rebuffs.

Other countries were far more open to persuasion. And Maxim set out at once to win them.

Before accompanying Maxim on his Odyssey, another incident must be related. The Germans had a slow burning cocoa powder which was highly valued as an explosive because it was comparatively safe. The British were eager to get it. The German manufacturer had no scruples about selling it, but he wanted £35,000 for the secret. The British were about to pay this sum, but fortunately they presented the problem to Maxim first. It is easy to analyse any gunpowder chemically, and the British chemists knew exactly the composition of the German powder, but they could not reproduce it. Maxim was given some of the powder and by means of the microscope he immediately uncovered its secret and duplicated the German invention.

Among the first to buy the Maxim gun were the Boers of South Africa. Maxim (and Vickers) probably knew that South Africa would soon be the scene of British conflict, but that did not prevent them from selling these guns. The Boers bought powerful guns which the African natives later named the Pom-poms from the sound they made. The name stuck. In the Boer War the British troops encountered stout resistance from the Dutch farmers armed with the Pom-poms. With a sense of pride Maxim records: " One Pom-pom manned by four Boers . . . would put a whole battery of British artillery out of action in a very short time." [3]

The march of triumph led next to France. Trials were held at Versailles and the Maxim gun emerged victoriously. Then came Switzerland. Here a competitive trial was arranged with the Gatling, the

AUTOMATIC DEATH—MAXIM'S GUN 89

Gardner, and the Nordenfeldt guns. The Maxim gun proved superior. On this occasion a great compliment was paid to the gun. A Swiss officer said enthusiastically: "No gun has ever been made in the world that could kill so many men and horses in so short a time." The Swiss gave an order.

Next on the list was Italy. Trials were held at Spezzia with the usual results. Here Maxim made an interesting connection. The Russian consul at Spezzia, Nicholas de Kabath, became an agent for the gun.[4] Maxim was satisfied with the Italian expedition. Everything passed off splendidly and he received a large order from the Italian government.

The next to see the light was Germany. Something must have closed the German mind to the excellencies of the Maxim gun, because it required a visit from the Prince of Wales and his recommendation of the gun to induce the Kaiser to inspect it. The trials were held at Spandau and the Kaiser was at once converted. He exclaimed: "That is the gun. There is no other." Since that time vast numbers of Maxim guns have been acquired by the German Military and Naval Services.[5] It was probably about this time that Krupp also saw the gun, and his admiration for his fellow craftsman was spontaneous and generous. He said to Maxim: "I do not believe any of your associates appreciate the great value of that invention." When, however, the Maxim-Nordenfeldt Company was formed the Maxim gun patents for the world were put in at £900,000, and the shares were subscribed for many times over in a few hours.[6]

Maxim's missionary labours next took him to Russia. This country amused him with its "superstitions." He was almost expelled because the Russians thought he was a foreign Jew. In Moscow he visited the "holiest shrine in the holiest city in the holiest country in the world." But his chief concern was the sale of his machine gun.

When he first exhibited it, the Russian military men ridiculed it. Russian officers, accustomed to any and all exaggerations, scouted the idea that it fired 666 rounds a minute. But he arranged for trials and he proved the efficiency of his gun. His performance was a great surprise to the Russians. Few of them were familiar with the new mechanism, and when they saw the bull's eye shot away they were most enthusiastic. From that time on, the Russian army used a number of Maxim guns, particularly in the war with Japan.[7] "It has been asserted by those who ought to know that more than half of the Japanese killed in the late war were killed with the little Maxim gun." With such achievements to its credit, no wonder Maxim was proud of his brain-child! His fame became so great in Russia that the Czar invited him to visit him, which he did. He was also decorated with Russian orders.

Other countries could not long ignore the Maxim gun. China heard of it, and Li Hung Chang at once set out for England to inspect it. His first words as he stepped off the ship on English soil were: "I should like to see Hiram Maxim." He saw and Maxim conquered. The machine gun was demonstrated to the Chinese at Eynsford. The Chinese were impressed.

Then the Danes decided to see the gun. The king himself watched the trials and after an inquiry as to its cost and maintenance, he declared: "That gun would bankrupt my little kingdom in about two hours."

Inquiries were then received from the Shah of Persia.

AUTOMATIC DEATH—MAXIM'S GUN   91

Persia would not be counted among the " backward " nations which did not appreciate the great advances being made in the Western world. A full description of the gun was sent, but Maxim was apparently too busy or the Persian market seemed too unpromising to repay a visit. Some time later the Shah visited England and saw the gun in action. But England knew her Shahs.

" In the meantime the Prince of Wales had sent word that the Shah would certainly ask me to make him a present of the gun, and this is exactly what happened ; but I was ready for him, and explained that the gun was not my property, but belonged to the company, and that I had no right to give it away."

Spain and Portugal had previously been visited, and a factory was established in Spain. Turkey was next to experience the blessings of civilisation. Maxim took ship for Constantinople, despite the fact that cholera was raging in the city. In Turkey he was constantly taken for a missionary or a teacher. His gun again won the hearts of the military, and the Sultan was so pleased that he gave much thought concerning the best way to honour this great benefactor of his country. Maxim was decorated with a Turkish order, and as a special sign of Sultanic pleasure he was to receive " one of the rare gems " from the Sultan's harem. Somehow this honour was evaded and Maxim again returned to his adopted country, one conquest more to his credit.

But the triumphs of Maxim were not yet ended. In the early '80's the British were having a lot of trouble with the Arabs of the Sudan. These fierce tribes frequently checked the British troops who were armed with the Gardner machine gun, which was operated by turning a crank. When the machine gunner saw the enemy approaching he frequently turned the crank so fast that the cartridges did not have time to fall into position; the gun jammed, and the British often suffered a cruel death from the sharp swords of the Arabs.

After this disastrous jamming had occurred several times, the Gardner gun was displaced by the Maxim. In the greatest battle of this colonial fighting, Omdurman, there was no jamming, and the newspapers reported that when the Maxim gun was turned on the Arabs, " a visible wave of death swept over the advancing host." Maxim was so proud of the work of his machine gun at Omdurman that he quoted Sir Edwin Arnold who wrote : " In most of our wars it has been the dash, the skill, and the bravery of our officers and men that have won the day, but in this case the battle was won by a quiet scientific gentleman living down in Kent." The German Kaiser said practically the same thing, and the American accounts of the death-dealing qualities of the Maxim gun were so lurid that Maxim recorded that " the English reports were not in it." [8]

Maxim's account of Omdurman is not an exaggeration. There is corroboration from many sources as to the terrifying effects of the Maxim gun in British colonial and imperialist wars. The significant thing is Maxim's pride in this fact.

Another interesting episode is recorded from the Spanish-American War. Some wild rumours had been circulated in America that Hiram Maxim would supply to the U.S. navy a gun of such tremendous power that the Spanish navy would be wiped out *instanter*. That was bad news for Spain, and the Spaniards immediately remembered that Vickers-Maxim had a factory in

Spain. Threatening moves were made against this British factory and great excitement prevailed because it seemed as though the factory might be destroyed. A telegram was immediately dispatched to Vickers in England informing the company of the threatening state of affairs. One of the Vickers' directors rushed right out into the night and roused Maxim from a peaceful sleep at two o'clock in the morning.

"Maxim," he said, "what in the world have you been doing? It is all right and highly commendable for a man to be very patriotic and do all he can for his country, but you are one of the directors of an English company; we are neutral; we cannot take sides."

Maxim was able to assure his fellow director that the whole story arose from a wild and baseless rumour, for no such gun existed as was described in the American papers, and that he had had no dealings with America these many years. A telegram was hurriedly dispatched to Spain explaining the situation, and the Vickers' works in Spain were not interferred with.*

But the most momentous adventure in Maxim's career took place in Vienna in the '80's. The Austrian government had expressed a desire to see the famous machine gun, and Maxim appeared on the testing ground in the Austrian capital before a large and distinguished audience. The Archduke William was greatly impressed and declared: "It is the most dreadful instrument that I have ever seen or imagined." Thus encouraged, Maxim arranged a little circus stunt at a second trial. The Emperor himself was present, and Maxim cut out the letters F. J. (Francis Joseph) on a new target at a shorter range. The monarch and many high officials were delighted, and a comic paper had an illustration representing Maxim firing a gun in the shape of a coffin making out the initials F. J. on a target with Death standing at his back holding a crown over his head.

But in spite of this feat and some help he gave the Austrian ordnance department in lightening the recoil of their big guns, he was not entirely successful. There was another and very famous salesman present whose glib tongue influenced the army officials against a whole-hearted acceptance of Maxim's product—Basil Zaharoff. When Maxim triumphantly called on the Minister after the trials, he got a rather cool reception, and received only a small order. In truth, the clever Yankee peddler had met his match in a man who has since become equally famous.

CHAPTER VIII

SUPER-SALESMAN OF DEATH

> I am a citizen of the world : my Fatherland is wherever I work and I work everywhere.—ALFRED NOBEL.

ABOUT the time when Alfred Krupp was being trained at the Gymnasium in *litterae humaniores* as a preparation for a life work which had so singularly little to do with humanity, a Greek family in Turkey was fleeing to Odessa. Greek patriots had proclaimed independence from Turkey and the Turks had responded with massacres. When the Ottoman fury subsided, the Zacharias family left Russia and returned to their home in a little Anatolian village where, in 1849, a child was born to them. He was christened Basileios, or Basil, Zaharoff.

Of course, " Zaharoff " was not an alias, although the chequered career of Basil Zaharoff and the fact that some of his most shady transactions as an arms salesman took place in the land of the Czars lent colour to the rumour. Like many other Greek refugees in Russia, the Zacharias family adopted a Slavic termination to their name—a simple explanation for what most people regard as a mystery. Indeed, of the many mysteries surrounding the life of a man who has well earned the title " The Mystery Man of Europe," it is the only one that is easy to clear up.

There is a sort of Biblical appropriateness in the fact that young Zaharoff opened his business career as a money changer in the bazaars of Constantinople. The Turkish capital was a clearing house of all races, a polyglot centre where French, German, English and the various Levantine and Balkan tongues mingled in infinite confusion. The young Greek money changer had to learn languages to get on, and he had to seek the protection of powerful compatriots to pursue his trade unhindered by the hostile Turks. This gave rise to a romantic love for Greece, which was to give an odd twist to his internationalist career.[1]

A scandal touching him arose at this time. Employed by an uncle in an importing business, he learned the details of commerce so rapidly that the uncle made him a partner. Suddenly he left for England with a sum of money from the firm's cash drawer. Haled into court in London on the complaint of his relative, he insisted that a share in the profits was due him and that he merely took money which was legally his. The exact merits of this case have never been fully examined, but it is well established that Zaharoff was acquitted. Innocent or guilty, he was tainted by the charge of dishonesty, and even now in Athens cafés it is accepted as a fact that the great world-figure took his first step on the ladder of wealth with the assistance of stolen money.

It was to Athens, however, that he returned from the Old Bailey, and there first displayed that lucrative preference for politicians which later marked his career. Etienne Skuludis, subsequently a powerful figure in Greek politics, gave him protection against the outraged murmurs of Greek society and even obtained for him his first job in the trade which became his *métier*. A Swede, who was the Athens agent for the Anglo-Swedish arms firm of Nordenfeldt, left his position and, on the recommendation of Skuludis, assisted Zaharoff in getting the vacant position.

It was just in time. The Russo-Turkish War of 1875-8 had just ended and the various Balkan kingdoms, particularly Bulgaria, had shown astounding military vigour. The Greek army, weak in numbers and equipment, stayed within its borders, and Greece failed to share in the spoils when the peace treaty was signed. It was a lesson to Greek statesmen, who resolved not to miss another such opportunity, and who forthwith engaged in the policy of raising the army from 20,000 to nearly 100,000. Out of a budget of 20,000,000 francs, Greece now allocated 16,000,000 to armaments.

The huge sums voted for arms by Balkan and Turkish ministers were to benefit Zaharoff and other representatives of small firms. Krupp, Schneider and the larger European war magnates were too busy supplying the great powers, and they were not organised to manœuvre in the treacherous waters of Balkan politics. Careful testing, calculating and auditing were the rule in connection with the purchases by larger states ; but in Greece deals were accomplished much more privately and deviously, especially since Ministers of War followed each other in swift and prosperous succession. Through his patron Skuludis, Zaharoff was able to make some very profitable sales for Nordenfeldt & Co.

Tosten Vilhelm Nordenfeldt was being sorely pressed by the competition of larger firms, and he needed such a wily contact man in the Mediterranean. Peace treaties, instead of ending armaments, increased the demands of defence ministries. There was a keen conflict of salesmanship, and Nordenfeldt supplied Zaharoff with a number of new improvements to lure buyers—such as the new base fuse, the eccentric screw breech, a mechanical time fuse, a quick-firing gun for light artillery, and finally the newest wonder of the world—the submarine.

Naval experts of the great powers had long felt the need of some such invention, but they were reluctant to accept Nordenfeldt's product until it had been proved practical. Thus Basil Zaharoff had the honour of selling the first submarine, and that to his native land. He was a staunch Greek patriot and he took great satisfaction in this deal. But another element in his business policy now appeared.

At this time, Turkey, the dreaded enemy of Greece, had a much more capacious treasury than her neighbour, and announced herself in the market for submarines. It was Zaharoff's business to sell, and sell he did, regardless of his patriotism. He placed an order from Turkey for two of the new submarines. As his biographer remarks: "If Greece, Rumania, Russia, or any other benevolent neighbour of Turkey should express a wish to enlarge their stock of ships by a submarine, the firm of Nordenfeldt and its agent Zaharoff were always at their service."

So well did he serve his master that he became salesman-at-large in Europe. In the '80's of the last century, Nordenfeldt was seriously worried by the progress of Hiram Maxim and his machine gun. Zaharoff reassured his employer, however, and offered to block the Anglo-American's triumphal march through the Continent. The curious little Yankee, as we have seen, appeared in Vienna with his extraordinary contrivance. Zaharoff was there too with the inferior Nordenfeldt gun, but also with an unsurpassed knowledge of the official mind and a linguistic ability which his adversary did not possess. In his autobiography, Maxim describes his own performance before the audience of Austrian officers and journalists, but he is evasive about Zaharoff's equally spectacular exploits on that occasion.

After the applause had died down following the sensational spelling of the Emperor's initials, a tall swarthy gentleman circulated among the journalists exclaiming, " A wonderful performance ! Marvellous ! Nobody can compete with this Nordenfeldt gun ! " " Nordenfeldt ? " asked one of the reporters. " Isn't the inventor's name Maxim ? " " No," replied the gentleman, who obviously knew all about the matter, " that is the Nordenfeldt gun, the finest weapon in the world." And in order that the foreign journalists present should be set right, he sounded the praises of Nordenfeldt in English and French.

After Zaharoff had thus established a new record for astute press-agent work, he talked to the officers, who were not likely to be so easily deceived. To them he appealed in the name of technical knowledge. " Nobody can compete with Mr. Maxim so far as this gun is concerned. But that is just the disadvantage of this great invention—that nobody can copy it. It is therefore nothing but a conjuring trick, a circus attraction." He proceeded to explain that everything about the apparatus had to be manufactured with the greatest precision, that a hundredth of a millimetre difference and the gun would not function, etc. All of this talk did so much to remove the impression that Maxim had made that when the inventor appeared in the office of the War Ministry he got a surprisingly cool reception. He was informed of the accusations against the gun by one of his competitors from London, and only by the greatest effort was he able to obtain an order for 150 guns.

The incident affected Maxim greatly. He saw that this cunning Greek could beat him at the game of salesmanship; that he himself was an inventor and needed leisure to work on his inventions, while some enterprising men like Zaharoff took charge of the selling. For his part, Zaharoff was enormously impressed by the spectacle of the amazing little gun; and so it was not long before we find Zaharoff, the Greek, joining forces with Maxim, the Anglo-American, under the head of Nordenfeldt, the Swede, in a most international armament firm. Later the mammoth firm of Vickers, which had been swallowing many of its competitors, amalgamated with the Greek and the Anglo-American, after Nordenfeldt, finding the alliance with the American uncongenial, had left to form his own concern in Paris.

As a result of his connection with Maxim, Zaharoff's commissions increased and his fortune grew. No wonder, for governments throughout the world were in a buying mood. Japan and China were involved in a war; the imperialist expansion in Asia and Africa had brought about numerous minor conflicts; and Greece and Turkey were again engaged in a dispute. Most important of all, the United States and Spain were fighting in Cuba and the Philippines. Zaharoff received some £5,139,270 worth of orders from Spain. In war and in love, Zaharoff found Madrid a very pleasant place, for he had become enamoured of a lady of the court and spent much time there.

Soon he had established himself as *persona grata* in courts and chancelleries, weaving his way into ministers' offices, insinuating himself into directorates of various foreign firms, and always emerging with handsome orders. In that *terra incognita* which is located between the representatives of the people and the firms which exploit them, he wandered with only an occasional glimpse vouchsafed to the curious. The journalists and pacifists saw him only through a glass darkly, and as the fragmentary rumours spread there was hardly a mystifying political scandal that was not connected with his shadowy figure.

Buried in the files of yellowing newspapers slumbers the once famous Turpin affair which rocked French politics in 1889-90. It was another of those " English scares " which were so prevalent at the end of the past century in the excitable French capital. The world has now forgotten how the British secret service was accused of appropriating the secret French process of melinite, a chemical used in explosives, and how there was a master mind supposed to be directing the conspiracy in the person of one Cornelius Herz.

But Zaharoff's biographers have not forgotten. Where was the Greek during these two years ? They can find no record of his movements in 1889 and 1890, and they note that there is a remarkable resemblance between Zaharoff and the descriptions of Herz, who disappeared after the termination of the affair. Was not Zaharoff also a minion of the English, and had he not, like Herz, intimate relations with that other shifty personality, Georges Clemenceau ? Zaharoff's Boswells have been unable to find satisfactory answers to their questions, and perhaps there was no connection at all between the two figures ; but these suspicions have not detracted from the air of mystery which still surrounds the figure of the world's most famous salesman of arms.

It was natural that in a land which nourished such back-stage characters as Rasputin, Zaharoff should appear at his best. He knew the Russian language and he was of the approved Orthodox religion. He could intrigue with the best of the members of the various factions. In order to gain the favour of a Grand Duke who was a powerful factor in granting arms contracts, he cultivated relations with the Duke's mistress. Among the aristocracy there were strange tales about the urbane Greek, and it is possible that Zaharoff inspired these stories to augment his power among the superstitious nobility. When he was once asked about these exploits he smiled significantly, and admitted that he had led a very adventurous life.

Russia, during and following the Russo-Japanese war, was a most active field for Zaharoff. As will be shown more fully in the story of the leader of the French armament manufacturers, the situation was complicated. The foreign arms merchants fought with one another, joined forces and then broke apart again —in fierce competition. The Nickolayeff naval shipyards on the Black Sea were the objective of a joint attack by both French and British firms, with Zaharoff in the midst of the mêlée. Zaharoff and his group scored a victory here.

Encouraged by this, Zaharoff steamed across the Black Sea to the shores of the Bosphorus, the scene of his earliest international *coup*. Turkish shipyards and naval ordnance had long been in the most inefficient condition, and the Turkish government readily gave a concession to Zaharoff to reorganise these yards. The futile cannonade of the British fleet in the Dardanelles a few years later, in 1915, was a well-deserved salute to the extraordinary feat of the most prominent of English arms merchants' commercial representative.

After aiding the Turks, Zaharoff returned to their enemies on the steppes, mindful of his recent promising experiences. A fertile field awaited him. The French had become too greedy and the Russian politicians were quite prepared for a man who offered to let them share in his enterprises, even if it cost their government a few hundred thousand roubles more than it would have done if they had dealt with M. Schneider.

The Russians were desirous of building a large artillery factory. Schneider insisted on building it far off in the Ural mountains where he had some holdings, and he wanted to make it an exclusively French concern. But Zaharoff pointed out the superior possibilities of a site rich in coal and iron on the Volga near the Donetz basin, and offered magnanimously to incorporate his new factory as a Russian firm—provided he got the bulk of the profits. So confident was he of the success of his offer that he bought the land for the factory three weeks before the date set for the letting of the contract.

He was not disappointed, and while M. Schneider withdrew, chagrined, the generous Greek gave more of his largesse to the accommodating Russians. British war "secrets" might be jealously guarded from inquisitive members of parliaments, but among Slavs and Anglo-Saxons there could exist no such niggardly spirit. Thus the *Morning Post's* Russian correspondent reported: "The English company is under contract to build and equip the Tzaritzine (Volga) works and also for 15 years to co-operate in the production of artillery and *has agreed to place its entire knowledge of the technical side of the work, all patents, improvements, etc., at the disposal of the Russian company and be responsible for their correctness."* ²

Much as he was away from Western Europe in these years, Zaharoff did not neglect to cultivate the powerful men of Britain and France. He was involved in the famous Marconi scandal in Britain. He was an associate stockholder and friend of the incautious Lloyd George, whose prestige suffered so much when it was revealed that he had speculated to a considerable extent in the securities of the Marconi Companies, to which his Cabinet had just let a lucrative contract. The Master of Elibank, who—in the same manner as some of the " mystery men " of American oil companies during the trying years 1924–28—found it convenient to stay away from his native land when the Marconi investigating committee was taking evidence, was Zaharoff's friend as well as Lloyd George's, and later on Zaharoff was not disinclined to put these friendships to good account.

Indeed, his alliances with all sorts of powerful figures in England and France offer exciting material for speculation. His agent in France was M. Nicolas Pietri, who appears on the directorates of Vickers in France. Through him he had connections with the Mexican Eagle Oil Company, of which The Master of Elibank was the principal director. The Mexican Eagle had a French affiliate which was to exploit the Algerian basins, and M. Pietri was prominent in that combination. Pietri was also on the board of directors of *Lait Berna*, in congenial proximity to M. Dutasta, relative and agent of Clemenceau. Nor did Zaharoff lack connections with one of M. Clemenceau's political rivals, M. Poincaré.

The Master of Elibank was his connecting link with this French politician. The French are flattered by gifts from rich men, be they Rockefeller or Zaharoff, and so we find Zaharoff endowing a chair of aviation in the Sorbonne. After this it would have been ungracious of the Gauls not to recognise officially the worthy Greek patron. The inevitable red insignia of the French Legion of Honour was pinned to his buttonhole in 1908, and again, with a promotion in that corps, in 1913—" For services rendered to the French Republic." A French senator was inquisitive enough to ask M. Poincaré to explain exactly the nature of these services, but the great man ignored the question. There were other Frenchmen who were equally suspicious of the swarthy benefactor. M. Albert Thomas said with some feeling in the Chamber of Deputies, at the time when Zaharoff was outwitting M. Schneider in Russia : " The Russian newspapers have described Zaharoff as the most active and enterprising agent of Vickers and the most important rival of Creusot."

It was most fitting that this *condottiere* of international business should endow the Prix Balzac, one of the numerous prizes granted each year to meritorious novels. For if ever there was a Balzacian character it was Zaharoff—a financial adventurer beside whom César Birroteau was a pigmy. What novelist save Balzac could conceive such a protagonist, combining such qualities of mystery and grandeur, romance and realism ? Rushing off to Madrid to court his inamorata, the Duchess of Villafranca, and to pick up an arms order, hob-nobbing with Grand Dukes in St. Petersburg, conferring with European cabinet ministers who were disinclined to admit the relationship, as much at home in Whitehall as he was on the Quai d'Orsay! Indeed a fascinating and mysterious figure.

Nor did he, in this mad whirl, neglect to honour the Fourth Estate. In 1910 the publishing firm of Quotidiens Illustrés were getting out a newspaper which was to seem almost as novel compared with the stolid journalism of that time as the publications of Alfred Harmsworth. It was not strange then that the progressive Zaharoff should acquire a large block of shares in the Quotidiens, nor was there anything very incongruous in the fact that the new *Excelsior* should become the outstanding Anglophile organ in the French capital. Whenever Vickers needed any defence in situations arising from the international squabbles of the arms makers, *Excelsior* was the most energetic apologist for the British firm.

By this time reporters who engaged in the pastime of naming the wealthiest men on the globe placed Zaharoff's name beside those of Rockefeller and Morgan. It was no wonder. His sumptuous house in the Avenue Hoche was one of the show places of the French capital. His summer palaces were scattered all through the beautiful French countryside, and he was not unknown in the social life of the metropolis on the Thames.

But his business ramifications became even wider. As if scenting the approach of a situation of much larger scope for holders of armament stock, he assisted in the organisation of a curious polyglot firm. The Société Française des Torpilles Whitehead was incorporated in France in 1913, to make torpedoes, mines, etc. The name was French, but the potent 51 per cent. was English, in the hands of the ubiquitous Vickers Ltd., with Zaharoff receiving enough shares to sit on the board of directors.

James Beetham Whitehead, English Ambassador to France, gave his name to the firm and held some shares. Vice Admiral Aubert represented the French navy. But it is most astonishing to find that this firm, founded to combat the menace of Von Tirpitz's submarines, numbered Frau Margareta von Bismarck of Friedrichsruhe, daughter of the late Iron Chancellor, as an important shareholder. Another director, Count Edgar Hoyos of Fiume, was an Austrian.

Besides this Fiume connection, Zaharoff held shares in other Austrian companies—the Teschen Steel Company, the Berghütten Arms factory and the famous Skoda works. In Germany he had stock in Krupp. Thus this Greek arms salesman had attained, just before the war, a dominating position as an international armament capitalist, the logical consummation of the policy he had started in selling submarines to both Turkey and his fatherland. He had advanced himself to the rôle of a sort of impresario for one of the largest polyglot organisations in the world, Vickers Ltd. It was as the director of the international performances of Vickers that he was best able to display his peculiar talents; and justly so, for Vickers manifested, in more diverse ways than any other, the multiple activities of the armament trust.

CHAPTER IX

STEPMOTHER OF PARLIAMENT

> "The Government of your country! I am the Government of your country, I and Lazarus. Do you suppose that you and half a dozen amateurs like you, sitting in a row in that foolish gabble shop, govern Undershaft and Lazarus? No, my friend, you will do what pays us. You will make war when it suits us and keep peace when it doesn't. . . . When I want anything to keep my dividends up, you will discover that my want is a national need. When other people want something to keep my dividends down, you will call out the police and military. And in return you shall have the support of my newspapers, and the delight of imagining that you are a great statesman."
> —UNDERSHAFT, the armament maker, in Bernard Shaw's *Major Barbara*.

OF course this diagnosis of the armament situation has that readable but exaggerated quality which has become known as characteristically Shavian. Only a very rash political theorist would undertake to prove that the armament manufacturers alone brought about the World War, nor is it possible to say that these magnates dictate orders to the government. Nor on the other hand do governments control armament manufacturers. The matter is not so simple as that. But that there is an intimate relationship between governments and the arms merchants is indisputable; and, to judge by the situation in England, the arms barons have woven a fine web of influence which enables them to condition if not to direct public policy. England may be the Mother of Parliaments, but it is fairly evident that Vickers Ltd. is the stepmother of Parliament.

Vickers did not spring, armed for the munition conflict, from the brain of Basil Zaharoff. Its history dates back to the early nineteenth century. Then it started as merely a general engineering and iron works, and, like most English firms of that day, it was the mentor of engineers of all nations. In the '40's Herr Krupp went to England to drink of the technical wisdom of the British. But a few decades later the term " Made in Germany " became synonymous with authority, and the rôles were reversed. Young Thomas E. Vickers served his apprenticeship in Essen and returned home so well armed with the precious German methods that he was able to take the lead over his British competitors.

At first, like Krupp, Vickers manufactured such prosaic articles as wheels for railway cars, cast steel blocks and cylinders ; but during the '60's he turned to arms making. He began modestly with the manufacture of gun barrels and armoured steel plates. Later, as the dividends grew, he branched out to include the production of entire guns. Designs of a lieutenant of artillery named Dawson brought Vickers large orders for guns, and it was not long before the firm was known as the most important manufacturers of cannon for the British navy.[1]

With the advent of Zaharoff in the '90's, the firm took on a more venturesome character. It acquired the Wolseley Tool and Motor Co., and then the Electric and Ordnance Accessories Co. Beardmore, the Glasgow firm of shipbuilders, combined with them ; and the consolidated firm obtained a subsidiary in Italy, the Terni company, which later took the name of Vickers-

Terni. Zaharoff shook Vickers out of the humdrum business of dealing solely with the British government. Cecil Rhodes was directing British policy in South Africa in such a way that it pointed ominously toward war, and Vickers took the first halting steps on the soil of arms internationalism with the sale of rapid-fire guns to the hostile Boer Republic. Maxim's machine gun, the " Pom-pom," now a Vickers property, was placed at the disposal of Oom Paul.

Other corners of the globe offered fertile soil for Vickers and their agent Zaharoff. Supplying the rickety army and navy of Spain was not unprofitable. The Sino-Japanese War brought heavy orders, and the war between Russia and Japan found Vickers sending munitions to both sides. The English firm was well launched on international roads to prosperity, and by this time it was offering to customers every lethal article from machine guns to warships.

In South America and the Far East, its principal competitor was Armstrong-Whitworth. This firm had a salesman, Mr. R. L. Thompson, who was less famous than Vickers' Zaharoff but no less energetic. He was particularly active in the '90's of the last century, but the world was unaware of it until he sued his employers in 1904 for salary and commissions which he claimed were due him. His counsel claimed that he held, with Armstrong-Whitworth, " a position somewhat analogous to that of a private diplomatic agent, or a sort of private ambassador." After a few days in court the action was settled, but not before some interesting revelations were made.

It seems that Mr. Thompson acted as special correspondent for the London *Times* while working for Armstrong-Whitworth. His first exploits were in

South America, where, during the tension between Argentina and Chile, he tried to sell to both republics; he was successful in the latter country, where he sold warships. Then he transferred his operations to Siam, China and Japan. Selections from letters which Thompson addressed to his employers, read at the trial, disclose his methods:

"I shall try to see the Mikado with regard to the model of your new battleship. In spite of all difficulties I shall also try and show the model to the Emperor of China."

"I intend, with De B——'s help, to make this (the increase of the American naval force in 1892) very clear to the Japanese; and I think they will go ahead in their naval preparations." [2]

In America it is often habitual to think of the era of business consolidation—when Roosevelt with his "big stick" was pursuing the "soulless trusts" and the "malefactors of great wealth"—as peculiar to the U.S.A. In fact the trust movement was also sweeping Britain. In 1901 Vickers became a part of a vast international armament trust—the Harvey United Steel Co. Albert Vickers, managing director of Vickers-Maxim, was its chairman, and on its board of directors were representatives of other British firms interested in the production of war equipment: Charles Cammell & Co., shipbuilders; John Brown & Co., also naval constructors; Sir W. G. Armstrong-Whitworth, Vickers' biggest competitor in the general arms industry; the firms of Krupp and Dillingen in Germany; Terni in Italy; the American Bethlehem Steel Co., and among the French, the powerful Schneider, the Chatillon Steel Co., and the St. Chaumont Steel Co.—all producers of arms. Other rings also became affiliated with this great trust—notably the Nobel Dynamite Trust and the Chilworth Gunpowder Co.— a formidable massing of forces on the side of Mars which covered all the great modern states, Great Britain, Germany, France, Italy and the United States.[3]

England did not lack its "trust busters." Philip Snowden, now safely shelved in the House of Lords, was then sowing his wild oats as a muckraker. In the House of Commons he revealed to England what accompanied this aggregation of forces: [4]

> "The First Lord of the Admiralty . . . some time ago said that the relations of the Admiralty with Vickers and another large firm in the trade are far more cordial than the ordinary relations of business. That might be one reason why the representative of these firms was received in audience at a Cabinet council. Patriotism is not one of the distinguishing features of the trade methods of this great combine. For instance, I find Messrs. Vickers have works at Barrow, Sheffield and Birmingham, but they do not confine themselves to this country. They have a yard in Placencia de las Armas in Spain; they have another place in Spezzia, Italy. They evidently take time by the forelock, they anticipate the promise of a Mediterranean squadron."

No wonder the relations between the departments of the government dealing with national defence and the arms firms were "cordial." The representatives of the arms firms were in many cases former army or navy officers, and the men they dealt with had the pleasing prospect, when they would retire, of augmenting their pensions with the salaries of the arms manufacturers. It was natural that these interests should want to obtain former officers of the government. They wanted men who "knew the ropes," and retired officers naturally kept in touch with their old comrades. As Mr. Snowden put it, "kissing undoubtedly goes by favour and some of these things might be characterised as corruption." Certainly the following list of honourable servants of their country's defence did not consider themselves as scoundrels. We find these men on the board of directors of Vickers: General Sir Herbert Lawrence, Sir Mark Webster Jenkinson, formerly auditor of the Ministry of Munitions, General Sir J. F. Noel Birch, Sir J. A. Cooper, formerly with War Office, Sir A. G. Hancock, formerly of Ordnance Committee. But the system had become so ingrained in the conduct of the Government and the industry that it was not regarded as corruption.

Sometimes there was a great rubbing of hands when a notable fire-eater and friend of the armament manufacturers attained a vantage point for the handling of munitions orders. Sir Charles D. Maclaren of John Brown & Co., a manufacturer of naval armaments, commented on the promotion of Sir John Fisher to the control of the Admiralty; Fisher was the Von Tirpitz of England, always thundering for greater naval armaments. At a meeting of the shareholders of John Brown & Co., Sir Charles allowed himself to gloat, as follows: [5]

> "The appointment of Sir John Fisher at the Admiralty is a fact of some importance to a firm like ours, and I am glad to see Sir John is prepared to go in for building battleships, because the heavier the work, the more of it goes to our firm. We are makers of armour plate, large marine shafting, and turbine engines, so that, when heavy work is about, we will get our share of it."

But the tentacles extended farther than this. In 1911 a British financial journal made the following analysis of the boards of directors of three of the leading British arms firms, classifying them according to rank and occupation:

	Vickers' Sons & Maxims	John Brown & Co.	Armstrong-Whitworth & Co.
Duke	2	1	
Marquess	2		
Earl, baron, or wife, son or daughter	50	10	60
Baronet	15	2	15
Knight	5	5	20
M.P.	3	2	8
J.P.	7	9	3
K.C.			5
Military or naval officer	21	2	20
Naval architect or government contractor	2		
Financier	3		1
Journalists (including newspaper proprietors)	6	3	8

It will be noticed that the nobility and titled classes were the largest groups represented on these boards. To those who are familiar with the influence which these classes wield in British politics, particularly in matters pertaining to the national defence, the list points a moral. But while it is not recorded on this chart, the First Estate was also present; several bishops were named as shareholders in these enterprises.[6]

While the friends of war were busy, the friends of peace were waking up. Increases in the naval estimates aroused their suspicions and some of them voiced their opinions as to who was responsible for this war-minded situation. Lord Welby, one peer who had withstood the attraction of armament shares—and who held the highest and most responsible position as permanent Civil Servant in the country—burst out in indignation:

" We are in the hands of an organisation of crooks.

They are the politicians, generals, manufacturers of armaments and journalists. All of them are anxious for unlimited expenditure and go on inventing scares to terrify the public and to terrify Ministers of the Crown."

Mr. Snowden brought up in the House of Commons the fact that the Member of Parliament for the Hallam Division of Sheffield was then a debenture trustee for Vickers and also for Cammell Laird & Co.; and, as his speech proceeded, he became more uncomfortably personal:

> "Now who are the shareholders? It would be too long for me to give more than a very short selection from the list, but I find that honourable members in this House are very largely concerned. Indeed, it would be impossible to throw a stone on the benches opposite without hitting a Member who is a shareholder in one or other of these firms. . . . The honourable Member for the Osgoldcross Division of Yorkshire . . . I congratulate him on his election last week as honourable President of the Free Church Council . . . is the great imperialist. I find that he is the holder of 3,200 shares in John Brown's and 2,100 in Cammell Laird's. Another of the Members for Sheffield figures in practically every list, as he figures in every debate in this House when there is a possibility of more money being spent on arms and ships. I refer to the Member for the Ecclesall Division (Mr. S. Roberts). He is a shareholder in John Brown's, a director of Cammell Laird, also a debenture trustee of the Fairfield Co., and a shareholder in the Coventry Ordnance Co." [7]

But the officials of Cammell Laird were not content to rely on their governmental directors. In 1909 they were very much concerned about the weak condition of the British navy—then the most powerful in the world. Would the growing menace of the German

116 MERCHANTS OF DEATH

fleet result in a *débâcle* for England? British arms magnates were determined that it should not, that the British government should be made to recognise the danger and forestall it by more dreadnoughts. And these guardians of the national safety were prepared to take all measures to see that this was done.

It was the famous " Big Navy Scare " of 1909.[8] Mr. H. H. Mulliner was managing director of the Coventry Ordnance Company, then partly owned by the great steel and ship works of Cammell Laird. A long time previous to 1910 Mr. Mulliner had displayed a touching solicitude about the British navy's international position. In 1910 he tells the story of his efforts in *The Times* under the heading " Diary of a Great Surrender." Here are two entries which provide an interesting sidelight on his work :

> " May 13th, 1906—Mr. Mulliner first informs the Admiralty of preparations of enormously increasing the Germany Navy." [This information was concealed from nations until March 1909.]
> " May 3, 1909—Mr. Mulliner giving evidence before the Cabinet proves that the acceleration in Germany for producing armaments, about which he had perpetually warned the Admiralty, was an accomplished fact and that large quantities of naval guns and mountings were being made with great rapidity in that country."

In the autumn of 1908 Mr. Mulliner was able to get the ear of a prominent British general who lamented in the House of Lords that a " terrible awakening is in store for us at no distant date." As a result of Mr. Mulliner's agitation, the navy estimates showed an increase of over two million pounds sterling ; and calculations on what Germany might be doing were so skilfully introduced into newspapers that there was much demand in Parliament for eight new cruisers with the slogan—"We want eight and we won't wait."

In the end they got four battleships and it was proved that Germany had been falsely accused of these alleged activities. But one of the first contracts was given to Mr. Mulliner's client Cammell Laird. The rest of Mr. Mulliner's career is not so brilliant. He boasted that he was the sole author of this scare and his indiscretion was a bit too much for the British public. His effectiveness as a contact man was so reduced as a result of his boast that he was replaced in the firm, quite typically, by a retired British admiral who had specialised in naval ordnance and torpedoes.

Mr. Mulliner's own personal career suffered, but his firm soon recovered from this exposure of their plot. One of the most cheering bits of news for the arms merchants in 1913 was the fact that Coventry was no longer in "coventry." True the company had received no orders from the government for some time after the confession of Mr. Mulliner, but no less a person than Winston Churchill gave them his absolution and welcomed them back into the fold. At a stockholders' meeting of Coventry, Lord Aberconway seemingly had no qualms about its future, when he made the following announcement : [9]

> "Coventry was improving, but it was a great drag on their finances and would be so for some time (he had reference to the Mulliner case). The place was not fully recognised by the Government as an essential part of the national armament works. Last autumn he went over to the Scotson works where they made the heavy naval mountings with Mr. Winston Churchill, who gave him an assurance—which he carried out—that Coventry would now be regarded as one of the most important

supplying firms for the Government, instead of being cold-shouldered as it has been for years past."

From these stories, it would seem that Shaw's Undershaft was perhaps not such a gross exaggeration, after all. Indeed, some of the opinions of arms merchants, uttered out of the range of meddlesome reporters' ears, could well be lifted from the dialogues in *Major Barbara*.

When the Hon. Louis Philippe Brodeur, Canadian Minister of Naval Affairs, in company with his colleague, Sir Frederick Borden, Minister of Militia, came to London before the war, they were lavishly entertained by Vickers officials at a banquet in the Carlton Hotel. The liberal Premier had been exploring the possibilities of disarmament and the hospitable arms makers were moved to complain bitterly about this anti-social and anti-financial policy. "Business is bad," confided one executive to M. Brodeur. "How could it be otherwise with a man like Campbell-Bannerman in office? Why, we have not had a war for seven years." While he was unburdening himself of these genial sentiments, one of his fellows went on in much the same vein to Sir Frederick, with complaints that "the Empire is going to the dogs for lack of a war and, worst of all, there is not even one small war in prospect." [10]

The pacific-minded Canadians were shocked by these remarks, but with Japanese buyers the Vickers salesmen had more congenial auditors. In 1910 Rear Admiral Fujii visited England as officer for the supervision of the construction of warships. The Admiral recommended Vickers' specifications and bid, and the Vickers firm got the business. Subsequently the Admiral fell foul of Japanese justice and it was proved that Vickers, in order to return Fujii's goodwill, had remitted to him large sums of money. No wonder they were large, for the Admiral had reported to his superiors that Vickers' bid and specifications were lower and better than any others.

As a matter of fact Vickers were not the only corrupters. Other firms added to the purse of the venal Japanese envoy. The Naval Constructor, Hanamoto Kaizo, visited the Yarrow works in England, and A. F. Yarrow showed him a new type of destroyer fitted for the consumption of oil fuel, the latest invention of that year. Fujii approved these specifications, and remittances were made later to him by Messrs. Yarrow. Arrol & Co. helped out this enterprising officer to the extent of £1,750 for an order of materials, and Wier & Co. sent him £1,000 for an order of pumps and machinery. The German firm of Siemens and Schuckert also attempted to bribe the Admiral, and perhaps were successful. But it was clear from the material brought to light during the trial that an elaborate system of bribery in connection with armament firms existed.

What a deplorable situation in Japan, said the world. But Japan, sensitive about these revelations, hit back at the conduct of other nations in an article in the *Japan Weekly Chronicle* of July 23, 1914:

> "There is no nation which can afford to throw stones at Japan in connection with the existence of bribery and corruption in State services. Only recently a series of scandals in connection with the supply of stores to British military canteens was brought into publicity in the courts, and the firm concerned . . . has been struck off the lists of Government contracts. In Germany and other countries there have been cases equally unsavoury, until it has been made clear that the 'profession' of arms has become as sordidly money-grubbing as it pos-

sibly can. It would seem that, in some countries, it is absolutely essential to resort to practices which, if not actually criminal, are grossly immoral, if any business is to be done by contractors anxious to get orders. Even when an order is obtained it is sometimes necessary to resort to further corruption." [11]

Corruption, influence of the press, directorates, share holdings, friendly members of Parliament—this was the cordon that was drawing tighter about Britain in the years before the war. While men like Philip Snowden were unveiling the true picture of the danger, Vickers waxed stronger. The great steel trust of which it was a member was dissolved in 1913, and thereafter began a keen and augmented competition for greater orders. It was a competition which grew more feverish for some years and found full play in the famous Putiloff case, which brought into the first rank of competition another gigantic firm.

CHAPTER X

SEIGNEUR DE SCHNEIDER

> If they are patriots, it is a new and singularly impartial kind—British on Monday, Russian on Tuesday, Canadian on Wednesday, Italian on Thursday, and so on, as orders may be got from China to Peru.—PERRIS, *The War Traders.*

DOWN in Burgundy there is a dark, sombre industrial town, its streets and houses black with soot and smut from the huge chimneys which tower over its factories—a marked contrast to the happy wine-making towns which lie north of it. Its narrow streets cluster about a hill on top of which, like a true medieval lord looking down at its vassals, is the Château de Verrerie, mansards and surrounding park and all. Symbolic of the factories below and of its owner, six bronze cannon crouch in its courtyard, their muzzles pointed at the grand portal. This is the home of M. Eugène Schneider, lord of this armament fief of Creusot and one of the most powerful cannon merchants in the world.

Although he bears a suspiciously Teutonic name, M. Schneider is French, and just as indisputably French as Mr. Vickers is English. His forefathers came from Alsace when it was still French territory; and, with the characteristic enterprise of Alsatians, the grandfather of the present owner of Creusot started as a clerk in a bank, became interested in engineering processes and much more than interested in methods of buying up defunct companies, for in 1833, when the foundries at Creusot, which had supplied iron products and arms to French monarchs since Louis XIV, went into bankruptcy, he bought Le Creusot.

Krupp was a business man of tireless industry and enterprise; Maxim was an inventor; Sir Basil was the high-pressure salesman; but the Schneiders were typical French industrialists, entrepreneurs content to till the field which they knew in France by the methods which were the common property of other French business men of the time. They offered nothing new in the development of the arms industry, but they appropriated very well the technique of other arms merchants in other countries.

The first Schneider, Joseph Eugène, was primarily a banker, with all of the aptitude of French business men for nourishing himself on the politicians who ruled the country. Without great technical ability, he became financially embarrassed as a result of his engineering enterprise and by 1850 was on the verge of bankruptcy. He had the foresight, however, to offer his support to Louis Napoleon, who was then planning his famous *coup d'état*, and when Napoleon cantered triumphantly down the Champs-Elysées M. Schneider was saved from destruction.

Napoleon III created, or at least gave the impetus of creation, to modern industrial France. Under him Baron Haussman changed the face of Paris, and other barons, lifted to nobility by their own commercial acumen and Napoleon's friendship, built railways, factories, ships, and wooed the money from the traditional sock of the French peasant to finance these enterprises.

Schneider participated in this great development. His factory was adapted to the making of rails, the pig iron and sheet iron which other manufacturers needed, and especially pile-drivers. There was also the imperial army which had to be built up and, as a member of Napoleon's subservient Corps Législatif, the cunning Alsatian won many contracts for war materials. Likewise, Schneider found the *débâcle* which sent his great benefactor into permanent exile even more profitable. The Franco-Prussian War brought into Creusot so many orders for cannon and ammunition that, when the humiliating peace was signed by the French, Schneider emerged with a tremendous fortune—outside of his plants and real estate holdings he had securities amounting to about 100,000,000 francs.

The latter decades of the nineteenth century were spent mending his political fences and consolidating his industrial power. Like many other Second Empire conservatives he was inclined to favour the monarchists after the republic was declared, but while the inflammatory Gambetta was challenging that royalist Irishman, Marshal MacMahon, he found that the electors of the constituency of Creusot were disinclined to place him in the Chamber of Deputies. He met with a humiliating defeat at the polls and had to suffer a Republican deputy at his doorstep.

However, the Republicans were good capitalists too, and so he found no difficulty when he sought to stifle labour unrest in his plant. Like Bernard Shaw's Undershaft, he could well boast " when other people want something to keep my dividends down, you will call out the police and military." Indeed, his opponents obliged him with troops when, in the radical 'eighties, communists challenged his power in Creusot. With the aid of the State and an elaborate spy system, he suppressed the unions and also recovered the political power he desired so greatly. His son was now carrying on, and by threats of dismissal to voting employees the younger Schneider was able to get the coveted post of deputy. From 1900 to 1925, Eugène Schneider was continuously in the Chamber of Deputies.[1]

Schneider had difficulty in breaking into the international armament business. At the beginning of this century he made strenuous efforts in South America, but everywhere he encountered strong opposition from the ubiquitous Krupp. In 1902 the Brazilian government was seriously considering buying some of Schneider's French '75's. The morning of the test day arrived, and both Krupp and Schneider were certain of victory, but on that very morning a great fire broke out in the storehouses where the French samples were kept and the '75's were rendered useless. The French accused the Germans of having started the fire, and the Germans retorted that the French had eliminated themselves because they feared the results of the test.

Again Schneider returned to the fray. New trials were ordered for 1903 by the Brazilian government. The Schneider guns arrived at a Brazilian port, but it was discovered that no steamship company would move them inland because they were dangerous "munitions." When the guns were finally brought to the testing ground, Brazil declared that it was too late.

Schneider did not yet concede defeat. He offered to pay all expenses for another test. Again Krupp swung into action. A German captain of artillery, Von Restoff, who was at Rio, released a story to the press that Peru was being armed by Schneider to fight Brazil. Brazil must meet this threat by immediately arming itself. Krupp was ready to help Brazil in this danger, if only Brazil would understand the situation in time. Brazil understood and Krupp got the orders.

The rivals moved on to Argentina in 1906. In that year Schneider was invited by the Argentine government to compete in a trial of rapid-fire guns; others taking part in these tests were Ehrhardt (Germany), Krupp, Vickers, and Armstrong. The contestants were informed from the outset that Krupp was now supplying this kind of gun and unless something better was produced there would be no change.

Schneider accepted the terms and entered the trials. Great advantages were granted to Krupp which the others did not enjoy. At any rate, the French complained that Krupp was permitted to rehearse Argentine gunners in the use of his guns before the tests; that when a Krupp gun exploded, he was not automatically eliminated but was permitted to replace the gun; that Krupp tampered with his ammunition to make it more efficient than the standard issue; that Krupp evaded the full test of his guns by pleading lack of ammunition.

The ordnance committee in charge debated the result of the tests a long time and finally in 1908 reported that Schneider guns had proved their superiority.[2] Krupp immediately set to work to counteract this report. An intensive press campaign was begun in the Argentine against Schneider. German diplomatic aid was enlisted and the Argentine parliament intervened. It appointed a new and special committee to look into the matter. This committee reported that Krupp and Schneider guns were equally good and they were given the same rating. Since Argentina was not making any changes unless better guns were demonstrated, Krupp retained Argentina as his customer.[3]

In 1908 Schneider was invited by the Chilean government to take part in the trial of special guns, particularly mobile field artillery and mountain guns. The tests were to take place in April, 1909. Schneider went to considerable effort to make special guns and was ready to ship them. Then, on January 11, 1909, a cable from Chile cancelled the gun trials entirely. The order had been given to Krupp without competitive trials. Schneider protested and demanded an indemnity for his expenses, but the Chilean government was silent. Schneider tried to exert diplomatic pressure on Chile, but without avail. Chile did not reply and Krupp had again triumphed.

But meanwhile the French manufacturer had sought other fields where French influence was stronger and where he hoped for better success. The French republic was bent on maintaining and solidifying its alliance with Russia, and French manufacturers of arms and other industrial products naturally expected trade to follow the flag. Indeed, the Russian situation provided exceptional opportunities for these merchants, for Russia was undeveloped economically and needed money.

Huge Russian loans were floated in Paris, and the cautious French investor was persuaded to back up the Czarist regime—to his bitter disillusionment some fifteen years later. But for the moment French manufacturers benefited from this political and financial alliance. When the Russo-Japanese war started, not only industrialists but also French politicians and journalists turned the alliance to good account.

The Russian Soviets have brought to light from the Czarist archives the reports of the Imperial Russian agent in Paris, Arthur Raffalovich. They provide fascinating reading for those who are interested in the condition of French journalism, and its bearing on national policy. Raffalovich's mission was to bribe the French press, so that reports of Russian revolutionary activities, the violent deeds of the Terrorists, the strikes and the industrial breakdowns would not frighten the French investors from buying the very necessary Russian bonds.

The great Havas Agency press was corrupted by the Russians. Ten thousand francs a month were placed at the disposal of this press association to doctor Russian news. But let Raffalovich's reports speak for themselves:

"Subventions of the (French) press began in February 1904 at the time of the panic provoked by the outbreak of hostilities in the Far East. Upon request of M. Rouvier, Minister of Finance (later Premier of France), the Russian finance minister opened a credit of 200,000 francs. Money was expended through the agent of the French ministry, M. Lenoir, and continued until the assurance of the 800,000,000 loan.... The internal events in Russia, disturbances, mutinies, and massacres, caused such an uneasy state of mind among French holders of our securities that if the press had been left to itself it would not have failed to upset public opinion still more.... The outlook was so threatening that the Banque de Paris put 50,000 francs at our disposition, which was issued as follows: 10,000 francs to Havas Agency, 7,000 francs to Hebrard of *Le Temps*, and 4,000 to *Le Journal* on November 30, and again as much on December 30. The costly sacrifice for Havas and *Le Temps* are absolutely necessary ... the support for a majority of the press is unfortunately indispensable until the loan is put through ... the papers have become greedier ... we must continue 100,000 francs for three months and look forward to paying Havas 10,000 for an even longer period."

In 1904 the bribes amounted to 935,785 francs, and in 1905 to 2,014,161. " In ten months the abominable venality of the French press will have absorbed 600,000 francs." In 1906 Raffalovich wrote to say that *Le Temps* had been bribed 100,000 francs in connection with that year's loan. Other items on Raffalovich's account indicated that a sum of 50,000 francs was distributed to *Le Temps, Le Petit Parisien, Le Journal, Figaro, Gaulois,* and Havas. Another list requiring 3,796,861 francs, including advertising, was distributed among the following : *Journal des Débats, Echo de Paris, Liberté, Patrie, Eclair, Rappel, Radical, Intransigeant,* and, curiously also, *La Vie Parisienne.*[4]

When Father Gapon led his proletarians up to the doors of the Winter Palace, when the Cossacks massacred these hungry men and the whole abortive revolution of 1905 startled the world, few connected these events with the barrage of Russian propaganda in France. Still fewer discerned any link between the participation in these riots of the Putiloff men with the enterprise of M. Eugène Schneider. The Putiloff factory was a Russian munitions factory in St. Petersburg, and its business had suffered so heavily from international forces that its unemployed workmen were ready for any agitation. Schneider-Creusot, on the other hand, was increasing its personnel, for very good reasons.

Following the *débâcle* of the Japanese war, Russia's army and navy had to be reorganised root and branch, its land artillery brought up to date and its navy completely rebuilt. The other member of the Entente, France, was also eager to have her ally equip herself to meet the growing menace of Germany ; and none were more eager than the arms makers. Accordingly,

SEIGNEUR DE SCHNEIDER

as money flowed out of the land of the Czars into the pay envelopes of the workers of the French republic, such firms as Putiloff found their business diminishing and their factory hands idling about the streets listening to radical agitators.[5]

It was an embarrassing situation for the Russian government, now struggling to be democratic with its new elective Duma. While the ruling classes which had sought French loans wanted to favour foreign supporters, the Duma and the bourgeois elements clamoured for greater participation of Russian business in the new spending programme. Finally, when all the revolutionary and labour disorders had been stilled and the " tame " Duma had been brought to a conciliatory mood, the Czar obtained from this body appropriations amounting to £127,397,260. But the pan-Slavic supporters insisted that this money should be spent in Russian workshops. " Russia for the Russians," was the popular cry.

A handsome slogan, but difficult to abide by, for Russia was not, in an economic sense, independent. She relied on England and Germany for coal, goods had to be brought from afar to the Neva in British bottoms, the securities market in Paris had to be conciliated to obtain loans, and raw materials had to be brought from all over Europe. Moreover, Russia, under the Czar, just as in 1934 under Stalin, needed technical advisers and skilled engineers to direct her industry. All her public services, particularly tramways and light plants, were manned by British and Germans ; her coal-pits were first exploited by a Welshman ; and, in general, this most nationalistic of states had a governing class employing foreign languages as a medium for polite and commercial conversation, schooled by an international corps of tutors and governesses, and permeated by an international outlook. Most important of all, in the manufacture of war materials, Russian plants were not equipped to turn out the highly efficient products of other European firms. No wonder Putiloff and other factories, in spite of Duma resolutions, had to rely on the aid of foreigners.

The most revolutionary polyglot invasion of Russia now took place, an invasion which was far more formidable and successful than Napoleon's famous attempt in 1812. To follow the analogy, the foreigners' ultimate retreat from Moscow did not come to pass until many years later, and its body blow was not the Muscovite climate but the radical programme of the Bolsheviks. But for the time being, it was a most fruitful mass attack.

The foreign firms, for the most part, concentrated their efforts on the new Russian naval building programme and so, in the various shipyards on the Baltic and Black Sea, there appeared a motley aggregation of European contractors. John Brown & Co., Vickers Ltd., Armstrong-Whitworth, Franco-Belgian Company, Augustin Normand of Havre, Schneider-Creusot, Karl Zeiss of Riga, F. Schuchau of Elbing—these names indicate the English, French, Belgian, and even German elements in the building programme.

The situation at the Nickolayeff shipyards on the Black Sea illustrates this very well. There contracts for three dreadnoughts were let to the Russian Shipbuilding Company and the Franco-Belgian Company. The former was a smoke-screen for a mixed foreign combination financed by the Banque Privée of St. Petersburg, which in turn was the subsidiary of the Société Générale, a Parisian bank. This parent bank had close connections with John Brown & Co. and Messrs. Thorneycroft, Vickers and other English firms who were to get most of this naval business.

But where was M. Schneider in this last combination ? In truth, he was not in it at all. For he was in league with another French bank, the Union Parisienne, which was a bitter rival of the Société Générale. The Union Parisienne had financed the Putiloff works in St. Petersburg, and naturally M. Schneider got the business there. But the Société Générale entrenched themselves on the Black Sea. Thus early in the struggle for contracts two factions among the invading interests formed their battle lines—on the one side Schneider and the Union Parisienne bank ; and on the other side the French bank, Société Générale, allied with English, Belgian and other French firms.

On another front Schneider was even less happy. The Russians proposed to build a large artillery plant, which would outfit the Slav army with the famous French '75. Naturally he would expect that French guns built with French money would come under his control. He was eager enough to plot to prevent the Russians from building their own arsenal operated by their own people. He therefore strove to get the new artillery factory placed in the Urals, at Perm, where he had valuable properties. But the agile Zaharoff circumvented him and persuaded the Russians to give his Vickers the Tzaritzine factory on the Volga, a much better site. Victory here for the English and their friend the Société Générale.[6]

Again the Russians returned to the fray, determined to get some part in this great building programme and to obtain some shipyards on the Baltic for Putiloff. Putiloff had already been financed by the Schneider bank to the extent of £1,000,000 and this bank was reluctant to advance more of its precious francs. Moreover, this bank, Union Parisienne, had become embarrassed by the freezing of its loans in the Near East by the Balkan War. So it had to refuse its favoured client at Creusot the money when he asked for it.

M. Schneider, determined to support Putiloff in its plan, went to the Société Générale, the rival organisation, which of course declined to finance Schneider. For were they not allied with the English interests? There was only one alternative for the harassed Frenchman. He had been working hand in glove with the German firm of Krupp in equipping Putiloff. The Russians, while favouring French light artillery, wanted the superior make of Krupp for its big guns, and so Schneider had bought the privilege of using Krupp patents in Russia. Krupp and its subsidiary Skoda in Austria were wealthy ; and thus we may see the curious spectacle of a Frenchman seeking German capital for the building of Russian armaments.

Skoda with the collaboration of the Kreditanstalt of Vienna agreed to underwrite one-quarter of a new Putiloff stock issue, with Schneider supplying the balance. Thus the alliance of the French bank Société Générale, and British firms faced a Franco-German combine. It was a gigantic conflict of international finance and industry and was the basis of the whole scandal which has become known as the Putiloff Affair.[7]

But the Société Générale was not bested yet. Its directors were aware of Putiloff's need of money and M. Schneider's embarrassment. They determined to make an effort to wrest control of Putiloff from

Schneider, who still had to raise the money to underwrite the two-thirds of the new issue. They made an offer to supply all the funds which Putiloff required. M. Schneider was in a melancholy position—rebuffed in the Urals, humiliated by the English occupation of Tzaritzine and now facing the loss of his last stronghold in Russia, Putiloff. He was ready for the most heroic measures to save his interests in Russia.

On January 27, 1914, the *Echo de Paris* printed a dispatch from St. Petersburg, as follows:

> " There is a rumour afloat that the Putiloff factory at St. Petersburg has just been purchased by Krupp and Company. If this news is exact, it will provoke much feeling in France. It is well known, in fact, that the Russian government has adopted French processes for its material of war. Up till now, the greatest part of this material has been constructed in the Putiloff factory with the aid of Creusot and the French personnel from Creusot."

There was indeed much " feeling " in France on the receipt of this news. The French capital was aroused as it had not been since the Dreyfus affair or the Agadir incident. What ? The devilish Krupp firm, the heart of Germany's menace to France, was buying out the Putiloff works, together with that important " secret," the design of France's famous light artillery ? The boulevards were aflame with indignation. Premier Doumergue sent a telegram to the French ambassador in St. Petersburg asking him to look into the matter at once. Caillaux admitted the " gravity " of the matter. Even M. Schneider, when questioned by a reporter from *La Patrie*, admitted that it was " grave." This reporter learned that M. Schneider knew only what he read in the papers.

REPORTER: "But, Putiloff manufactures for the Russian army material of war invented by Frenchmen?"

M. SCHNEIDER: "The Putiloff factories are indeed constructing material of war on plans furnished by us, and we have representatives from our factories at Creusot with them."

REPORTER: "But if the House of Krupp has really bought these factories, will the Germans then have access to our own secrets of manufacture?"

M. SCHNEIDER (making a vague gesture of impotence): "It's very grave."

REPORTER: "Very grave!"

M. SCHNEIDER: "This news surely must be inexact." (Same gesture of impotence.)

What eloquence there was in this shrug of the shoulders for the excitable French readers of the newspapers! They saw in the whole affair a conspiracy between Germany and the treacherous Russians, to whom they had paid out countless millions for the equipment of armies which would, they hoped, defeat the Germans in the next war. Again France had been duped and by its trusted allies. It is difficult to say whether French ire was greater toward Germany than toward Russia. Krupp, indeed, denied that they had anything to do with the matter, but this only increased French suspicions. The *Echo de Paris* added more fuel to the fire by alleging that the treacherous English were in with Krupp on this scheme. More denials, this time from the representatives of Vickers.

Perhaps in revenge for this unwarranted suspicion, the St. Petersburg correspondent of the London *Times* wired his paper and gave his "inside" view of the situation. He said:

"The whole question of Franco-Russian relations in respects to armament orders is raised. There are complaints that French industry has not received its proportion of orders, especially in matters of naval construction, to which it is entitled in view of the financial and political connections of the two countries. During the last few months, it is asserted that orders for the Russian navy have been given to the extent of 69,000,000 roubles to the Germans, 67,000,000 roubles to Great Britain and only 57,000,000 roubles to the French."

Pursuing his indiscretions further, the following day, this correspondent reported that the Russians wanted about £2,000,000 for their Putiloff works, and as Schneider was reluctant to unloose the purse-strings again, a "feint" was being made to get German capital; moreover, that [8] "there will be an endeavour in Paris to improve the occasion in order to assure larger French participation in orders from the Russian Ministry of War and from the Admiralty"; on the other hand that the Russian government was about to raise a new loan for which it would require the good will of the Paris market: that "there are nowadays, except in naval construction, few if any real 'secrets' in manufacturing materials of war. The admirable French field-gun is being manufactured for the Italian navy, and independently of this fact, it is well known that the German military authorities have long been familiar with it."

The Times correspondent did an excellent but rather belated job of "debunking" when he stated the facts about war "secrets." But he was rather misleading when he declared the wily Slavs were feinting toward Germany to get a loan from Schneider. If he had followed up his news about the projected Russian loan to be floated in Paris, he would have come to the root of the matter; for it was in this loan, which as a matter of fact had already been arranged, that the sorely tried M. Schneider found his remedy, the shining path out of his difficulties, the means by which he could defeat his enemies the Société Générale and the English firms. He had indeed conspired well.

This loan was the immense Railway Loan which Russia needed very badly and which the diplomats and financiers of the two countries had carefully prepared for the Parisian market. To underwrite this, all the French banks had to combine to float the issue on the Bourse. As we have seen in the great corruptions of 1905 and following years, the press had to be effectively managed so that no news of scandals, mutinies or revolutions would frighten the French investor who would buy the Russian bonds. A careful conditioning of French public opinion was started with ceremonial visits of premiers, princes of the blood and other notables, and the prospective bond buyer stimulated by these affecting sights would presumably rush to the banks to get the bonds.

He would, of course, unless disastrous news like Krupp's purchase of Putiloff intervened. M. Schneider was well aware of this psychological background for the loan and he saw his opportunity. His paid retainers in the press were therefore given orders to send the false news from St. Petersburg to the *Echo* and the result, even to his cunningly arranged and delivered interview with histrionic gestures and exclamations of apprehension, was most satisfactory. The news, as M. Schneider put it, was indeed grave, but grave principally for the Russians and the French bankers who had agreed to sell the bonds. The Russian Railway loan was in grave danger of foundering.

The Franco-British combination which was going to take over Putiloff so easily and defeat M. Schneider was aghast. They had, it is true, excellent material for an exposé of Schneider's own dealings and alliance with the Germans. If it were revealed that Schneider, in league with the villain Krupp, was prepared to sacrifice " French secrets " to the enemy, this patriotic combination of the orthodox *entente* of France and England would conceivably profit. But if this was disclosed, public opinion in France would be even more upset and the Railway Loan would certainly fail. And the Société Générale would suffer as one of the participants of this loan.

Naturally, there was much hasty conferring behind the scenes and Schneider was not far away from these conferences. The Société Générale saw that, rather than jeopardise the loan, it was better to concede defeat in their scheme to oust Schneider from Putiloff. Events moved rapidly, and within three days of the crucial telegram to the *Echo* a consortium of French banks, including the Société Générale, agreed to underwrite the necessary capital for Putiloff, with Schneider left in control of this much disputed factory. Thus the Franco-German combination had routed the Anglo-French. It was a spectacular triumph for the crafty Alsatian, for he had not only retained his stronghold in Russia, but also forced his rivals to put up the money for its maintenance and expansion.

When the consortium reached this agreement, the turbulent French press was stilled as completely as the stormy waves under the magic trident of King Neptune. On the 30th of January, the *Temps*, which had quickly followed the *Echo* in sounding the tocsin a few days before, admitted that " the scope of the whole matter had been greatly exaggerated." M. André Tardieu, who to-day makes so much capital out of French fears of the results of disarmament, wrote in *Le Temps* as follows: " The secrets of manufacture are, in our epoch, somewhat confused; we may cite, as a single example, the standard French cannon which we are constructing for the Italian army." Nothing could be more authoritative than this on the subject of war " secrets," and on February 2 Premier Doumergue pronounced the funeral oration of the famous Putiloff affair with these words, " The incident was handled for the best interests of France." [9]

The London correspondent and M. Tardieu were right. Italy, that temperamental ally of the Central Powers and therefore the potential enemy of France, had for some time enjoyed the use of the exclusive '75. Indeed, her light artillery was largely composed of this make, supplied by the French.

M. Schneider had learned well the technique of the international arms commerce. He had done a nice piece of business with Bulgaria. A photograph of Ferdinand of Bulgaria, inspecting the Creusot factories under the personal guidance of M. Eugène himself, tells the story. In 1906, this Balkan prince came to the Burgundian mecca to buy guns. He had the collaboration of the French government in the matter. The order which Ferdinand gave Schneider was so large that the Bulgarian parliament, the Sobranje, called their prince before the Bulgarian Financial Commission and, after hearing him, refused to grant the appropriations. There was a Bulgarian loan pending at this time from France, and the French government now intervened and declared that if the Sobranje did not ratify the appropriations the loan would not be authorised.

Seigneur De Schneider

The Sobranje took their medicine and ratified the appropriations; the loan was granted, and M. Schneider profited by selling guns which were used some years later in Macedonia against General Sarrail's men.

But M. Schneider's activities went further. Turkey wanted some of his guns. In 1914 Turkey had received a loan from France for this purpose; and, after being led in state through Creusot, the Turkish Minister of Marine witnessed a demonstration which was so gratifying that he gave an order. He had the money to pay for it, but unfortunately this visit took place late in July 1914. War broke out and the order could not be filled, but the Turk departed through Switzerland, and on his itinerary to Constantinople were Essen and Pilsen. He stopped off at these factories and spent French money on guns which were later used against France and her allies.[10]

Thus by the outbreak of the World War, Schneider-Creusot had attained its majority as an armament firm. It had fought gamely through the discouraging contest in South America. It had won its spurs in the famous Putiloff affair. And 1914 found it gathering business from potential enemies of its country. It had reached this stature by certain methods: by cultivating governmental connections, by playing the complicated game of international banking, by stimulating war scares and by manipulating the press. These were the instruments not only of Schneider but also of the armament business in general, and only by examining them in detail is it possible to arrive at a just appreciation of the extraordinary power of this business in creating a situation tending toward war.

CHAPTER XI

THE EVE OF THE WORLD WAR—THE ARMS MERCHANTS

> An ordinary firm may utilise all available means for securing business on profitable terms. Ordnance manufacturers, in the nature of things, adopt a similar policy; but because the transactions are with the home and foreign governments, special objections are taken to methods which find numerous parallels in ordinary commercial life. A firm must study its customers and must maintain the closest possible touch with probable requirements. Some people will never understand business.—*Arms and Explosives*, journal of the British arms industry.

THE modern armament manufacturer is the result of the Machine Age. Rapid technological development and mass production in the arms industry raised the problem of markets and business methods. The sales methods which the arms merchants evolved in the course of time are fundamentally the same as those employed by Big Business everywhere. But because the arms merchants dealt so largely with governments, and because their activities so frequently involved both national and international politics, their business methods have been subjected to a much closer scrutiny. Many of these methods have already been touched upon; they will be summarised here for purposes of emphasis and further elaboration.

Choice of Directors.

The selection of directors is important in any business. In modern corporations the board of directors is, as a rule, chosen, not for detailed and expert knowledge of the business, but for "influence" and for "window dressing." The president of the board of a powerful American bank recently declared that he knew personally less than half of his fellow directors of whom there were eighty-four.[1] Their names, their connections, and their influence were to bring business and to inspire confidence.

The armament manufacturers follow the same practice, due regard being had to the special needs of their industry. In Great Britain they choose their directors from the nobility and from members of Parliament, the Army, or the Admiralty. These names will aid them in securing business, in establishing a front of respectability, and in silencing criticism.

In France, the armament manufacturers' boards are made up largely of the great industrialists and bankers. All of these maintain very close relations with important members of the Chamber of Deputies. Many French political leaders are outstanding corporation lawyers, and this makes the tie between the arms makers and their best customer even closer.

In the United States the banker is the all-important person in industry. Hence, while few cases are known where an important government official or a member of Congress has been a director of an armament firm, all arms makers have important financial connections. In the Morgan group will be found the Du Pont Company, the Bethlehem Steel Corporation, the U.S. Steel Corporation, together with copper, oil, electric appliances, locomotive, telephone and telegraph interests. This tie-up also leads over into the great banks, including the National City, Corn Exchange, Chase

National, etc. It is the Morgan group of corporation clients and banks which dominates the American arms industry.[2]

The most significant development in directorates, however, was the internationalisation of many boards of control. The recently published volume by Launay and Sennac, *Les Relations Internationales des Industries de Guerre*, deals largely with this subject. Alfred Nobel, for instance, the inventor of dynamite, located his companies in almost all parts of the world, from Sweden to South Africa, from Japan to South America. Most of these scattered interests were gathered into two huge trusts, the Nobel Dynamite Trust Company, which combined the German and English companies, and the Société Centrale de Dynamite, which united the French, Swedish, Italian, Spanish, and South American companies. The boards of these two trusts were made up chiefly of Frenchmen, Englishmen, and Germans, but each country represented had one of its nationals among the directors.[3]

The Harvey United Steel Company was governed by a board made up of Germans, Englishmen, Americans, Frenchmen, and Italians.[4] The Lonza Company of Switzerland was German owned, but had French, Austrian, Italian, and German directors.[5] Dillingen, a German firm, had German and French directors.[6] The Whitehead Torpedo Company had a French, British, and Hungarian directorate.[7]

These international trusts insured the arms merchants against all possible developments. In peace time they could solicit business everywhere, because their local directors would make the proper contacts. Since most of the larger companies also maintained branch factories abroad, the plea of " home industries " could frequently be made. In war time a separation of some kind might become necessary, but this could readily be patched up again when peace returned. Thus the Great International, which political idealists and labour strategists have sought for so long, was actually taking shape in the armament industry.

Maintaining Close Relations with Governments.

The relations between the military departments of governments and the armament industry are always very close. This is attributable just as much to governments as it is to the arms makers. All governments still believe in military preparedness as an essential of national life; hence they foster and aid the arms makers and co-operate very closely with them. Armament makers, on their part, woo the government and its officials, so that their particular company may be favoured when government contracts are given out.

To illustrate, the armour-plate industry was introduced into the United States because the U.S. Navy urged the steel makers to establish a native industry in this field. The Du Pont Company has recently declared that it has " been requested and encouraged by our Government to maintain facilities for the production of munitions." [8] The aeroplane industry announced recently to a Congressional committee that the government had urged it to continue its development in the interest of national defence.[9]

On the other hand, the individual arms company does all it can to " keep in close touch," so that it may obtain government orders. In Great Britain it has become an established practice of the armament men to place retiring admirals and generals on their boards. The reason for this was well expressed by *Arms and Explosives*: "they know the ropes."

In the United States, Du Pont got his first government orders because of the friendship of Thomas Jefferson, President of the United States. Furthermore, the Congressional representatives from the arms-producing states frequently appear as champions of the industry. A particularly interesting illustration of this was recently afforded by Congressman E. W. Goss of Connecticut. Mr. Goss was formerly an officer of the Scovill Manufacturing Company, a firm which, in addition to other products, produces brass cartridge cases and fuses. Five members of the Goss family are closely associated with the firm. When the House Foreign Affairs Committee held hearings on the resolution to declare an embargo on arms in time of war, Representative Goss appeared against the resolution.[10]

The activities of Krupp were described by an American newspaper correspondent in 1911: "Hence we find that King Krupp of Essen has ambassadors of his own in every great capital of the world, from Tokyo to Constantinople, and from St. Petersburg to Buenos Aires. He has even in Sofia a representative who knows more about local politics and has a larger acquaintance with politicians than all the legations put together."[11] Krupp also placed high military officials on his pay-rolls and kept himself fully informed on government plans through his agents.

Bankers.

Armament work must be financed, and the operations frequently demand large sums and impose the utmost secrecy. Hence armament makers either get control of powerful banks for themselves or they find bankers whom they can trust. In every great country certain banks are known as the "armament banks." The Banque de l'Union Parisienne takes care of Schneider's finances, the Deutsche Bank was the banker for the Germans, Morgan takes care of the Americans, the Oesterreichische Kredit-Anstalt für Handel und Gewerbe and the Ungarische Allgemeine Kreditbank did the financial work of Skoda.

The work of the arms merchants frequently involved the necessity of granting international loans, and there again their close connections with both bankers and governments were very valuable. Sometimes the bank would undertake to float such a loan, sometimes the armament manufacturer's government would advance funds to the foreign state. The complications into which this might lead are shown by the Putiloff affair in Russia and the Bulgarian armament orders of 1913. In post-war days, France has cemented her friendships and alliances with Poland and the Little Entente with heavy loans, many of which were earmarked for payment of armaments "made in France." Loans to China by various governments frequently stipulated similar conditions.

How important these governmental loans might be for the arms merchants is illustrated by an incident from pre-war Serbia. Krupp and Schneider were in competition for the armament contracts of Serbia. A competitive test was held in which Krupp easily emerged as victor. But he did not receive the orders. A French loan had recently been negotiated by Serbia, and it was expressly specified that it must be used in part for French armaments.[12]

L

The Press.

The press is too powerful and important to be neglected by the arms makers. Hence none of the great arms merchants are without their press connections. Sometimes a newspaper is bought outright; sometimes a controlling interest is sufficient; sometimes influential newspaper men or owners are put on the pay-rolls or on the directorates of the armament makers.

The Du Pont Company, for instance, controls every daily in Delaware; Krupp owned three great dailies, and, moreover, the powerful press and moving picture " czar," Hugenberg, was a Krupp director. Hugo Stinnes owns or controls 19 newspapers and magazines in Germany, Austria, Hungary, and Norway.[13] The French press has generally been for sale to anyone willing to pay the price, as Raffalovich has revealed. Indirect contacts are also valuable. Morgan is the banker for the American armament industry, and it is also represented on the Crowell Publishing Company which publishes a number of widely read magazines.[14]

In practice the control and use of the press works out in various ways. Newspapers live from advertising. Now armament makers seldom advertise their military wares, although this has happened. It is much better to advertise their ordinary industrial products, such as railway tracks, machines, construction materials, etc. But the same purpose is frequently served by this kind of advertising. Where the press is venal, the journal may be paid for a series of articles on "the dangers of disarmament" or similar subjects.

The press is useful also in suppressing news or in refusing paid advertisements against the arms makers.

During the World War, for instance, almost complete silence was maintained by the French press when great industrialists were accused of treason for trafficking with the enemy. After the war, *Le Temps* refused to accept an advertisement of Mennevée's book on Zaharoff, the mystery man of Europe.[15]

The arms merchants have likewise put the moving picture into their service. The Barrow works of Vickers-Armstrong have their own cinema theatre where prospective buyers may see exhibitions of tanks, warships, machine guns, etc. in action. These special films of the arms makers are also taken on tour to various nations in order to demonstrate before the very eyes of the purchasing agents what effective killing machines are for sale.

A report of one of these foreign showings appeared in the *North Mail* on December 5, 1931:

> "A special exhibition of British films was given to the King and Queen of Yugoslavia in their new palace at Dedinje. The films were productions made by a British firm of armament makers. There were tanks of all kinds, as well as field guns of all calibres and tractors. A firm of shipbuilders also showed a film of the launching of a Yugoslav warship."

Here is a publicity and sales medium which the arms merchants have only begun to exploit.[16]

War Scares.

When international relations become strained, the business of the arms industry generally improves. Hence when nations manage to get along with a minimum of friction, the armament manufacturers have sometimes not hesitated to stir up trouble. Every nation has "natural" or "hereditary" enemies.

The arms makers need do no more than to point out the increasing armaments of the " enemy " and the virtual " helplessness " of the " threatened " country, and before long there is vigorous action for " preparedness," which in turn means business for the arms merchants. Sometimes it is sufficient to sell to the " enemy " the latest engines of war and then to apprise the other government of that fact.

The Mulliner war scare in Great Britain has been considered. The Gontard affair in Germany is just as instructive. Paul Gontard was (and is) one of the mightiest men in the German armament industry. As director of the Ludwig Loewe Company he was eager to get orders for machine guns from the German government. Accordingly he sent a letter to his Paris representative suggesting that an article be inserted in *Figaro* declaring that the French government had decided to speed up its machine gun programme and to double a recent order. The fact that it was taken for granted that such a notice would be inserted in this French journal speaks for itself.

The procedure suggested by Gontard was too crude for the French press, particularly since the story was not true. Another approach was found. A number of French papers, including *Figaro, Matin*, and the *Echo de Paris* carried articles reporting the superiority of French machine guns and the advantage these gave to the French army.

Hardly had these articles appeared when the Prussian delegate in the Reichstag, Schmidt, an ally of the armament manufacturers, read them to the assembled Reichstag members and demanded to know what the government proposed to do about it. After a patriotic flurry the government began to increase its orders for machine guns very considerably. This happened in 1907, and during the three following years (1908–10) Germany spent 40 million marks for machine guns.[17]

Military Missions.

The "backward countries" of the world have frequently sought the aid of their Big Brothers in training them for war. Hence the system of military and naval missions, to which now are being added aviation instructors. The by-product of this arrangement generally is armament orders for the country from which the mission hails.

In pre-war days the British had a naval mission in Turkey, while the Germans trained the Turkish army. Armament orders were divided between the two countries. Japan's modern navy was trained by the British, who also furnished many battleships and vast naval armaments. The United States maintains naval missions in various South American countries, and the American armament men consider this field so promising that they issue their catalogues also in Spanish. China has of late been the scene of American aviation activity. The American companies have furnished an air mission and are selling aeroplanes to the Chinese at the same time.

Shares in Armament Companies.

The utility companies are not the only ones who know that their shareholders may win them important friendships or aid them, particularly if they are "widows and orphans," in making public pleas. The arms merchants in some countries use this device very effectively. The last German Kaiser was one of the largest shareholders in at least two arms companies, and these two naturally got most of the German government orders. The British have probably developed this technique more fully than any other group. Among the thousands of shareholders of the British companies were representative people from every walk of life and also " common people " in plenty. Among those listed as shareholders in 1914 were Lord Balfour, Lord Curzon, Earl Grey, Lord Kinnaird, president of the Y.M.C.A., Sir J. B. Lonsdale, Sir Alfred Mond, the bishops of Adelaide, Chester and Hexham, as well as many other distinguished personages.[18]

Bribery.

The charge of bribery has frequently been made against the arms merchants. To be sure, " graft in business " is not limited to the armament industry, as Gustavus Myers, Upton Sinclair, John T. Flynn, and others have shown. The American National Association of Manufacturers recently embarked on a campaign to wipe out bribes in business, which it estimated at about a billion dollars a year.[19] But somehow the arms makers seem to attract more attention in their bribing practices.

After 1908 the Young Turk government was in control at Constantinople, and the fires of nationalism were said to have burned out all traces of corruption for which the old régime was notorious. To the armament manufacturers, however, this was simply a legend. One of them confided to a friend that the only difference between the two régimes was that the Young Turks demanded higher bribes.[20]

Just before the war, Clemenceau charged in a series of articles that the German armament manufacturers were so successful in South America because they bribed so well.[21]

"A story is told of an Englishman who went out to execute a contract for a cruiser which a branch establishment of his firm had procured from the government of a European power. On his arrival he began to pay 'commissions' to various folks, great and small, who were interested in the contract. At last to an officer who came with an exorbitant demand the Englishman cried: 'How can I build the cruiser?' The reply was: 'What does that matter, so long as you get paid and we get paid?'"[22]

Sabotage.

This practice is hard to prove and probably occurs seldom, but the charge appears at times. The Russian government in pre-war days had an important cartridge factory in Poland which manufactured much ammunition. This factory was burned down by an incendiary and was never rebuilt. The newspaper *Novoe Vremya* charged that the conflagration had been started by German armament manufacturers in order to increase their Russian business.[23]

A significant by-product of the business methods of the arms merchants is the virtual elimination of military secrets, as far as the manufacture of armaments is concerned. Spies may ferret out strategic plans, naval bases and fortresses, and other military information,[24] but the normal industrial and commercial procedure of the arms industry makes most espionage as to actual implements of war unnecessary.

The arms industry practises public testing. Krupp's proving ground at Meppen was open to the ordnance engineers of all nations. The purpose of the test was to demonstrate the efficiency of the new invention and to sell it; hence secrecy could hardly prevail.

After a successful test, the new device or weapon was offered freely to all. Whoever was willing and able to pay a licence fee and a stipulated royalty could secure exclusive rights of manufacture in his country. Krupp's armour plate is the classic example of this.

Furthermore, most of the technical problems of the arms industry are problems of engineering and chemistry. As might be expected, the journals in these fields also deal with the developments in the arms industry. Even a casual examination of such journals as *Engineering*, *Cassier's Magazine* and the *American Machinist* reveals that all the latest guns, cannon, and war machines are fully discussed. Detailed drawings are generally given showing the construction and operation of these new inventions. Secrecy is impossible under such conditions.

Another standard practice of the arms industry is to exhibit its products wherever possible, especially at world's fairs and industrial exhibitions. From the middle of the last century to the present there was hardly a large exhibition in any part of the world, from London and Paris to South Africa and Australia, which was not attended by the arms makers. And their exhibits received widespread attention and were carefully and fully reported in engineering journals.[25]

An interesting illustration of the publicity attending a world's fair exhibit of armaments is a report made to the U.S. Government in 1867.[26] This was the year of the Paris Exhibition, and all great arms makers were represented. The United States sent two observers to Paris to report on the armaments exhibited. Their report was embodied in a huge volume, fully illustrated, telling of latest developments in all forms of armament from guns and cannon to battleships. The observers were also able to report that they had seen and examined the famous German needle gun, which was supposed to be a closely guarded secret. This gun had not been on public exhibition, but private collections contained it and there was no difficulty in securing access to it.

Many armament manufacturers established branch factories in other countries or they contracted to build arms factories for other governments. In either case all the patents and processes of the company were transferred to the other country, particularly since there was generally a clause in the contract binding the foreign company to that very thing.

How there can be any secrets as to the structure and operation of military implements under these circumstances is difficult to see. Yet arms makers every now and then make a great ado about their "trade secrets" which they pretend are invaluable to them. In 1915, for instance, when the United States government was planning to erect its own armour-plate factory, because it believed it was being consistently overcharged by the private manufacturers, it appointed a committee to gather all the information it could on the subject. The committee approached the armour-plate makers, asked them about their processes and organisation, and about 75 per cent of their questions remained unanswered, because they could not reveal their trade secrets.[27] In view of the general practices of the arms industry, it does not seem far-fetched to surmise an entirely different reason for their failure to reply to the committee's questions.

As a matter of fact, new inventions in arms generally make their way round the world in a very short time, due largely to the ordinary business methods of the arms industry. This will explain what has frequently been considered a mystery or the clever work of spies, how certain new developments spread so rapidly in spite of the efforts of governments to keep them secret. One incident is worth telling here. The British had for long been seeking a smokeless powder suitable for all climates. The British armies were to be found in blistering deserts and near snow-clad mountains, hence their need for this kind of explosive. Finally, in the early 1890's, they succeeded in perfecting an explosive which was called cordite. It was exactly what they had wanted and they were elated. Naturally they wished to keep its ingredients a secret. Imagine their surprise and consternation when, in the very next year, a British military man discovered that cordite was already known in Russia, where a climate-proof powder was also sorely needed.[28]

On the eve of the World War, then, it was clear to all observers that the " next war " would be a gigantic and terrifying affair. The prophets of doom foresaw a titanic conflict in which armies of millions would face one another with countless new and monstrous death machines, developed and sold indiscriminately to all nations, by the arms merchants. They foretold deaths by the millions, the exhaustion of world economy, the pauperisation of nations, and a grave threat to human civilisation. Unfortunately, the prophets, for once, were right.

CHAPTER XII

THE WORLD WAR—THE WAR IN EUROPE

> Great armament firms have no national or political prejudices; they are concerned not with the ulterior objects of war, but with the immediate means by which victory may be secured; and the value of such abstract ideas as justice and liberty they leave to the discussion of idle and metaphysical minds, or employ the terms as convenient euphemisms by which the real objects of statesmen may be cloaked and the energies of a people directed.—Biographer of Sir William White.

THE World War was waged by 27 nations; it mobilised 66,103,164 men of whom 37,494,186 became casualties.[1] Its direct costs are estimated at £42,739,726,712, its indirect costs at £31,164,383,561.[2] And these figures do not include the additional billions in interest payments, veterans' care and pensions, and similar expenses which will continue for many decades to come.[3] The world had never before witnessed so gigantic a conflict.

Not only were the number of combatants and the financial costs of the war without precedent, but the number and variety of death machines had never been equalled. All the sinister engines of war invented and perfected in the previous half-century were used in the fighting, and, naturally enough, there was a further development of these during the war itself. The machine gun was improved, artillery was motorised and its range became longer, sights and fire-control apparatus became more scientific and more accurate.

Many new implements of war were also invented. The tank, generally acknowledged a British invention, was first used at the Somme. Hand grenades were supplied to the trenches, and rifle grenades increased the range of these deadly missiles. The aeroplane gave its first prophetic demonstration as a war machine, and aviators learned to drop bombs and to fire machine guns from their lofty perches. Poison gas made its first appearance, spreading the gruesome "silent death."

In the trenches soldiers wore helmets to protect them from flying fragments and gas masks to guard them against the 63 different kinds of death-dealing chemicals. Trench periscopes enabled them to see without exposing themselves to the rifles of sharp-shooters.

In naval warfare the submarine created a radically new situation involving changes in naval policy, battleship construction, sea fighting, and international law which even now remain unsettled. The first ships had a very limited cruising radius, but constant improvement made them extremely dangerous. Many new devices were evolved to fight this menace, including submarine chasers, depth-charges, anti-submarine walls, specially constructed mines, and various highly ingenious scientific instruments to reveal or dispose of the under-sea enemy.

The prevailing pre-war international traffic in armaments made it inevitable that many of the armies and navies were met by guns and armaments which had been manufactured and sold to the enemy by their own countrymen. Germany and Great Britain, in particular, had sold arms to virtually all countries, while France and Austria lagged only a little behind.

The Germans had armed Belgium, and the German army marching into Belgium was met by German-made guns. They had helped to re-arm Russia, building part of its fleet and its artillery factories; German soldiers marching into Russia were confronted by German-made cannon. Krupp armour plate had been supplied to all the great navies of the world; in every naval engagement of the war the German fleet had to face armour-plated vessels made by Germans or from German patents. Just before the war Germany had supplied to England, Japan, and Russia some of her very successful dirigibles, particularly the smaller Parseval type. The British order had been filled by a company in Bitterfeldt in 1913. From this model the British developed their own small airships, a type of craft which proved especially useful against submarines. The English Parsevals accompanied ships as convoys, readily sighted the hiding submarines and summoned the patrol. No ship accompanied by a Parseval was ever sunk by a submarine.[3] Finally, the Germans helped to arm Italy, and German-made arms were turned on the Central Powers when Italy threw in her lot with the Allies.

Great Britain had sold as widely as Germany, but it was her good fortune that she was faced by no more than four hostile nations, two of which supplied most of their own armaments. Maxim and British arms companies had introduced the modern machine gun to all of Europe, and though Maxim patents had expired, the Maxim principle underlay all the new developments in machine gun construction. The British had established a torpedo factory at Fiume in Austria-Hungary; if the Austrian navy had been more formidable, these British-made torpedoes might have done considerable harm to the Allies. The British had built the Italian fleet in two great yards, Vickers-Terni and Armstrong-Pozzuoli; only Italy's defection from the Triple Alliance prevented the use of this British-built fleet against the Allies. The British, finally, had helped to build and train the Turkish navy, and the disastrous Dardanelles campaign found British ships foundering on British-made mines and crippled by British cannon.

France had also helped to arm her enemies. Italy and Bulgaria were both equipped with the best mobile artillery, the French 75 mm. gun. The fortune of war placed Italy on the side of France and Bulgaria on the side of the Central Powers. French troops in Bulgaria were later repulsed by the French '75's. France's arms traffic worked out still another way. Both Bulgaria and Rumania had bought French armaments. When these two countries met as enemies in the war, both of them fought with French guns.

Austria-Hungary, finally, with its well-known Skoda factory, had helped to re-arm Russia, and the Russians turned these Austrian-made guns against the Austrian armies. Other countries in the Balkans and Belgium also had received some of their arms from the Austrians.

All these complications arose through pre-war sales of arms. After war was declared, the great armament companies were kept busy day and night supplying their own governments and its allies. With millions of men engaged and battle-fronts running for hundreds of miles, the demand for arms and munitions was staggering. Every available man and woman was put to work in war activities, all resources of the various countries were strained to the limit.

It is impossible here even to outline the colossal activity of the armament industry during the war.

The subject has been studied in a series of monographs published by the Carnegie Endowment for International Peace. It is feasible, however, to include some figures on the profits of the great armament makers. The following tables throw a vivid light on this subject. Great as the net gains of most of these companies appear, in reality they were even greater, for increasingly heavy taxation cut into these profits and in every country there have been charges of rigging reports by various tricks of bookkeeping with the express purpose of making net gains appear smaller. Even these doctored figures show how profitable war is for the arms merchants.

Net War Profits of Some European Arms Companies [1]
(add 000)

	Average last 3 Peace Years	Average first 3 War Years
Germany (Marks)		
Krupp	31,625	66,676
Rhein. M. & M. F.	1,448	9,568
Deutsche W. & M. F.	5,467	10,778
Koeln. Pulverf.	4,329	11,921
Austria-Hungary (Kronen)		
Skodawerke	5,607	11,325
Poldihuette	1,360	3,615
Waffenfabrik Steyr	2,749	14,269
Hirtenberger Patronenfabrik	1,709	6,967
France (francs)		
Schneider-Creusot	6,900	10,405
Hotchkiss	—	8,026
Commentry Fourchambault	4,792	6,663
Usines á Gaz	8,776	11,536
Usines Metallurgiques de la Basse Loire	2,836	6,777
Trefiloires du Havre	4,321	8,475

Of the great arms merchants comparatively little is known during the period of the World War. They kept themselves hidden from public view. Two revealing incidents are told about Basil Zaharoff. The first occurred at the outbreak of the war. When Jaurès was assassinated, one of the first acts of the French government was to throw a guard around the house of Sir Basil—an act which was far more than a perfunctory tribute to an important personage.[5] The second is derived from one of the critical periods of the war, when peace sentiment was making headway among many of the war-weary Allies. Then it was that the great arms salesman declared himself in favour of carrying on the war " to the bitter end " (*jusqu'à bout*). His sentiment uttered in the council of the mighty, must have become pretty well known, for Lord Bertie records it in his diary.[6]

Little as the arms merchants and the war contractors attracted public attention, yet they were busy as usual. Numerous incidents have become known which show the vast power of these groups and their " trafficking with the enemy " in the midst of the war.

Take, for example, the story of the Nobel Dynamite Trust. This huge international trust combined German and English companies and it was found expedient at the outbreak of the war to dissolve the trust. This was done and the shares of the company were distributed between German and English shareholders. The strange part of this transaction was that both governments permitted it. Any other company would probably have come under the provisions of the law by which enemy property was confiscated.[7]

The international solidarity of the arms makers is shown in another incident. The great iron mines of the French armament industry are in the Briey basin. This is the veritable home of the *Comité des Forges* and the *Union des Industries Métallurgiques et Minières*. But these mines are geologically so closely related to the German mines in Lorraine that Briey was partly owned by German steel makers. Early in the war the Germans took control of the Briey basin and they immediately began to work the mines for themselves. A German map had fallen into the hands of General Sarrail on which the great mines of the French arms industry were marked with the notation " Protect these." These orders had been carried out, and the Germans took over the properties virtually intact.[8]

One would suppose now that the French would bend all their efforts to destroying the advantage the Germans had gained in the Briey basin. No such thing. The region was never effectively bombarded, either by guns or from the air, though sham attacks took place. And practically all through the war the Germans were extracting valuable ores here for the prosecution of the war.

This fact became known to several people and they tried persistently to bring the matter to the attention of the proper authorities. They approached the French G.H.Q. and told their story, but their documentary evidence was returned to them and no action was taken against the Briey mines. Curiously enough, the officer at G.H.Q. with whom they dealt happened to be an official of the *Comité des Forges*. Finally the matter was taken up by various journals, including the *Correspondant*, the *Echo de Paris*, *l'Œuvre*, and *Paris Midi*. The government replied that it dared not bombard the Briey basin and stop the German exploitation of its mines, because if it did the Germans would certainly bombard the mines operated by the French at Dombasle (Meurthe-et-Moselle), now virtually the chief source of iron ore of the French war forces.

Here then was the situation. By a kind of supernational power the arms makers of France and Germany had brought it about that their sources of supply—and profit—were not disturbed. Had both Briey and Dombasle been destroyed, the war would have ended much sooner; but the hand of destruction which dealt so ruthlessly with human life, with famous cathedrals, libraries, and art treasures, was stayed when it approached the iron mines of the arms merchants.

The press of the armament manufacturers was also busy during the war. Any fool could have told the arms merchants that their interest lay in prolonging the war. The stock market was very sensitive to peace talk. Every time news of peace feelers was published, the stock quotations of the armament manufacturers plunged immediately. In 1917 France was tired of the war. Even the army longed for peace. This natural reaction to years of slaughter and superhuman exertion was promptly labelled "defeatism" and stern measures were taken to suppress it. The pacifists shot by the French during the war far outnumbered the victims of the famous French Reign of Terror of 1793.[9]

This situation alarmed the French armament press. It immediately branded the entire movement for peace as inspired by the Germans and paid for by German money. On the face of it this was ridiculous, because the Germans were far more concerned with decisive victory than with a negotiated peace. But the armament press scored and the desire for peace was henceforth outlawed as treason and pro-Germanism.

THE WORLD WAR—THE WAR IN EUROPE 163

Then the armament press took another step to prolong the war. In both Germany and France there was suddenly an outbreak of almost fantastic plans for annexation. The German plans, fostered by the Pan-Germans, among others, included a great expansion of German territory, the crippling of France, and the creation of various protectorates in Europe to insure German hegemony in Europe and German dominance in world affairs. These German " peace plans " were immediately paralleled by French ones, which demanded, among other things, the left bank of the Rhine, German colonies, and the destruction of the " German menace."

The result of both these press campaigns was to destroy utterly all efforts for peace. Each side professed fear and horror at the other's plans for annexation, and both were stimulated into further desperate efforts to carry on the war.[10]

A most significant and important phase of the World War was the widespread and continuous international trade in war materials, even among enemy powers. Consider the situation concretely. Germany was effectively cut off from the rest of the world by the British fleet. Theoretically, according to international law, Germany could buy from all neutrals whatever she wished, but contraband goods were subject to confiscation and had to run the blockade. France and Great Britain, on the other hand, needed certain materials for which they had hitherto depended on Germany. Would it not be possible in some way to supply to both groups what they needed? The solution of the problem lay with the neutrals round about Germany, especially Switzerland, the Netherlands, and the Scandinavian countries.

At this point a very troublesome feature of modern war entered into the situation, the problem as to what really constitutes war material. Many raw materials invaluable in carrying on war are also very useful in ordinary industrial processes. Many chemicals, for instance, are basic in the production of fertilisers; they are also used to make poison gas. Aluminium may be made into cooking utensils and also into submarines. Electrical power has a thousand peace-time uses; it is likewise necessary in a hundred processes in the arms industry, among others, in extracting nitrates from the air. Cotton is used in textiles and also in gunpowder. This situation paved the way for an extensive and highly important commerce in war materials almost straight through the war. The details of this trade are very interesting.

Rear-Admiral M. W. W. P. Consett was British naval attaché in the Scandinavian countries during the war. After the war he published a highly sensational volume, *The Triumph of Unarmed Forces*, on the events which he had witnessed. Among the matters discussed by Consett are the following:

The various nations in the war soon learned the importance of fat, because glycerine, so vital in the manufacture of explosives, was derived from it. In the British army, for instance, all scraps of meat were carefully collected, and whatever fat remained was used for glycerine. The need for fat produced one of the most astonishing stories of German atrocities—since disproved—that the Germans derived some of their glycerine from the dead bodies of their soldiers. It was relatively easy for the Allies to secure all the fats they needed, because their vessels sailed the seven seas with little interference. But what was Germany to do when her borders were almost hermetically sealed? Germany's situation was so serious that Consett declares that a really air-tight blockade in 1915 and 1916 would have compelled her to sue for peace before the breakdown of Russia and the entry of Rumania into the war.

That this blockade was not enforced was due to the British merchants. When they received orders for vegetable oils, fats, and oil-cake from Denmark, they did not inquire into the ultimate destination of these products, even though the orders far exceeded the normal demand of Denmark. They forwarded similar orders to the British possessions in the Far East where they were filled with the aid of British shipping. For almost three years this trade went on undisturbed, and all through this period the Germans had no difficulty in making their explosives.

Consett tells further of the shipment of copper to Germany from the United States, via Italy, Norway, Sweden, Denmark, and Switzerland. The Germans were badly in need of this metal, as may be seen from the fact that they appealed to their own people to turn in all their copper cooking utensils and from their confiscation of almost everything made of copper in Belgium. Now the British merchants came to their aid. They delivered copper to these various neutrals, whence it was immediately transhipped to Germany. The statistics for Sweden and Norway alone show an export of copper to Germany (in metric tons) as follows: 1913, 1,900; 1914, 4,366; 1915, 3,877; 1916, 2,563; 1917, 202. The vigorous protests of Consett finally put an end to this traffic.

A similar story concerns the supply of nickel to Germany before and during the war. The chief sources of nickel in 1914 were Norway, Canada, and New Caledonia, a French colony. The British rigorously controlled the Canadian nickel supply, refusing to permit sales even to the United States, unless its use in this country was proved. They also made an agreement with the Norwegians contracting for most of their output. Still there was some traffic in nickel between Norway and Germany which barely exceeded 1,000 tons a year.

The situation was different in regard to French nickel from New Caledonia.[11] The French company, Le Nickel, was controlled by the French bankers, the Rothschilds. Its board of directors included two Germans closely associated with Krupp and with the *Metallgesellschaft* of Frankfurt, of which the Kaiser was a large shareholder. Already in 1910 Krupp felt the war-clouds ominously drawing closer, and he began to lay in an adequate supply of nickel. The normal German demand for nickel is about 3,000 tons a year. From 1910 to 1914 Krupp received from New Caledonia about 20,000 tons. More of it was under way when the war broke out.

Now nickel is extremely valuable in the manufacture of various armaments. In Great Britain it was immediately placed on the list of contraband materials, and a steamer flying the Russian flag loaded with nickel destined for Krupp was confiscated. The story was significantly different in France. On October 1, 1914, a Norwegian steamer loaded with 2,500 tons of nickel from New Caledonia, consigned to Krupp, was stopped by the French navy, taken into Brest harbour, and claimed as a prize of war because it carried nickel. Immediately an order came from Paris to release the ship. The local authorities and the prize court were surprised and questioned the decision, but it was at once reaffirmed and the shipment of nickel proceeded to Hamburg. It was not till May, 1915, that nickel was declared contraband by the French and that the export from New Caledonia was controlled. By that time, Le Nickel and the Rothschilds had adjusted their affairs—and Germany was well supplied with nickel for several years.

But not for the entire war period. Uncertain as to the duration of the war, the Germans decided to make sure of their supply of nickel. The commercial submarine, the *Deutschland*, made its sensational and dramatic trip safely to America carrying cargo of much-needed chemicals. It returned with 400 tons of nickel valued at $600,000. This nickel was supplied to the Germans by the American Metal Company, a firm closely allied with the *Metallgesellschaft* of Frankfurt. Where did it come from? Not from Canada, because that source of supply was closely supervised. The only other place of origin was again New Caledonia. Export figures show that there existed a lively trade in nickel with the United States, and apparently some of this French nickel was carried back to Germany by the *Deutschland* and helped to prolong the war.[12]

A similar story concerns the lead of Spanish Penarroya. The Société Minière de Penarroya controls the most important lead mines of the world. The annual production of these Spanish mines is about 150,000 tons, that is, one-eighth of the world total. Since 1883 the French bankers, the Rothschilds, have controlled these mines, but in 1909 the Rothschild Bank entered into an alliance with the *Metallgesellschaft* of Frankfurt, the company in which both the Kaiser and Krupp were heavily interested.

This international partnership was to continue until December 31, 1916. It was very profitable to both sides. The Rothschilds did not reveal that they were allied with the Germans in this company until the fact was about to be disclosed by hostile informers. Thus this company remained under German and French control for about two years of the war. At the outbreak of hostilities 150,000 tons of lead were shipped from these mines to Germany, via Switzerland. Meanwhile France had to wait for its lead. When shipments into France were resumed, the price of lead was raised to such an extent that it more than doubled the figure which the English paid for their lead.

Spanish lead from another mine also was jointly controlled by Germans and French in the Société Française Sopwith. A German, Hermann Schmitz, was on the board of directors. In May, 1915, he was finally relieved of his position, " because under present circumstances he cannot effectively discharge his duties." [13]

This sort of thing was not the prerogative of the British and the French. The Germans also knew their way about. Senator Possehl of Luebeck was a German steel king, whose possessions lay in Sweden, Norway, and Russia. His chief factories were in Fagersta in Sweden. Possehl was a very patriotic German and made a great display of his patriotism. He was proud of the German " boys " and rarely missed an opportunity of seeing them off at the railway station when they left for the front. His great problem was the disposition of his Russian factories. If he continued to operate them, he would be aiding the Russians in the war ; if he should attempt to shut them down for the duration of the war, the Russians would confiscate them. He solved his problem by declaring for " business as usual." That is, his Swedish factories supplied raw materials to his Russian factories, where they were used to produce war materials for the Russians. The German military authorities heard of Possehl's strange patriotism and charged him with treason. He was tried, but the courts accepted his contention that he had merely forestalled the confiscation of his properties by the Russian government. Even the Kaiser rejoiced at this verdict. Meanwhile the man on the street and the German soldier wondered why the products of Fagersta might not have been diverted to the Fatherland or why a loyal German should not prefer to lose his Russian factories rather than supply the enemy.[14]

The rôle of Switzerland during the World War as an intermediary for enemy trade was very important. Switzerland found itself hemmed in by warring nations, all of which were desperately in need of valuable war materials, and ready to pay handsomely for them. The temptation was too great, and before long the little mountain country was the centre of a very profitable international trade. In fairness to the Swiss it must be added that they were threatened with reprisals of various kinds if they failed to comply with the demands of their warring neighbours. Officially there was an embargo on war materials, but smuggling and a loose interpretation of terms encouraged an active traffic.

The details of this business were frequently very curious. Germany needed chemicals for explosives and bauxite for aluminium ; France, deprived in part of her iron resources, was sorely in need of iron and steel. The Swiss engineered this matter for both parties. For a long time during the war the Germans exported an average of 150,000 tons of iron and steel every month into Switzerland. In some months a peak of

250,000 tons was reached. It went in the form of scrap iron and manufactured products, such as railway tracks and barbed wire. The German trade-mark was removed from steel rollers in Switzerland. The German companies carrying on this trade were accused of treason, but their defence was that they were merely fulfilling their part of what was virtually an international bargain by which France and Germany supplied vital materials to one another during the war. Their contention was accepted by the court and they were found not guilty.[15]

The French also lived up to their part of the bargain. A great fuss was made about the *affaire des carbures* when it became known in 1917. It happened in November, 1914. The Lonza Company was a Swiss industrial firm, owned by Germans, which had one of those international boards of directors so typical of the armament manufacturers. It was made up of French, Italian, German, and Austrian nationals. Under the pretext of paying a debt, the French Société Commerciale des Carbures delivered to the Lonza Company in Switzerland 300 tons of carbide-cyanamide, a chemical which is readily converted into saltpetre, which in turn is an essential of gunpowder. The French company did owe money to Lonza, but the value of the chemicals delivered was very much greater than the debt.[16]

When this story became known in 1917, there was great excitement in some quarters. A trial was ordered for the great industrialists who were charged with treason. Immediately a great " hush " fell over the entire affair. Hardly a word concerning it appeared in the press. Only the radical papers knew that a scandal had broken. The accused protested that they had merely paid a commercial debt and that they had believed the chemicals were to be used for—fertiliser. Of course, this was possible. At that point mysterious influences began to make themselves felt in the trial, supposedly set in motion by Poincaré, a close friend of the great industrialists. The entire prosecution had been carried on reluctantly and half-heartedly and the final acquittal surprised nobody.

French bauxite also entered Switzerland freely during the war, was there manufactured into aluminium, and then shipped into Germany for the construction of submarines. The Swiss delivered about 20,000 tons of aluminium annually to Germany and 200 tons to the Allies. As to saltpetre, it is reported that the Swiss supplied annually to Germany enough for 56 billion rifle shots or 147,000,000 grenades. In 1917 alone Germany produced with the help of the Swiss 300,000 tons of saltpetre. Before the war, the *world* production had been 214,000 tons a year.

The Swiss were not only intermediaries between the warring nations; they also supplied to both sides vast amounts of electrical power, useful especially in the new process of extracting nitrates from the air. The lack of coal during the war compelled the Swiss to develop their hydro-electric resources. All along their frontier, facing Germany, France, and Italy, great power houses sprang into being, using the vast water power of the country. It was an easy matter to transmit this current to the three neighbouring countries. The export of electrical power reached enormous proportions: 382,000 h.p. to Germany and 76,500 h.p. to the Allies.

The profits of this war traffic in iron, bauxite, chemicals, and electric power were colossal. Swiss statistics for the period are utterly unreliable; in some cases they are only 25 per cent. correct.[17] Swiss aid to both belligerents, given under tremendous pressure, undoubtedly did much to prolong the war.

Various other stories are told about the international commerce of the belligerents during the war. The German Zeiss factory was famous for its lenses and optical instruments which were in demand throughout the world. Armies and navies everywhere used Zeiss instruments for gun sighters and firing directors. The British needed the Zeiss products during the war and they managed to get them. Stories differ as to how they did it. One account declares that they reached England via Holland.[18] Another has it that the British got hold of some Zeiss workmen and " persuaded " them to produce these instruments in the Vickers factory in England.[19] Whatever the method employed, there seems to be no doubt that the British fought the battle of the Skagerrack with Zeiss instruments acquired after the beginning of the war.

The Germans came to grief elsewhere through materials manufactured by their own countrymen. In the terrific fighting around Verdun, Fort Douaumont was repeatedly a bone of contention. It changed hands several times. In one of the attacks, the Germans ran into some barbed-wire entanglements which only two months previously had been shipped into Switzerland by a German factory, the Magdeburger Draht-und-Kabelwerke.[20]

The most important matter relating to the World War was the colossal demand for arms and munitions and the vastly profitable business of the arms makers. This fact will stand out in even sharper relief when the rôle of the United States in the war is considered.

CHAPTER XIII

THE WORLD WAR—ENTER OLD GLORY

> As a result of the war, a million new springs of wealth will be developed.—FRANK A. VANDERLIP.
>
> A corporation cannot live on patriotism. Our stockholders must have dividends.—GEORGE D. BALDWIN.

WHEN the World War began in 1914, the President of the United States advised his fellow countrymen to remain neutral even in thought.[1] When the armistice was signed in 1918, there were 21,000 new American millionaires, Du Pont stock had gone from $20 to $1,000 a share, and J. P. Morgan was said to have made more money in two years than the elder Morgan made in all his life.

At the outset, Europe was convinced that the war would not last long and that it would be able to supply its own ammunition for the duration of the conflict. For almost a year Europe did manage to fill most of its needs from its reserves. When it became evident, however, that a long war was probable, new sources of supply were eagerly sought.

The one great power which had remained neutral was the United States. Theoretically, according to international law and the Hague Convention of 1907, both sides in the conflict were permitted to buy from a neutral, and the neutral was privileged to sell. It was not a new situation. In many wars the neutrals had sold to both sides.

Now, however, a new factor entered the picture. Germany was blockaded, at least in theory, and the Allies would not permit neutral commerce to pass the blockade. The list of contraband articles was extended until an absolute blockade existed, and, despite the irritation of the United States, the Allies persisted in this policy. In reality, therefore, the United States was arming and supplying only the Allies.

There was no great and important buying of war materials in the United States by the Allies until the second half of 1915. Then the traffic began in earnest. The Allies established a central purchasing bureau in the States which soon spent on the average of $10,000,000 a day. Between August, 1914, and February, 1917, more than $10,500,000,000 worth of goods were shipped out of America.[2]

Munitions played a prominent part in this traffic. In 1914, exports amounted to $40,000,000; in 1915, they totalled $330,000,000, and in 1916 they piled up to $1,290,000,000. From 1914 to 1918 the Allies bought $4,000,000,000 worth of munitions in the United States. But munitions were by no means the only item of commerce. In a long list of exports, the following are included: Iron and steel, explosives, cotton and cotton manufactures, wheat, copper, brass, leather, chemicals, firearms, automobiles, wheat flour, metal-working machinery, corn, horses, wire manufactures, shoes, railway cars, mules, barley, wool manufactures, tyres, aeroplanes, motor-cycles, etc.[3]

The war year 1916 was by far the most prosperous in the entire history of American industry and finance. The enormous volume of foreign trade created something like a shortage at home, and as a result domestic prices began to skyrocket. The golden harvest reaped from American pocket-books far outweighed the profits from the traffic with the Allies.[4]

There was only one cloud on the horizon: the war might end. Every time there was talk of peace, munitions stocks went down by 5 to 40 per cent. War had brought prosperity, peace threatened to bring calamity. Gradually other worries began to trouble American industry and finance. Suppose the Germans won—what then? No, that could never happen. We have the word of A. D. Noyes, financial editor of the New York *Times*, that Wall Street picked the Allies to win at the very start and never wavered in this firm belief.[5]

Still, one could never tell. The Germans were making an astonishing stand and in many ways they had a decided military advantage. Suppose the war should end in a stalemate, suppose a " peace without victory " should be concluded? Thoughts like that made Wall Street shudder. American finance had placed its bet on the Allied horse, and if that should fail to reach the post first, the stakes were so enormous that none dared even think of what might happen.

The terrible years wore on. The seas were crowded with vessels rushing supplies of all kinds to the Allies. Then another nightmare began to trouble Wall Street. How were the Allies to pay for these goods? The credit of the Allies was virtually exhausted. The United States had grown from a debtor nation to one of the greatest creditors of the world. At the beginning of 1917 the Allies had little more to offer than their IOU's. Some of the vast loans already made had virtually been unsecured and the announcement was actually made that henceforth Allied loans would have to be wholly unsecured. No wonder Wall Street was worrying. All the beautifully embossed notes which it held might turn out to be just so many " scraps of paper." The year 1916 had taken American business and finance to the dizziest peaks. Would 1917 find them shattered and broken at the bottom of the abyss ?

But this hour of darkness was also the beginning of the dawn. On April 6, 1917, the United States entered the conflict, and the heart-beats of the war traffickers became normal again. It is not contended here that the United States fought in the World War solely because of its armament makers and their financiers. There were many other factors in the situation. Yet the question of Hamilton Fish, Jr., is more pertinent than is generally admitted : " Is it not a fact that the World War was started by the shipment of munitions ? . . . Was not the cause of the war our continued shipping of munitions abroad ? "[6] American commitments with the Allies were so enormous that only the entry into the war saved the U.S.A. from a major economic collapse.

In 1917, on the floor of Congress it was charged that as early as March, 1915, the Morgan interests had organised and financed a huge propaganda machine, including 12 influential publishers and 197 newspapers, for the purpose of " persuading " the American people to join the Allies. Furthermore, the French historian and politician, Gabriel Hanotaux, tells in his history of the war that in 1914 he and a member of the Morgan firm had drawn up plans for a great war-scare campaign in the United States in order to embroil the country in war. He adds that France was ready for peace in 1914, but that the Morgan partner dissuaded French leaders from talking peace at that time.[7]

When war was actually in the offing, the war

traffickers rejoiced. President Wilson had just made his war address to Congress and Wall Street replied. "It was exactly right," said Judge Gary of the Steel Trust. "It was 100 per cent. American," said Frank Vanderlip of the National City Bank. "The speech breathes the true spirit of the American people," said Martin Carey of the Standard Oil Company. "The President's address was magnificent," said James Wallace, head of the Guaranty Trust Company.

Wait a few days for the break in diplomatic relations. Hardly had the news reached Wall Street, when, according to the New York *Times*, "Wall Street was bright with the Stars and Stripes floating from banks and brokerage houses. Figuratively, the street gave a concerted sigh of relief." On the Produce Exchange 300 brokers sang *The Star-Spangled Banner*. And stocks went up immediately.

The United States was in the war from April 7, 1917, to November 11, 1918. During this period it spent $22,625,252,843 and advanced another $9,455,014,125 to the Allies. Just as important for Wall Street was the absolute guarantee of Allied credit by the American government. All the reckless financing of the war years was now saved and, above all, the United States had now joined the Allies in placing war orders.

It is really impossible to get an adequate picture of what $22,000,000,000 means. It required two heavy volumes for the Director of Munitions merely to outline the colossal buying of the American government in 1917 and 1918. Spending like this cannot be paid for by a single generation. Nor were these government orders the only factors in the situation. To this $22,000,000,000 must be added the rise in prices of all goods and commodities. Wheat reached $3.25, most of which went to others than the farmer, who was paid only $1.30 a bushel for that crop. Cotton touched the highest point in forty-five years. It was the same story with everything that was sold throughout the country.

Exactly what the profits of the American arms merchants and their allies and financiers were in the war will never be accurately known. They realised very quickly that it would never do to let even the approximate amounts of their net gains be known. The Federal Trade Commission characterised the business methods of these groups as " inordinate greed and barefaced fraud." It " exposed many tricks of bookkeeping by the great corporations . . . Costs were fictitiously enhanced by account juggling. Officers' salaries were increased. The item of depreciation was padded. Interest on investment was included in cost. Fictitious valuations of raw materials were resorted to. Inventories were manipulated."

Despite all this, the profits reported were simply colossal. Du Pont paid a dividend of 100 per cent. on its common stock in 1916. The earnings of the United States Steel Corporation for 1917 exceeded by many millions the face value of its common stock, which was largely water. In 1916 this same company reported earnings greater by $70,000,000 than the combined earnings of 1911, 1912, and 1913. Bethlehem Steel paid a stock dividend of 200 per cent. in 1917. U.S. Treasury figures show that during the war period 69,000 men made more than $3,000,000,000 over and above their normal income.

Almost immediately the cry of profiteering went up. The Federal Trade Commission was put to work to

THE WORLD WAR—ENTER OLD GLORY 179

investigate, but the minute it began to reveal damaging facts it was called off. It did publish a 20-page report which suggests what a rich mine this was for an able and fearless investigator to work, but it never even scratched the surface.[8] Later some Senate committees went to work, but they, too, proved abortive. The technique of "whitewashing" consisted in asking the Attorney-General to take over the investigation and to make a report.

In spite of all, it would be possible to fill scores of pages with statistics showing the enormous profits of the arms merchants, the war contractors, and the bankers in the war years. The following table of net profits is suggestive.

Net War Profits of the U.S. Armament Industry [9]

(figures in dollars—add 000)

Company	Average last four Peace Years	Average four War Years
U.S. Steel	105,331	239,653
Du Pont	6,092	58,076
Bethlehem Steel	6,840	49,427
Anaconda Copper	10,649	34,549
Utah Copper	5,776	21,622
American Smelting and Refining Co.	11,566	18,602
Republic Iron and Steel Co.	4,177	17,548
International Mercantile Marine	6,690	14,229
Atlas Powder Co.	485	2,374
American and British Manufacturing	172	325
Canadian Car and Foundry	1,335	2,201
Crocker Wheeler Co.	206	666
Hercules Powder Co.	1,271	7,430
Niles-Bement Pond	656	6,146
Scovill Mfg. Co.	655	7,678
General Motors	6,954	21,700

So much for the picture as a whole. Of the individual arms companies and their activities during the war period, a number of significant incidents can be told. Du Pont manufactured 40 per cent. of the ammunition used by the Allies during the war, and it continued to be the chief source of supply for military explosives for the United States government.[10] Its employees increased from 5,000 to 100,000.[11] In 1914 it produced 2,265,000 pounds of powder; in 1915 contracts from the Allies began to appear and the company produced 105,000,000 pounds of powder; this figure rose to 287,000,000 in 1916; and when the United States entered the war, in 1917, production jumped to 387,000,000 pounds for that year and 399,000,000 pounds for 1918. A few years later a Congressional committee showed that the government had paid about 49 cents a pound for powder while the cost of production was estimated at 36 cents. No wonder Du Pont stock increased 5,000 per cent. in the war period.[12]

The war also brought a red-letter day to Du Pont, such as few companies ever see. It had been filling Russian orders and one day there came to the company a cheque. They looked at it and smiled. It was made out for $60,000,000, one of the largest cheques ever written.[13]

Du Pont did very well during the war. Winchester Repeating Arms Company, manufacturers of rifles, bayonets, and ammunition, could hardly complain of bad business. In its 1921 Catalogue, the company reports on its war work.[14] During the war period it sold almost 2,000,000,000 separate units made up of guns, rifles, bayonets, shells, and cartridges.

> " In addition, Winchester Arms produced large quantities of spare parts and accessories, many millions of shot shells and small calibre rifle cartridges and many guns of sporting models for the use of the Home Guards

and in training camps, gallery practice, and protection of life and property all over the country.

" Not a single lot of Winchester products was rejected by the United States government during the World War. Including cartridges made for foreign governments before the United States entered the war, there was an uninterrupted flow of 700,000,000 cartridges produced without rejection of a lot."

The company's own estimate of its war work is then added :

" This bare summary of the war activity of the Winchester Repeating Arms Company is given here simply to show cause why we believe we have kept the faith in time of stress and as a merited acknowledgment of the patriotic services rendered to the country and to us by our nearly 22,000 employees during the war period."

There is no mention of war profits or of the rise of Winchester stock.

The poison gas industry also prospered in the United States during the war. Since poison gas had been introduced into the war, the Americans manufactured it also. Before the war ended, American chemists had evolved 63 different kinds of poison gas and eight more were ready to be put to use. The arsenal at Edgewood, Md., and its tributaries manufactured 810 tons of poison gas every week. This was a larger output than that of any other nation. France, for instance, showed a weekly production of only 385 tons, Great Britain produced 410 tons, while Germany lagged far behind with only 210 tons a week.

For the Americans this 810 tons was really only a beginning. Just before the war ended they were ready to increase production to 3,000 tons a week. The government had appropriated $100,000,000 for chemical warfare and 48,000 men were to be employed in this undertaking. But before the world could be given this convincing demonstration of American efficiency, the armistice was signed.[15]

An exciting story with many ramifications, nationally and internationally, is that of the advertisement which the Cleveland Automatic Machine Company carried in the *American Machinist* of May 6, 1915. This company had a shrapnel-making machine which it was anxious to sell. The death-dealing qualities of the shrapnel manufactured by this machine apparently surpassed those of any other, for it was a poison gas shrapnel which would cause death within four hours "in terrible agony." The advertisement which was published in the *American Machinist* read as follows:

"The material is high in tensile strength and VERY SPECIAL and has a tendency to fracture into small pieces upon the explosion of the shell. The timing of the fuse for this shell is similar to the shrapnel shell, but it differs in that two explosive acids are used to explode the shell in the large cavity. The combination of these two acids causes a terrific explosion, having more power than anything of its kind yet used. Fragments become coated with the acids in exploding and wounds caused by them mean death in terrible agony within four hours if not attended to immediately.

"From what we are able to learn of conditions in the trenches, it is not possible to get medical assistance to anyone in time to prevent fatal results. It is necessary to cauterise the wound immediately, if in the body or head, or to amputate if in the limbs, as there seems to be no antidote that will counteract the poison.

"It can be seen from this that this shell is more effective than the regular shrapnel, since the wounds caused by shrapnel balls and fragments in the muscle are not as dangerous, as they have no poisonous element making prompt attention necessary."

This advertisement attracted immediate attention.

It was roundly denounced in many circles and the *American Machinist* was severely criticised for publishing it. Among those who censured the journal was the Secretary of Commerce, Redfield.[16]

This advertisement was promptly forwarded to Germany and became widely known there. A copy of it was placed on the desk of every member of the Reichstag and a bitter discussion ensued. The American Ambassador in Berlin, Mr. Gerard, reported the incident to the State Department and added his own surmise that the advertisement was a clumsy forgery designed for anti-American propaganda. But the advertisement was authentic enough, even though it furnished excellent material to German agitators.

When all this stir was made about this advertisement, the Cleveland Automatic Machine Company finally got round to "explaining." It was all a mistake, a misunderstanding. The company had sent to the journal, along with its copy for the advertisement, an article on shrapnel machines, a topic which then frequently appeared in the *American Machinist*. Part of the article had through some error been included in the advertisement and this unfortunate substitution had caused all the uproar. The New York *Times* and various other journals took up the case and valiantly defended the advertiser and the journal with a dozen evasive arguments. That all of these found little credence is readily understood, particularly since the responsible officials in Washington rebuked the journal for publishing the advertisement.

A more successful use of the press was that of the Bethlehem Steel Company. This company was one of the Big Three which had for years supplied armour plate to the U.S. navy. There had long been dissatisfaction with the price charged for armour plate. Perhaps the high price was partly the government's own fault. For under the "Father of the American navy," Theodore Roosevelt, a deliberate policy of virtual subsidising had been followed in regard to armour plate. For some years the Midvale Steel and Ordnance Company had underbid its competitors in this field, but it had not been able to get the government contracts until its prices were identical with those of the other armour plate manufacturers. Midvale finally "learned the ropes" and discontinued underbidding its competitors. After that it shared armour plate orders with Carnegie Steel and Bethlehem Steel. The whole procedure appears to have been an attempt by the government to aid and foster a native armour plate industry in the country.[17]

The belief that the government was being heavily overcharged grew to such proportions that Congress decided to build a government armour plant. It appointed a committee to investigate the costs and it proposed to spend $11,000,000 to circumvent the "armour plate ring."

Consternation reigned among the armour plate makers. What could they do? If the government built its own plant, they would lose much of their business, and on top of that they would probably have to reduce their prices. They protested in Washington, but Congress persisted in its undertaking. Then Bethlehem Steel remembered the power of the press. It inserted paid advertisements in 3,257 newspapers setting forth the "folly" of the government's plans. These advertisements were followed up by 26 bulletins spread in millions of copies throughout the country.

Bethlehem declared that the action contemplated by

Congress interfered with business. It was pure waste, because armour plants already existed in the country. It was very expensive, because the government could never produce as well and as economically as private manufacturers. Finally, it was a threat to national security, because the government could never expect to keep informed on the latest developments in the field, and thus the American navy would be built of inferior materials.

The press was not slow to see the point. Before long, Bethlehem Steel was able to quote a long series of editorial comments from all parts of the country which all agreed that the government's plans for an armour plant were very bad and an outrageous waste of the people's money.[18]

In its press campaign Bethlehem Steel also undertook to answer the charge of intriguing and profiteering. Since 1887 it had supplied to the government 95,072 tons of armour plate at an average price of $432.62 a ton; that is, its government business had amounted to about $42,000,000. During that same period it had sold 5,331 tons of armour plate to other countries, about two-thirds at higher prices than in the United States, and about one-third at lower prices. Now it was ready to furnish armour plate to the government at the lowest prices it had ever asked. Why should the Congress waste the people's money and build a government armour plant?

Thus it went on in endless variation, citing the press, denying lobbying activities, emphasising its patriotism. Only two things remain to be added: The government armour plant was never built and, when naval contracts were awarded in 1916, the Bethlehem Shipbuilding Company, a subsidiary of the Bethlehem Steel

Corporation, received orders for 85 destroyers at a cost of $134,000,000.[19]

Remington Arms was also very busy during the war. Its great expansion at this time is described by an enthusiastic chronicler:

> "Early in 1914, the two plants at Ilion and Bridgeport employed about 3,700 workers in peace-time operations. Then demands came rushing in from England, France, Russia, and Servia for rifles, small arms, ammunition, bayonets and large shells such as the famous French 'seventy-fives.' Existing plants were enlarged with emergency buildings, a huge new armoury added at Bridgeport for Russian rifle production, a 12-story factory erected at Hoboken, New Jersey, for making Russian cartridges and bullets, and a plant at Swanton, Vermont, was taken over for the manufacture of French rifle cartridges."[20]

When the United States entered the war, "figures for firearms soared from thousands to millions; for ammunition from millions to billions. The plants turned out amazing quantities of Browning machine-guns, Model 1917 Service Rifles, ·45 calibre automatic pistols, bayonets, and trench warfare materials."[21] At the height of war activities the Remington factories were producing in half a day materials which would have required four months' work in peace time.

A curious sidelight on the international activities of the American arms industry is shed by the story of the Enfield rifles. Remington Arms had received orders from the British for a huge consignment of Enfield rifles; it delivered 700,000 of these to the British during the war. Now the Enfield rifle was by no means the best rifle known in the war period. The American Springfield, which had been evolved after much experimentation, was considered a much better weapon.

THE WORLD WAR—ENTER OLD GLORY 187

The British Enfield was in fact a sort of transition rifle; that is, the British themselves in 1914 were not satisfied with it and were seeking to displace it. They retained it only because their experimental work with a new rifle had not yet been completed.

When Remington (and Winchester) received the British orders for Enfields, they found it necessary to spend some months in reorganising their workshops, adjusting their machinery and introducing new machines. When the United States entered the war, it tried to place huge orders for its own Springfield rifle with these great small-arms factories. Very shortly it was discovered that so much time would be lost in again reorganising the shops and readjusting the machinery that months would pass before the government would receive its Springfields. The only way out was for the American forces to accept the inferior British Enfield rifle which the American factories were prepared to manufacture on short notice. This was done and American soldiers fought in the World War with both the Springfield and the Enfield rifles. This incident was used by a Congressional committee to refute the arguments of the arms makers that foreign orders "kept them in practice" for an American emergency. In this case, foreign orders crippled the equipment of the American army.[22]

Another arms company which prospered in the war was the United States Cartridge Company. It never did better business than during these war years. To supply cartridges to the Allies, a new auxiliary plant was built at South Lowell, and when the United States entered the war, the huge Bigelow carpet plant in the heart of Lowell, which had been idle for some years, was quickly converted into an up-to-date cartridge factory. The personnel grew from 1,200 in 1914 to 15,000, and the rate of production was speeded up enormously. From 1915 to 1919 the company filled cartridge orders for the British, the Russian, the Dutch, the Italian, the French and the United States governments. Its total output reached the remarkable figure of 2,262,671,000 units in war material.[23]

Over against all these "successes" of the arms makers and the war contractors must be placed a certain number of dismal failures. They are summarised in a letter of President Harding, dated August 29, 1921. The President wrote in part:

> "Our government . . . expended between five and six billion dollars for the manufacture of aircraft, artillery, and artillery ammunition. To show for this expenditure, it has been officially testified that less than 200 American-made aeroplanes or 200 American-made cannon ever went into action on the fighting front of the war, while not more than one per cent. of the ammunition expended by American artillery was, according to the same testimony, of American manufacture. Approximately $3,500,000,000 has been poured out under the direction of the Shipping Board, yet I have from the War Department the curious bit of information that only one vessel built by the Shipping Board ever carried any American troops to fight in Europe. This was a cargo boat, the *Liberty*, which, according to War Department records, in October, 1917, carried approximately fifty soldiers to Europe." [24]

The great failures were particularly in artillery, in aircraft, and in shipping. This is readily understood. The American arms industry has always been outstanding for its small arms and ammunition. In these it excelled in the war. It was also efficient in producing small mobile artillery and it turned out successfully large orders for the French '75's. Heavy artillery had never been its forte and it could rely on the Allies for these materials, meanwhile using all available shipping for the transport of troops.

As for aircraft, the explanation of failure lies with inexperience, bad judgment, and possibly graft. The aeroplane was still in its infancy and, while the Allies had made rapid progress, the Americans continued to make the crude De Haviland 4's, which the fliers called "flaming coffins," because they caused battle fatalities three times as great as those of other planes. Over a billion dollars were expended on aviation up to June 30, 1919, yet not one American-built pursuit or combat plane or one American-built bombing plane reached the front.[25] As for shipping, the cause for failure was largely the lack of time. Americans are fair enough shipbuilders, but the rush of events was so rapid that the Shipping Board only began to deliver when the war was over.

Many other similar matters were examined in detail by the Graham Committee on War Expenditures some years after the peace conference. These voluminous reports are a veritable mine of important information as to the conduct of the war. Of one thing there can be no doubt: it was profitable for the arms makers.

CHAPTER XIV

PLUS ÇA CHANGE—

> Articles against peace are written with pens made of the same steel as cannon and shells.—ARISTIDE BRIAND.

"THE more it changes, the more it's the same old thing," say the French, and the French ought to know. They are the countrymen of the cynical Clemenceau, the facile Tardieu, and the scheming Poincaré. No matter what new things the American Moses, with his "new decalogue," the Fourteen Points, might insist upon at the peace conference, the makers and interpreters of the peace treaty would see to it that nothing was changed fundamentally. In the name of self-determination of peoples the map of Europe and the Near East was carved up into a new geographic pattern with many small new states. This new arrangement frequently served to emphasise the old system of rival alliances, secret diplomacy, irredenta, etc. "Mandates" were established as a move against the old colonialism, but before long every nation looked upon its "mandates" as national possessions or protectorates. The "reparations system" proved even worse and more disturbing internationally than the old practice of military plunder and indemnities. Peace treaties were written which contained a dozen causes for friction, dispute, and war. And finally a League of Nations was established as a herald of a new era in world affairs, but all too often this body proved to be little more than a buttress for the peace treaties.

If a deliberate attempt had been made to create a situation in which the arms merchants could flourish, nothing better could have been devised. After the "war to end all war" was concluded, Schneider, Vickers, Skoda, and even the crestfallen Krupp were literally "at it" again.

Indeed the peace conference was still in session when a war between the Greeks and the Turks broke out. A ruthless Mohammedan massacre of Christians was enough to set going the ambition of Venizelos and his soldiers. The English supported the Greeks; and Vickers arms, through the kind offices of Sir Basil Zaharoff, were amply supplied to the Hellenes as they advanced into Asia Minor. But the French were also interested in the Levant and they did not restrain Schneider from arming the Turks.

And so immediately in this "new world" there is the old and familiar phenomenon of two friendly, in fact allied, states, supporting respectively two other warring countries. The World War was over, but the arms factories were still geared up for mass production and they were grateful for any outlet for their wares. The Greeks, whether through bad generalship or because of the inferiority of Vickers products, were put to flight by the Turks and were soon streaming back over Anatolia in great disorder. An American correspondent told the tale :

> "First I saw the retreat of the Greeks. They left behind artillery and machine-guns, all of which bore the marks of the English firm of Vickers. Then I witnessed the triumphant entry of the Turks into Smyrna. They brought with them magnificent guns made by Creusot.

On that day I understood what the *Entente Cordiale* meant."[1]

The word "mandate" also appeared almost at once virtually synonymous with war and rebellion. The French were made "guardians" of Syria; but the turbulent Druses and Emir Feisal contested their claim, and with no little bitterness, for the British had promised this territory to the Emir. Schneider, of course, supplied the arms and ammunition with which General Sarrail bombarded Damascus and the "street called straight." As for the Druses' equipment, it was surprisingly up to date for desert tribesmen, and it was rumoured that it all came from Birmingham and Leeds. Yet Downing Street, just as in the case of Anatolia, was at peace with the Quai d'Orsay.[2]

A short time later it looked as if the Quai d'Orsay was at war with itself. Down in Morocco the French had something more authoritative than a mandate, a prosperous colony. Their possession of this was suddenly challenged by that valiant sheik of North Africa's wild mountains, the hero of all the scattered Mohammedan tribes, Abdel Krim. This leader of the Rif went on the war path and talked ambitiously of a Rif republic. His first encounters were with the Spaniards whose possessions included part of the Rif. Huge Spanish armies were routed and the Rif republic was beginning to be more than a fantastic dream. Now the French must be driven out also. So formidable was the threat of this mountain chieftain that the French found it necessary to send to Africa one of their best soldiers, Marshal Lyautey, with something like 158,000 men. The Rif uprising was finally put down and Abdel Krim was banished from his native mountains.

FLASH AND THUNDER *[Copyright Acme*
A super-dreadnought costs £6,000,000 to £7,000,000. Its annual upkeep is about £400,000. A single salvo, as pictured, sometimes costs £5,000

THE VIOLET CROSS
Civilians of Paris prepare for gas raids—members of new Violet Cross organisation for universal use of gas masks

[*Copyright "Wide World"*]

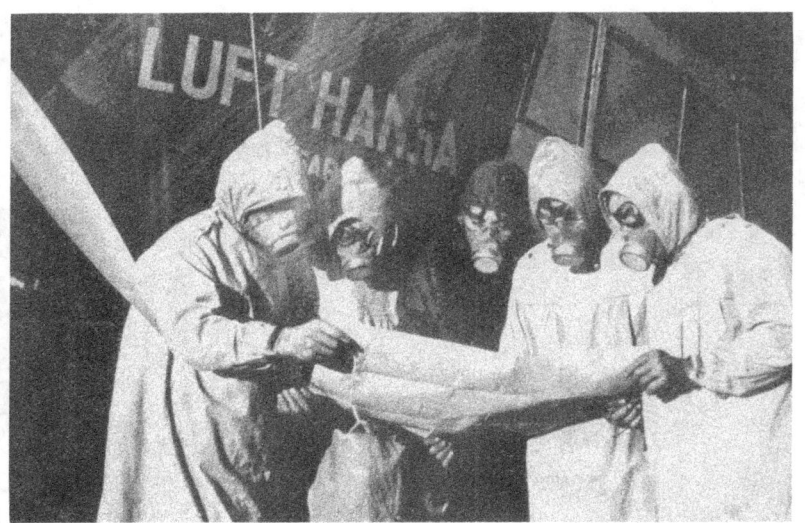

HARPIES—NEW STYLE [Copyright "Wide World"
German pilots before attack, study area to be gassed

JOLLY TARS—NEW STYLE [Copyright "Wide World"
British sailors receive instruction at Royal Navy Anti-Gas School

MORE WORK FOR VICKERS
British submarine, with one of the few submersible seaplane hangars

[Copyright "Wide World"]

MORE WORK FOR BETHLEHEM
Big guns of U.S. cruiser span a seaplane and its catapult

[Copyright Acme]

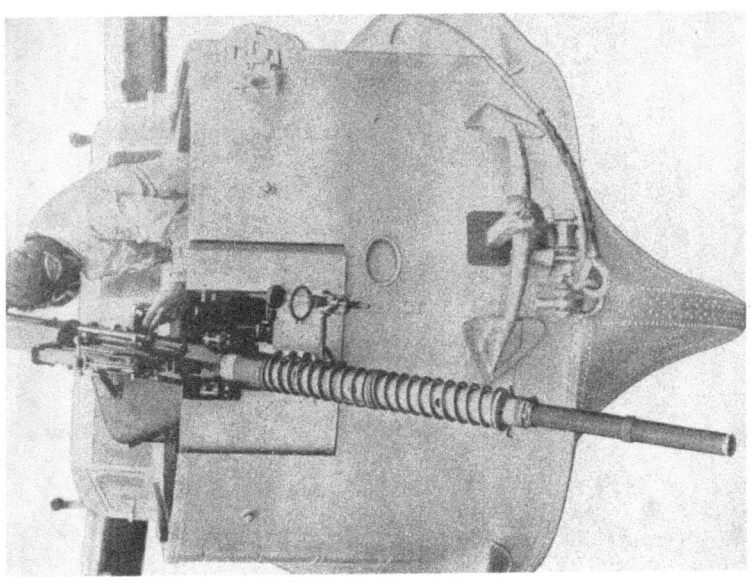

"—AND THERE RAINED A GHASTLY DEW—"
New quick-firing gun for British seaplane
[Copyright "Wide World"]

Soviet anti-aircraft gun
[Copyright International]

AMPHIBIAN
Vickers tank with speed of 40 miles an hour and 6 knots enters and leaves water without any preliminary adjustment

HEIL SCHNEIDER!
160,000 Nazi Troopers—armed? Hitler received funds from directors of Skoda, a subsidiary of Schneider-Creusot

[Copyright "Wide World"]

THE INTERNATIONAL AT WORK
Division of Bofors, the Swedish firm in which Krupp has an interest

Plus Ça Change— 193

What surprised all observers and participants in this colonial war was the modern equipment displayed by the Rifians. Even at the final surrender these tribesmen were found in possession of 135 cannon, 240 machine-guns, and more than 40,000 rifles.[3] Where did these come from? Some of them were captured from the Spaniards, but that was not the only source of supply. It was shown later that the corruption in the Spanish army was so great that the Spaniards had even sold their own arms to the Rif. More important than either of these sources was widespread gun-running. There are many rumours as to the origin of these contraband arms and the nationality of the gun-runners. It seems well established that French soldiers captured from the Rifians machine-guns, ammunition, and even aeroplanes which were obviously of French manufacture, but a discreet silence in official and journalistic quarters stifled comment on this discovery.[4]

These were great days for French politics and the French armament industry. French influence spread all over Central and Eastern Europe and Creusot waxed strong and hearty together. No longer had M. Schneider to suffer the humiliating rebuffs that were his lot during the Putiloff affair. The adept chicanery that was his salvation in that affair was now employed not in defence but in attack. France rose in power; and nothing is more evident than that cannon follow the flag.

Schneider had an old acquaintanceship with the famous Skoda works in Bohemia. After the war, the Skoda business languished and its financial structure became endangered. In 1920 Schneider came to the rescue, through the intermediary of a holding company,

L'Union Européenne, which was the creature of Schneider's bank, L'Union Parisienne. Schneider became one of the " principal participators," as he phrased it, in Skoda, and he was moved to boast that after completely modernising her industrial processes he enabled Skoda to attain " an extremely rapid cadence." [5]

This cadence became so rapid that within a few years Skoda got control of the motor industry—Laurin-Klement—of Masaryk's republic, the cable company of Kablo, the aviation concern known as Avia, the power plants of Brno-Donat, and the road construction firm Konstruktiva, and then it overflowed the frontiers of Czechoslovakia. Skoda's subsidiary in Poland is the arms firm Polskie Zaklady. In Rumania it had another munitions factory, the Ploesti, and in Yugoslavia Skoda reorganised the railroads and participated in the power company of the Central Electric. These were the countries of the Little Entente and Poland, but Skoda did not stop within these limits. It crossed the frontier of political alliances and entered Hungary and became interested financially in the Kreditanstalt of Budapest.[6]

The scandal growing out of the activities of Skoda's agent Seletzky (or Zelevski) in Rumania has been noted. Equally devious were Schneider's dealings in Hungary, a potential enemy of France. The Treaty of Trianon forbade Hungary to arm, yet Schneider had loaned money to Hungary. When the loan fell due, the Magyars could not pay. But the French government could, and so a French official loan was arranged for Hungary. The loan was just enough to cover the Schneider debt, and it was transmitted to Hungary not by the regular channels of the Bank of France but by

Schneider's bank, the Union Parisienne. This was revealed in the Chamber of Deputies by Paul Faure, Socialist deputy from Creusot, at the same time as it became known that Hungary had been able to rearm so well that it could put 300,000 troops in the field at short notice.[7]

So complex has this manipulation of loans and political alliances behind the scenes become, that the comment of a French journalist, Charles Reber, is rather illuminating. "Schneider and his Skoda, a state within a state, first of all have heavily profited from the conflict between Hungary and the Little Entente, by opposing the Beneš plan for a Danubian federation. At that time it was a question of supplying armaments to these small nations. Next, when the crisis appeared, it was the same Schneider and his Skoda which, always in the shadow of Tardieu and Flandin, extorted hundreds of millions from the states in which they operated, shutting off credits in Paris from those which resisted, so that finally, finding it impossible to thaw out their frozen credits, a revised Beneš plan was conceived, now called the Tardieu plan, which Schneider had long before projected."[8]

Schneider's and Skoda's rôle in aiding Hitler and in rearming Germany are considered elsewhere. From the arms makers' point of view these were good investments. French friendship with Japan, however, has caused some surprise. The link is not far to seek. On the board of the Franco-Japanese bank is M. Saint Sauveur, a relative of M. Schneider, and the president of this bank at one time was Charles Dumont, once Minister of the Navy. Schneider's factories have been turning out huge masses of war material for Japan, and perhaps for China also. Pierre Cot, a French journalist, suggests that there was more to these Japanese orders than just the Japanese need for arms and munitions. " Japan has no need for the material ordered, but she needs the influence of the house of Schneider." [9] Another French journalist points the answer to Cot's statement when he asks whether there is nothing disturbing about the sympathy that has been aroused by certain French newspapers in behalf of Japanese aggression.[10]

Indeed there is a connection which explains the extravagant sympathy by French editorial writers for the imperialist ventures of Japan. As previously noted, the leading organs of Paris are controlled by M. Schneider. *Le Matin*, *Le Temps*, and *Le Journal des Débats* all take their cue from the French arms maker. Thus orders from Japan to Schneider also insure a favourable press in Paris for the Manchurian expedition of the Japanese.

More important than all this, however, to the French arms merchants, loomed the whole question of disarmament. Obviously it was a menace which must be combated. Here again the press proved useful. *L'Echo de Paris* is a prominent daily with a vast reading public. Together with *Matin*, *Temps*, the *Journal des Débats*, and the *Petit Parisien*, it has formed a consortium allied with the powerful and reactionary Havas Agency, the Associated Press of France, to mould public opinion. Through the *Echo's* columns recently an appeal was launched for funds for a campaign against disarmament, with the heading " The Struggle against Disarmament." On the subscription lists one notices several anonymous contributions of 25,000 francs, 50,000 francs, and 100,000 francs. Who were these modest contributors who did not wish to give their

PLUS ÇA CHANGE— 197

names ? Some hint may be gained from a cynical advertisement opposing disarmament which this paper ran on July 15, 1931, paid for by the S.O.M.U.A. Investigation showed that this is the Société d'Outillage Mécanique et d'Usinage d'Artillerie, an artillery firm connected with Schneider.[11]

In this campaign against disarmament Geneva has naturally been a salient against which the forces of Schneider and his allies have concentrated—and not in vain. The 1932 session of the disarmament conference was most unsatisfactory for the friends of peace. The reason is not far to seek. On the French delegation the arms merchants had their own spokesman, Charles Dumont, vassal of M. Schneider ; and, inasmuch as his master manufactures submarines, it was not surprising that Dumont insisted on the recognition of the submarine as a legitimate instrument of war—one of the rocks on which the conference foundered. To complete the picture it may be added that Colonel F. G. C. Dawnay, brother of a Vickers director, was among the English delegates. Apparently the arms merchants have adopted the Communist practice of boring from within.[12]

One thorn remained in Schneider's side. Paul Faure, Socialist deputy from Creusot, continued his exposures of the arms merchants in the Chamber of Deputies. He it was who read to his colleagues a document emanating from the House of Creusot in which it was recorded that 1,000 kilograms of powder were sent for Mauser gun cartridges to the Mauser firm in Leipzig, Germany, and another shipment to the firm of Paul Capit in Baden. He made some researches into the history of Schneider and regaled the deputies with photographs of Schneider and the German Kaiser on a yacht, of Schneider escorting King Ferdinand of Bulgaria on his inspection trip of the Creusot factories, and other similarly revealing pictures. Under fire now from the representatives of the people, a spokesman for Schneider offered the rather ingenious explanation that the powder shipped into Germany was intended for the Skoda works in Czechoslovakia and had passed through Germany merely " in transit." The spokesman did not comment on the photographs.[13]

Here was a leak that had to be stopped. Foreign governments, foreign industry, French industry, the French press, the French government, even the French disarmament commission were " fixed." It remained only to get rid of this Paul Faure. In its early history the House of Schneider had intimidated its workers at the polls and had harvested big majorities for its deputies. Why should it not repeat that performance now? In 1932, Faure again stood for office in the Creusot constituency and now, by the same old methods of intimidation and influence, he was defeated. Thus one of the most powerful voices raised against the cannon merchants was deprived of its forum.[14]

It looked as though it was a case of " Creusot über alles." Certainly it is on the Continent. Vickers, while still fighting bravely for its place, underwent some reverses—at least for a time. Unlike the French, the British have lent one ear to peace advocates. The practice started with the Washington Naval Conference of 1921, when Charles Evans Hughes proposed that the fleets of Great Britain, the United States, and Japan should be limited in the case of capital ships to the ratio of 5–5–3. The British Stock Exchange, that delicate register of international currents, imme-

PLUS ÇA CHANGE—

diately translated this news into a fall in the prices of Vickers securities.

Vickers appealed to the government, asking if it would submit to these disastrous propositions. After some delay the Admiralty replied that it considered the maintenance of the armament works of Vickers as "necessary and desirable," but this resulted only in a temporary rise in Vickers shares on the exchange.[15]

More heroic measures than encouragement from the Admiralty were needed. Vickers had expanded prodigiously during the war, and England had not arranged for any gradual reduction in the armament business after the Armistice had shut off orders. To save itself Vickers had to launch into other lines of business. It branched out into the construction of railway carriages and electrical equipment. It subscribed more capital and took a factory in Poland for the manufacture of war materials. It even built a shipyard on the Baltic, altered its Italian Terni factory to take care of electrical orders, and took over some mines in Ponserrada, Spain. But the more it struggled the more unwieldy it became.

It was obvious that the electrical and allied enterprises would not supply the expected business, and the depression in Britain had not lifted. Credit allowed to Continental states had been lost through inflation, and it was apparent that Vickers was in extreme danger. A committee of bankers and industrialists set up an investigation of its affairs with a view to reorganisation. The upshot was that assets were revalued and its capital stock was reduced to one-third. It was a painful measure for shareholders, but they faced the possible loss of all their holdings and the result was that Vickers, while taking a smaller place among world trusts, was saved.

It was another one of those cases where peace meant disaster, particularly since Vickers' great rival, Armstrong, also came to grief. It had attempted to follow Vickers' lead in embarking on a course of diversification of its products and it was in much worse condition than Vickers. There were reorganisation committees sitting on its fate with the inevitable consultations with bankers, and, as usual, a radical operation was prescribed. Sir Basil Zaharoff appeared from his eyrie on the Mediterranean in one of his last and most shadowy missions. It was said that he put pressure on the banks which held the fate of Armstrong's in their hands and that they ordered Armstrong's to combine with Vickers at a huge loss or to take the consequences. The fact is that they did combine, with Vickers getting the lion's share of the reorganisation and merger.

Perhaps it was this triumphant *dénouement* of Sir Basil's career in international finance that inspired Vickers to present him with a golden cup with the following inscription: "*Presented to Sir Basil Zaharoff, G.C.B., G.B.E., by the chairman and directors of Vickers, Ltd., on the completion of fifty years' connection with the company and as a mark of their great appreciation of the valuable work he has done for them and of their sincere gratitude and high esteem.*"

In spite of this distressing picture of both Vickers and Armstrong, the combined company exists to-day in no diminutive form. Its combination in England includes four firms: Vickers-Armstrong, English Steel Corporation, Metropolitan-Cammel, and Vickers (Aviation) Ltd. Its subsidiaries are almost as extensive as the British Empire. There is a Vickers-Ireland, which, during the Irish revolution, is said to have supplied the Irish in their fight against the Black and Tans; in Canada and New Zealand there are Vickers Corporation and Vickers Ltd.; in Spain are the Sociedad Española de Construcción Naval and the Placencia de las Armas company; in Rumania are the Usines Metallurgiques de Resita and the Copsa-Micu; and in Poland it has holdings in the Société Polonaise de Matériel de Guerre. In the two last countries—Rumania and Poland—its factories are shared with Schneider-Creusot.[16]

One of Vickers' most interesting ramifications is in Germany. After Krupp bowed to the Treaty of Versailles and discontinued the manufacture of arms, he transported part of his armament industry across the border to Holland where he has a factory; another famous armament manufacturer, Rheinmetall, has a Dutch factory; and Vickers is interested in both. Vickers is also interested in the Nederlandsche-Engelse Techniese Handelsmij at The Hague and in the Fabrique de Munitions Hollandaise.

More significant is its connection with the Dutch firm of aeroplane makers, Fokker, which is a subsidiary of Pintsch of Berlin. For this Pintsch house, which is ostensibly a manufacturer of gas apparatus, actually produces war material, and English engineers have worked there. But what is even more interesting is that Pintsch is also mentioned as one of the subsidisers of Hitler.

But to proceed with the ramifications of Vickers across the map of Europe and Asia—Vickers have interests in the Swiss firm of Brown-Boveri and in Italy Vickers-Terni supplies Mussolini and through him Hungary. Meanwhile, Sir Herbert Lawrence, director of Vickers, is also director of the Bank of Rumania, a strategic position when arms orders are given out in

King Carol's country. In far-off Japan Vickers has an interest in the Japanese Steel Works, and an English M.P. has accused Vickers of being "one of the principal supports of the Manchurian conflict." Thus the old employers of Sir Basil Zaharoff, while suffering reverses for a time, have nevertheless retained their place in the sun.

But what has happened to this Greek spearhead for Vickers' attack on national sales resistance? The World War was a splendid climax to his career, the results of years of hard work, and he was proud of his achievements. However, the fatal *hybris* of his people visited Zaharoff, now by grace of King George, Sir Basil Zaharoff, Knight of the Bath. Decked with orders and decorations like a Mexican general, and his purse flowing with the prodigious profits of the war, he apparently felt that he could indulge himself in some less directly commercial activities. Even when retailing submarines to the Turks, the Greek had doubtless felt the twinges of patriotism, and now that he was powerful, now that his political friends were in the saddle and his native land under the rule of the iron Venizelos, he foresaw a Greater Greece at the expense of a defeated Turkey.[17]

He became the angel for the Greek war of expansion in Anatolia. Indeed, Mr. Lloyd George gave him the British benediction and Clemenceau did not raise opposition. He put up some £4,000,000 for the support of the Greek army, and if it had not been for unexpected French antagonism—the power of Clemenceau was waning—and a sudden revolution in Athens against Venizelos, he would possibly have seen his dream come true. But the Greek statesman fell; the Turks, armed with French cannon, defeated the Greek forces, and, worst of all, Lloyd George failed him.

As the Greek army streamed dejectedly back over Asia Minor, severe attacks were made against the alliance between the famous Zaharoff and the Welsh politician. The war-weary British public asked why Lloyd George was so willing to drag their countrymen into such an uninteresting land, and Mr. Walter Guinness, M.P., hinted that the Greek was "the power behind the throne." Englishmen decided that no munitions maker could dictate policies to their premier and the government of Lloyd George had to resign.

It was the end of Lloyd George's power in English politics and it was the end of Sir Basil's prestige in the chancelleries of Europe. By departing from the impartial international code of the arms merchants, this great exponent of the code went down to defeat. He still, however, had one realm over which he could rule supreme. His friend Clemenceau had arranged that the principality of Monaco should be free of French interference, and Zaharoff obtained a controlling interest in the Casino at Monte Carlo. He married the Duchess of Villafranca, one of the royal Bourbon house of Spain, and settled down as potentate over roulette and baccarat.

One year later his bride died and Zaharoff retired from the Casino. He retired also from active business and politics. His Vickers shares had caused him heavy losses, but his oil holdings were so large that he was still tremendously wealthy. And he is still the man of mystery. Every now and then the wires are agitated with reports of his death—for he is now over eighty years old. More interesting are rumours that he has written his memoirs. Finally, the announcement that he had founded a hospital at Biarritz for war-wounded will no doubt furnish excellent material to the cynical —and to others.

Zaharoff in retirement, Vickers just saved from bankruptcy, and Krupp put out of business by the Treaty of Versailles—in many ways this seems like a true *Götterdämmerung* of the arms merchants. But it did not last long. Vickers survived and showed signs of recovery. And even Krupp has made a singular resurrection. Krupp's great cannon factories had been forbidden, by the terms of the Versailles treaty, to make arms. Reorganised Vickers and triumphant Schneider might continue the merry game of selling to their countries' friends and enemies, but legally Krupp and his German *corpsbrüder* could not participate. Indeed, Krupp's suit against Vickers for the royalties of his grenade fuse looked as though the old business man had decided to balance his books and to close out his accounts in arms once and for all. But not for long.

Krupp had to go out of the arms business—in Germany. But there was no stipulation in the treaty about foraging through the intermediary of other countries. In Sweden there is Bofors. Bofors is more than a firm; it is a country, just as Essen used to be almost a sovereign state, just as Creusot is to-day. But Krupp obtained an important block of shares in Bofors, and Bofors employs his patents. Moreover, there have been charges that the ubiquitous Schneider has attempted to acquire a share in this company. Thus while King Gustav, most pacific of European monarchs, rules in Stockholm, and while the countrymen of Alfred Nobel award the famous Peace Prize, in their very midst shells are being timed, guns bored, and grenades manufactured by a new consortium of arms merchants.[18]

Plus Ca Change—

So the new world which was to arise out of the ashes of the World War turned out to be very much like the old. Political and territorial disputes still continued, nationalism went on unabated, and the peace treaties, having sown dragon teeth, produced a huge crop of bitter fighting men. It seemed in many ways an even better world for the arms merchant than that preceding the war. Adjustments had to be made, to be sure, because the volume of business created by the war could not be maintained in times of peace. But the future, on the whole, looked bright. The greatest menace was the growing demand all over the world for disarmament. The insistent cry of the peace forces, of labour, and of the common people groaning under the burden of taxation, forced the governments to call international conferences at which world disarmament was discussed. Should these conferences succeed, the business of the arms merchants would certainly suffer. But the arms manufacturers were equal to this emergency.

CHAPTER XV

THE MENACE OF DISARMAMENT

> I will challenge anybody to say that any representatives of the Bethlehem Steel Company have ever been in Washington attempting to influence legislation as to size of naval or military programmes. That is not our business. Our business is to serve the U.S. Government. . . . We are here to serve you when you have decided what you want. Please do not cast any such reflections on us. It is unfair.—EUGENE GRACE, before the House Naval Affairs Committee, March 22, 1916.

ON the graph of human affairs two lines converged in the year 1927 : one the red, wide band of war, the emblem of the arms merchants, rising intermittently from the days when the Liégeois armed the Duke of Alva to the time when Sir Basil arrived in Athens, then ascending steeply to the last decade ; the other a mere thread of the serene blue of peace, indistinctly wavering from the earliest times, curving upward with the founding of the Hague Peace Palace and finally reaching its highest point in another edifice on the shores of Lake Geneva.

There in 1927 gathered the Naval Disarmament Conference in which Great Britain, the United States and Japan participated. The friends of peace were present in the persons of Lord Robert Cecil—tall, distinguished, the flower of British Conservatism, a staunch advocate of disarmament—and of Hugh Gibson, American diplomat of long standing, voicing the desires of the American people for peace and smaller armaments. The

Japanese shared politely and enigmatically in the proceedings. There were others—stern blue-coated men like Lord Jellicoe and Admiral Sir Frederick Field and a group of American sea-dogs who were reluctant to see any more scrappings of battleships. But there was another person in Geneva at that time, wholly dissimilar to Lord Robert or Mr. Gibson, and unattired in the professional blue of the navy, yet on most congenial terms with the latter.[1]

Mr. William Baldwin Shearer might have served as a model for Sinclair Lewis' Babbitt—expansive, good-natured, cordial to all, back-slapping, hand-shaking, a true salesman type. Another super-salesmen of death? Well hardly in the tradition of the famous Greek. There was mystery about him, but mystery of a rather Gilbertian nature. Who could tremble before a man who flourished credentials from the Native Sons of the Golden West and the Daughters of the American Revolution? And who, especially if he were an American newspaperman, could withstand this genial personality when he extended an invitation to dinner—" a real American dinner "—at his sumptuous home not far from the League of Nations palace?[2]

American he surely was. Did he not answer a " Who's Who " enquiry with the statement, " I am a Protestant and nationalist "? But he had a record abroad. He claimed that he had introduced the first night club into England and that he had been interested in prize-fight promoting and dramatic productions. He bet on horse-races and in this connection he had some trouble. To a question, " Were you ever arrested in connection with it "? Mr. Shearer answered, " I was taken in Paris on the charge of the British Embassy and then returned £125 and that was the end of it." In the United States, he admitted that he was "taken" in connection with a liquor charge and forfeited a $500 bond.

As the Geneva conference in 1927 drew near, Mr. Shearer was prepared for it. He had already performed some publicity work in connection with an earlier conference, and his views on the danger of naval armament reduction and the menace of the British navy were pronounced. These patriotic views seemed to interest three American gentlemen—Mr. Bardo, president of the New York Shipbuilding Company, Mr. Wakeman of the Bethlehem Steel Company, and Mr. Palen, vice-president of the Newport News Shipbuilding Company. After some preliminaries Mr. Shearer was hired by these men to go to Geneva; according to his own story, to see that the United States should "get out their side of the story," at the conference, to obtain a treaty of parity, if possible, but failing that—no treaty at all.

The consideration was $25,000 a year, and with some of this money Mr. Shearer went to the capital of the League of Nations, took a flat in the exclusive Champal quarter and set to work. He betrayed a most unusual modesty about the identity of his backers, and referred only to the Daughters of the American Revolution and other patriotic organisations. The New York *Times* correspondent present, Mr. Wythe Williams, said, "He was silent as to his sources of revenue." But his credentials must have carried no little prestige, for, according to Mr. Williams, "The first day of the conference when the proposals of the three powers were first submitted for public consideration, Mr. Shearer managed to obtain a seat in the famous glass room of the League secretariat where the meeting was held—no mean feat—where he was able to make copious notes of the session."

He lost no time in fraternising with that most gregarious of creatures, the American newspaper man. Technical data on gun elevations or diameters were naturally rather difficult for these scribes to understand. Mr. Shearer was able to provide "handouts" for the press on these questions, and few of the correspondents were inclined to refuse to consult these papers which clarified matters thoroughly. According to Mr. Williams, he prepared a "tremendous amount of elaborate data," and he also prepared and gave to correspondents weekly brochures under his own signature which were, Mr. Williams said, "violently and tactlessly anti-British."

It was no wonder that Mr. Shearer was better informed about such details than the inexpert members of the Fourth Estate. According to his own statement, he had secured from the U.S. Navy Department, under official ægis, a more or less confidential document dealing with naval statistics. He conversed, he claimed, with about a dozen admirals, as many captains and every commander and lieutenant commander in the Navy Department before he went over to Geneva. No wonder that he could assert that he talked with all of the American naval delegation at Geneva with the exception of Admiral Jones. No surprise then that, when he took a trip to Rome, the Naval Intelligence office thought so much of him that a telegram was sent to the Ambassador at Rome heralding the great man's approach. When he arrived, Ambassador Fletcher and the naval attaché received him and discussed the Mediterranean situation with him.

He could well assert that he had worked vigorously

and well at this famous tri-power conference. Mr. Pearson testified, "I frequently saw Shearer around the lounge of the hotel with members of the delegations." In his sumptuous residence, with the aid of his wife, he entertained newspaper men, and from one of these we obtain a picture of him—" in precise staccato tones, he dictated clearly and thoroughly an opinion on the disadvantages for the United States if British terms were accepted." [3]

The world knows now that the conference of that year was a failure. The armament interests had a worthy agent. Shearer was indeed the lion of the conference. He was known among European journalists as "the man who broke up the conference," and when a newspaper item painted him in these flattering colours, he took the trouble to clip it and send it home to his backers.[4]

Flushed with victory, the hero returned, but he was not to rest idly on his laurels. He received no testimonial to his valuable success from his late backers, but the fact that Mr. Wilder, of the Brown Boveri Company, controlling the New York Shipbuilding Company, hired him, in 1928, for more publicity was evidence that he had made no little impression. As a statistician and entertainer he had done well; now he turned to literature. Dr. Nicholas Murray Butler had criticised Herbert Hoover's speech of acceptance, especially the portion dealing with the navy and merchant marine. Mr. Shearer, in the pay of shipbuilders, wrote a reply to Dr. Butler and prepared other propaganda papers which the publicity bureau of the Republican National Committee accommodatingly sent out. These releases were well inflated with demands for a big navy and merchant marine;

they cast reflections on the patriotism and intelligence of peace advocates, and they were admirably conceived to catch the Irish vote by denunciations of perfidious Albion—to use Mr. Shearer's own words, " to fool the simple Irish."

Success again attended Mr. Shearer's efforts, but not for long. His candidate was elected, but the evil poison of peace propaganda had infected Mr. Hoover; so Mr. Shearer was again engaged for publicity on the 15 cruiser bill in Washington in 1929. And another gentleman, unrelated to the shipbuilding interests, but as resoundingly patriotic as the hero of Geneva, was now exercised about the evils of disarmament and such dangerous proceedings as the League and the World Court. Mr. Hearst engaged Mr. Shearer for publicity along the line which Hearst newspapers have long made familiar to their readers.[5]

Now, at a salary of $2,000 a month, he launched strong attacks on the League of Nations and the World Court; his duties included writing articles, speaking and organising patriotic societies. But he had other allies than the Hearst organisation in this congenial work. His pleasant manner and bristling knowledge of naval facts led him into the welcome sanctums of the American Legion. He assisted Commander McNutt in preparing a speech which voiced the Legion's approval of the construction of more cruisers.[6]

Mr. Shearer became well known as an adviser and writer on patriotic topics, but his experience with the methods of the Fourth Estate had given him wisdom about the fearsome libel laws. So while he dealt rather charily with the word " treason," he was not averse to careful innuendo. Advocates of peace and disarmament, he believed, were menaces to the safety of the United States, and he was not at all hesitant about lumping them with communists, anarchists and other dangerous characters. One of his finest flights of belles-lettres was entitled *The Cloak of Benedict Arnold*. It sought to discredit individuals and societies which favoured the League, the World Court, and the limitation of arms. *Imperialistic for Peace* was another pamphlet from his hand, nicely calculated to place in one category all enemies of a big navy, a strong army and national isolation.

> " From October 1914, the weight of internationalism and communism was developed, the members of which, pacifists, defeatists, radicals of many hues, and foreign agents, communists, I.W.W. and socialists, included in this merger, and a dozen or more organisations with impressive names designed to fool patriotic Americans and lend aid to the enemy. Associated with these agents and organisations of these anti-American bodies were statesmen, Senators, bankers, lawyers, actors, directors, and writers, men and women of American birth who were used to fight the existing government of the United States. . . . All names, records, cheques from prominent people in this country, instructions from Moscow, speeches, theses, questionnaires, indeed the workings of the underground organisation, working secretly through 'legal' bodies in labour circles, in society, in professional groups, in the Army and Navy, in Congress, in the schools and colleges of the country, in banks and business concerns, among the farmers, in the motion-picture industry, in fact in nearly every walk of life—this information and authentic documentary proof of a colossal conspiracy against the United States were seized by Federal officials and are in possession of the authorities." [7]

This particular composition was sent out when Mr. Shearer was still on the pay-roll of the shipbuilders.

THE MENACE OF DISARMAMENT

But so far as its readers were concerned, its author might conceivably be just another fussy old patriot, perhaps a sympathiser with the D.A.R., or even a Native Son of the Golden West. If it was suspected that he was in the pay of Mr. Hearst, there was nothing much to be said against that either—for had not Mr. Hearst by this time almost the sanctity of an institution?

In the summer of 1929 Mr. Shearer appeared in the newspapers in another rôle—that of a worker demanding his just wages. There must have been some confusion in the agreement which Shearer had with his industrial subsidisers preceding his embarkation for Geneva. He claimed that while he had demanded $25,000 for ten years, they had refused, but had promised that he would "be taken care of." Inasmuch as he had worked diligently at the Geneva conference, thus insuring a chance for more shipbuilding, and had made great success in the 15 cruiser fight, Shearer could well claim success in gaining, as he declared, in the prodigious speed of two years, all the objectives which his employers had estimated would take ten years. He felt that he was entitled to $250,000, and when the shipbuilders declined to make out a cheque for this amount he sued for payment.

The public now became interested to know more about this strange alliance of patriotism and business. Senators and representatives and, most important of all, President Hoover, who had suffered from vitriolic attacks for his negotiations for disarmament, displayed curiosity. Senatorial investigation was decreed. It called Mr. Palen and Mr. Bardo, and Mr. Wilder, and Mr. Grace of the Bethlehem Steel Company and Mr.

Grace's superior Mr. Charles A. Schwab—and it did not have to summon Mr. Shearer. He appeared voluntarily, eagerly, and insisted that he be heard.

A strange spectacle followed. It was odd, indeed, to observe how these titans of American industry sought to portray themselves as bungling, inefficient executives, as innocent but stupid employers. It was extraordinary to observe how readily they admitted that they had employed a man about whom they knew nothing; and how they had sent him to Geneva for a task about the nature of which they had only the faintest idea—and that they had paid out $25,000 for this nebulous enterprise.

Mr. Bardo was particularly vague as to why he had consented to the hiring of Mr. Shearer. He admitted that he knew nothing about the man, and conceded that by so doing he had violated one of the principal rules which he had always followed as an employer. He was equally obscure in his understanding of the objective which this strange employee was to work for. According to this president of the New York Shipbuilding Company, Shearer was sent to Geneva simply as an observer to report the "trend" of the conference so that the shipbuilders would have more information than was available in the newspapers. The results of the conference, he declared, did not possess interest for him; the "trend," not the "result" was what he was interested in—whether the conference ended in an agreement or not.

SENATOR ROBINSON of Arkansas (questioning Mr. Bardo): It (a failure) might aid you, and yet you are interested in the trend but not the result.

MR. BARDO: But not in a disagreement. Please do

not get those two terms confused. We were interested in the trend but not in a disagreement.

SENATOR ROBINSON: You have made a distinction which I confess my poor mind is not able to grasp, but perhaps you will make the effort to explain just why you were interested in tending toward disagreement, but in no wise interested in disagreement itself.

MR. BARDO: Because one indicated a trend, the other indicated a result.

Mr. Bardo tenaciously held to this somewhat dialectical view, but one of his associates, Mr. Palen of the Newport News Shipbuilding Company, was a bit more definite, after much long cross-examination.

SENATOR ALLEN: You really did want something more than plain observing done?
MR. PALEN: Yes. . . .

As to Mr. Shearer's credentials, all admitted that they had neglected to ask for them.

SENATOR ROBINSON: You made no inquiry concerning Mr. Shearer whatever when you employed him and sent him on a confidential mission for your company?
MR. BARDO: We made no——
SENATOR ROBINSON: No inquiry concerning Mr. Shearer; no investigation of him?
MR. BARDO: I did not.
SENATOR ROBINSON: Is that usual?
MR. BARDO: Not ordinarily.
SENATOR ROBINSON: Why did you depart from the usual practice in this case?
MR. BARDO: Well, in the first place we did not have time. (Here Bardo referred to the fact that

Shearer had reservations to sail for Geneva within a few days.)

Mr. Bardo admitted that his business judgment had been disarmed by Mr. Shearer's " apparent familiarity and knowledge of the question." Mr. Wakeman admitted " I was jazzed off my feet on that proposition, if you want to know. I do not like to make the acknowledgment." [8]

The head of the Bethlehem Steel Company, Mr. Charles M. Schwab, made many noble statements such as the following :

> " I was interested in a way that I wanted to see peace come to the world and especially to this own great country of ours ; no entanglements of war. Not only was I interested as a patriotic American citizen, but I may say that I was selfishly interested from a prosperity point of view of this great country, particularly as an industrial country under peaceful conditions."

As to naval work, he said :

> "We do not care whether we ever do any of that work in the future."

Yet Mr. Schwab's right-hand-man—" his boy " he called him—Mr. Eugene Grace, only remarked that it had been " unwise." [9]

The defendants in the suit Shearer *v.* Bethlehem Shipbuilding Company, *et al*, were vigorously critical of Mr. Shearer's accomplishments ; yet while the latter was giving out releases and sending propaganda to America against limitation of naval armament, none of them took steps to stop him. Nor did they, after presumably condemning his anti-peace propaganda, visit their wrath on him by denying him employment thereafter. For in 1928, as we have seen, Mr. Shearer was employed by one of them in his merchant marine legislation, and in 1929 in lobbying for the 15 cruiser bill.

Indeed, Mr. Bardo, who was so contemptuous of Mr. Shearer's abilities, was party to another affair which involved lobbying, this time by means of a Congressman. Together with another of Mr. Shearer's late employers, Mr. Wilder, he was interested in a land and shipping enterprise to develop Montauk Point, Long Island, as a seaport, the terminus of a line of four-day vessels across the Atlantic. One of the firms sponsoring the venture, The Montauk Point Development Corporation, had a stockholder in the person of Hon. Fred Albert Britten, Chairman of the House Committee on Naval Affairs. Mr. Britten also owned some land at Montauk Point. In order to show that the new port was capable of admitting large vessels and proving a good harbour, the representative of the people promised to have one of the U.S. naval fleets use it. And he made good. In the following year, vessels of the navy anchored off the Point. But the officers and men objected to the place as a base, and their dissatisfaction was communicated to the New York papers in whose columns Mr. Britten became the object of much irony. It was hinted that the fleet had been brought to this place solely to help out a money-making enterprise.

Mr. Britten declared in rebuttal that the Navy Department had ordered the fleet to Montauk without " the slightest pressure or suggestion from me or anyone else," and he gave an inspired and lyrical reason as to why the fleet had really been brought to this point. It seems, according to Mr. Britten, that Mr. F. J. Libby of the National Council for the Prevention of War had made some pacifist speeches on Long Island, and that "one of the main objects of bringing the fleet was to counteract the propaganda." [10]

The activities of individuals like Mr. Shearer illustrate the lengths to which armament companies will go in trying to further their business. They have perceived that the burden of armaments is growing rapidly, that this alone is sufficient to move governments to take drastic measures—to curtail naval building programmes, to cut appropriations and to join disarmament conferences. This threat to the armament manufacturers' business is growing, and, while these powerful interests will hesitate to repeat the performance at Geneva in 1927, it seems unlikely that they will refrain from assisting "big navy" publicity in the future.

CHAPTER XVI

FROM KONBO TO HOTCHKISS

> I had hoped that the page of future history might record the great fact that in one spot in the Eastern World the advent of Christian civilisation did not bring with it its usual attendants of rapine and bloodshed; this fond hope, I fear, is to be disappointed. I would sooner see all the treaties with this country torn up, and Japan returned to its old state of isolation, than witness the horrors of war inflicted upon this peaceful people and happy land.—TOWNSEND HARRIS, first American consul-general to Japan.

THE "well-oiled" military machine of Japan, to employ the newspaper jargon, has crushed all opposition in Manchuria and has even moved into Jehol. It is, indeed, well lubricated by the industry, efficiency and progressiveness of the Japanese. Less than three-quarters of a century ago these people were dependent on medieval instruments of war; and, considering the way they have handled all the lethal apparatus of 1933, their adaptability is astonishing. But the monster which they have so ably harnessed manifests most of the customary traits—and some others which occidental countries have not yet developed. How the Japanese reached this high stage of machine gun culture is a fascinating story.

The first firearms beheld by innocent Japanese eyes were blunderbusses in the hands of the Dutch who landed on the islands in 1540. The Dutch received a rather singular welcome; they were overwhelmed with a politeness never seen by Westerners, but they were firmly requested to stay at a safe distance on a tiny island off the coast. For centuries the Japanese consented to trade with the Europeans in this distant manner. They took the Western traders' novel articles; in their intelligent way they even copied some of them; and among these was the unwieldy musket of the time. But the Nipponese took it no more seriously than any other trifle from Amsterdam or Rotterdam.[1]

True, their own weapons could easily be improved upon, according to European lights. They had the *konbo*, a long stick made of iron and wood, which was the weapon of the varlets, and the broadsword, which the high-born Samurai used. But according to the doctrines of the Bushido (Way of the Warrior), honourable warriors had to meet their adversaries face to face with cold steel; and a blunderbuss, however defective its aim might be at hundred paces, was decidedly bad form for any Samurai. Tradition was all against the new and cowardly device.

Beside the *konbo* and the broadsword there were the *naginata* or long-handled falchion, the bow and arrow, and those elaborate suits of armour that are now the amazement of the museum visitor: these were the equipment of Japanese soldiers until the nineteenth century. The Japanese tinkered with firearms and employed them in winging birds, but that was about all. Factories for the new fowling pieces did not exist, for the Japanese were accustomed to making their medieval weapons in various shapes and designs according to their individual fancies and ideas. Mass production of arms was, of course, still in the womb of time.

Amid these backward habits Japan drowsed until

1807. In that year a Russian expedition landed forcibly on the main island and in the following year a British ship threatened Nagasaki. The dreamer stirred a little, but was not fully awakened until " four black ships of evil mien " anchored off Tokyo in 1853. It was Commodore Perry, U.S.N., who had come to obtain a commercial treaty with the Japanese and to make arrangements about shipwrecked sailors of American whaling vessels. The Commodore had an exquisite sense of the theatre, and with the aid of a brass band and four tall negroes from the ship's crew —they towered a foot and a half over the diminutive islanders—he made such a profound impression on the Japanese that they fled to their temples to pray for deliverance. Perry's gifts of firearms, a toy railway, telegraph instruments, books, champagne, and many barrels of whisky dispersed some of the original terror, but the American was unable to complete his treaty negotiations until his return in the following year.[2]

For centuries the Shogun, greatest of feudal lords, ruled Japan from his capital Yedo, and kept the Emperor in virtual captivity in Kyoto as a mere ceremonial and religious official. Now the advent of the strange trousered white men, with their death-dealing cannon, stirred up one of the more progressive Shoguns, who felt a desire to study and import Western methods just to be on the safe side in case the visitors should turn belligerent. The young heir to the throne, too, was eager to imitate the occidentals; and so a *rapprochement* was effected between the up-to-date Shogun and the royal house.

The Western intruders did show their teeth in 1863 when three Englishmen, who were so incautious as to ride their horses into a ceremonial parade, were summarily cut down. Thereupon a British fleet appeared demanding a large indemnity. The Shogun refused, and the British bombarded the town of Kagoshini. The game was up. The Shogun realised that his precious palace overlooking the harbour was at the mercy of the British guns and he paid the indemnity.

The game was up, likewise, for the backward shogunate. The majority of the feudal lords had become so " civilised " and unwarlike that all they were good for was to sip rice wine and paint wall screens after the manner of Hokusai. The progressive members of the clans determined to restore the Emperor to power as a symbol of enlightenment. In 1867 the old order fell, and in the following year the most " go-getting " Son of Heaven in many a century ascended the throne which was now dominant over the shogunate.

All progressive Japan rejoiced and rushed hurriedly into the business of importing new customs and discarding old. But the American consul-general, a farsighted man named Townsend Harris, wrote in his diary: " Half-past two p.m. To-day I hoist the first consular flag ever seen in this Empire. Grave reflections. Ominous of change. Undoubtedly the beginning of the end. Query: if for the real good of Japan." [3]

In the decade which followed Japan was too busy to ask such metaphysical questions. The new era was militaristic from the start, but at first the Japanese had to be content with rather elementary weapons. The Dutch had been there first, and it was their *Gewehr* which was copied in the first factories established on the islands. The guns of Commodore Perry had awakened the medieval Japanese, and good guns have been their concern ever since. Already in 1858, in the commercial treaty with the United States, they had definitely stipulated that they might purchase ships of war, arms and munitions in the United States and employ American experts to train them in arms making.[4] The inefficient Dutch guns were soon discarded in favour of the French " *minie* " rifle, and for some time the French military technique and tactics were followed. Foreigners were, of course, imported to organise the armament industry, and simultaneously that phenomenon, Hashimuro Togo, the " Japanese schoolboy," appeared in Western universities, diligently engaged in absorbing Western culture.

But these were only sporadic efforts. The greatest impetus to the Japanese munitions industry came after the civil war of 1877. A Japanese general, who wished to be considerably more progressive than his fellows, started an insurrection in that year, and all the power of the Empire was brought to bear before he was put down. He committed hari-kiri, but the arms industry rose in greater strength from his ashes. During the insurrection, orders had poured into the arms factories in such huge quantities that even women had to be pressed into service to speed up production. It was the first appearance of female labour in Japanese industry. It was a sign of the times, and the government, to prevent another such shortage in arms, decided to accelerate the development of the arms industry.

Grinning politely, Japanese students now spread to all corners of the Occident. They were seen at Essen, at Creusot, at Wilmington, wherever the accommodating forges of the arms makers flared. Representatives of these firms paid return calls, and business in the arms industry became very brisk. So quick were these eager Japs to pick up the new technique that in

1880 a Major Murata Tsuneyoshi designed a rifle which was so effective that it was adopted officially by the government. With the coming of the Murata, the brand "Made in Japan" appeared for the first time in the international arms traffic.[5]

Naval construction had advanced, too, but more slowly. The first warships owned by the Japanese were—ironically—presented to them by the Russians, in gratitude for help given to a shipwrecked Russian squadron. All through the sixties and seventies the Japs studied in foreign shipyards and imported English naval architects. Sir William White, afterward chief designer of the British navy, was one of those most responsible for the successful construction of Japanese men-of-war.[6]

Sir William, who late in his career was attached to the British Admiralty, had spent some time in the employ of the firm of Armstrong. He was not unworthy of his hire. He it was who saw the advantage of exploiting the Far Eastern situation for the best interests of the armament company stockholders. When, in connection with the Franco-Chinese war in Tonkin, Admiral Courbet cruised up and down the South China coast throwing shells into bamboo villages, Sir William made his report to Armstrong's: "Orders can only be taken when the Chinese are in the humour and the destruction of their men-of-war the other day, instead of depressing them, I am quite sure will stir them up to further endeavours." He was correct; the Chinese were so stirred up that they gave Sir William the orders he wanted.

This was an excellent opportunity to point out to the Japanese the growing menace of the Chinese fleet, built as it was by so good a firm as Armstrong's. China meanwhile had been gazing apprehensively across the Sea of Japan, anxious over the growing military power of its island neighbour. Sir William's adulant biographer summarised this gratifying situation very neatly:

> "White was not unwilling to play the part of *honnête courtier* by pointing out the growth of the Japanese navy to his Chinese clients, or of the Chinese to their indomitable rivals. In doing so, he was careful to insist on the confidential nature of his designs and the daily progress of our scientific knowledge. By such means he was able to increase the profits of the great company which employed him, to extend what is perhaps the most important of national industries, and to kindle in the hearts of two Asiatic peoples the flames of an enlightened and sacred patriotism."

Nor did the benevolent Sir William neglect the patriotism of his own people in this affair. He reported to his superiors in London—and it is hardly possible that they kept the Admiralty in ignorance—" They (the Japanese) will receive in the next few years a very great accession of strength which obviously must have a direct bearing on the types and numbers of ships of the Royal Navy required for the defence of our interests in Eastern seas." [7]

The Japanese certainly did agree with Sir William's biographer that arms were the country's most important industry. What had impressed them first and most about the Westerners was their arms, and they believed these to be the secret of their power. When they began to " westernise," therefore, arms, modern, up-to-date efficient war engines, were first on their programme. At first they had to buy finished arms from the West, but after a time they decided to have their own arms industry. The manufacture of armaments was the first Western industry to be introduced into Japan and in many ways it remained the most important. Other industries arose as auxiliaries to this, in order to supply raw materials or accessories. The arms industry was built as the very foundation of Japanese economic life; all other industries were built round it; its prosperity or decline was a reliable index to the economic life of the islands. Furthermore, the budget expenditures for arms exceeded those for any other purpose and the government loans for war and armaments were vastly in excess of those for any peaceful, industrial or social developments.[8] In short, Japan made the logical deductions from her observation of the West. Military power, she believed, had given dominance to the West; hence her people became soldiers, her first and chief industry was the manufacture of armaments, and her entire economic structure was erected with the purpose of serving as a war arsenal.

Nor was industry alone in this military philosophy. The political scheme of things also was oriented toward war in this rule of the new Samurai. Japanese generals and statesmen had travelled abroad and some had stopped in Potsdam to gaze appreciatively at the dominating figure of Bismarck. The lesson was not lost on them and one of these travellers was so enthusiastic over this new *Kultur* that he paused on the way back through the United States to deplore the fact that Abraham Lincoln had not been intelligent enough to see the wisdom of making himself dictator. But when these wisdom-seekers returned to the shade of their cherry blossoms, they arranged the Cabinet to suit the taste of the most military minded. The positions of Minister of the Navy and Minister of the Army were henceforth filled by high ranking officers of these two branches of government. The legislative bodies were given very little power in fact, however much they might have in theory. The war-making power was in the hands of the Emperor who decided issues of this kind with the advice of his "Cabinet." The Emperor Meiji, who gave his name to this era— the new Era of Enlightenment it was called—was fully in harmony with these arrangements. He had all the instincts of a Prussian Junker, believed in military dominance, and when he could not ride at the head of his cavalry, he practised the equestrian arts on a wooden horse in his palace.[9]

Sir William White received the warm congratulations of this governing group after the Sino-Japanese war of 1894. Admiral Ito wrote to tell him how splendidly two cruisers, which the Englishman had designed, fought in the famous battle of Yalu, where the Chinese warships had been badly defeated. To quote the quaint English of Ito, "the behaviour of the cruisers was in all respects unblamable." In fact, this signal success of Japanese valour and Armstrong's cruisers obtained for Japan loans which the big bankers of London and Paris had hitherto withheld. The American banker, Jacob Schiff, was so impressed that he organised a consortium of American and English banks in the first large loan to the Japanese government. The Japanese incidentally got more than money as a result of this war; they obtained possession of Formosa and various important islands—the beginnings of Japanese imperial expansion. Only the intervention of the Western powers prevented them at this time from gaining a foothold on the Chinese mainland.[10]

Townsend Harris must have shaken his head with

all the satisfaction of a successful prophet in 1904, when Japan startled the world with her defeat of the Russians. The destruction of the Russian fleet in the Sea of Japan by Admiral Togo was an epochal victory. Together with the correspondingly great victories of the army at Port Arthur, it placed Japan in the front rank of military powers. Even if she did have to depend on the willing ministrations of Messrs. Vickers, Krupp, Schneider, and Bannerman during the war, she had demonstrated that she was able to make good use of the implements and organization of the modern industrial era.

From medieval primitiveness to modern industrialism in less than a half-century—that was a record of achievement. The first daily newspaper in 1871, the first railroad built by the British in 1873, baseball introduced by American missionaries in 1876, horse cars two years later, Hotchkiss guns right after that, etc., etc. That is a brief recapitulation of the stages of her progress. She was now almost as fully organised as the Kaiser's Germany or Lord Fisher's Britannia.

The Japanese arms industry did not follow exactly the Western pattern. At the beginning, the progressive Shoguns and the new imperial power had to set the wheels going, so it was inevitable that government arsenals should manufacture all arms. During the nineteenth century there were no Japanese counterparts of Krupp or Vickers, no private industries of war at all. After the Russian war, however, it was seen that these arsenals could not keep up with the demand when a real conflict was in progress. As a result of this observation, the government permitted the founding of the Japan Steel Works, with the assistance of army and navy specialists, the first and only privately owned arms factory in the country. It was capitalised at 15 million yen and a considerable block of shares was acquired by Vickers. The factory turned out gun barrels, carriages, torpedo tubes, steel castings, and machine work of all kinds.[11]

The year 1913 found the Japanese spending 33 per cent of the national budget for arms—arms which were most useful in the following years when Japan captured Germany's Eastern possessions. But the richest harvest came during the World War, when Japanese factories and arsenals worked night and day supplying arms and ammunition to their Western allies. Just as in America, huge profits were earned, and by the end of the war the island empire was bursting with money.

But the arms industry, which was the lodestar of the industrial development of Japan, now became something of an incubus. It had indeed, as the focal point around which all other machines were placed, greatly stimulated the development of Japan. But now Japanese experts were forced to admit that the economic structure of the country was decidedly lopsided. Capital, which otherwise would have been spent for the good of industry as a whole, now flowed into the arms industry. One of these experts declared:

> "The gradual decrease in the capacity of the nation in economy and general industry occurred thus. The profits which the military industry will bring to the national economy, hereafter, by its expansion, will amount to nothing if the loss caused by same be set off—rather the latter might be greater."[12]

With such a voracious industry still growing, it is not surprising that China became a good customer of her enemy neighbour. In 1930 Japan supplied 37·5 per cent. of the arms used by China. How much these arms and the Japanese arms interests had to do with the military unrest and internecine strife in China—strife which Japan has seized as pretext for her own territorial expansion—cannot even be estimated.[13]

This Chinese situation has fascinated students of the arms merchants for some time. One observer summed up the picture as follows:

> "For twenty years this immense country has been the prey of a dozen rascals, real fomenters of war who raise mercenary armies. These armies have European equipment, and if anyone wants to know where the equipment comes from he has only to follow in the newspapers the visits of their officers to Creusot, Saint-Etienne, Krupp, and Vickers. The big armament firms provide them abundantly with cannon, machine guns, and munitions, and are paid with the proceeds of the pillage of the provinces. Every general has his sleeping partner whose name can be found in the banks of Hong Kong, Paris, New York, Yokohama, or even Moscow. Simple shifts of capital determine the separation or fusion of armies. The sleeping partners change generals or the generals change sleeping partners. This system has unleashed all the horrors of the Thirty Years War on this unfortunate country." [14]

This gives an excellent background for the recent Japanese venture in Manchuria. As the clouds of war gathered, Shanghai became a large centre of the arms industry. Japanese factories, as noted, sold munitions to the Chinese there. Schneider and Skoda and other leaders in this traffic acquired a huge building in the International Settlement. From this centre public opinion in Japan and China was influenced and made ready for war. Three great journals, one in English, one in Japanese, and one in Chinese, amply supplied by advertising from the munitions makers, began to shriek for war. The English paper, the *Shanghai Post*, was cynical enough to remark that "a war would undoubtedly be very helpful to many branches of industry." [15]

Hamburg soon became the shipping centre for German, French, and Czechoslovak armament manufacturers. The extent of the traffic may be gauged by the following facts. On February 2, 1932, two ships departed for Japan loaded with grenades, dynamite and aeroplane parts; on February 7, Skoda sent 1,700 cases of ammunition; on February 8, a Norwegian vessel called for 1,000 cases of explosives destined for the Far East; on the same day the French sent machine guns valued at 100 million francs. That is the record for one week.

Many of these shipments were disguised. Poison gas, which was unloaded by men wearing gas masks, was marked as "Exterminator for the protection of plants," and munitions were packed in huge crates and neatly labelled "Pianos." Night and day work was reported from many arms factories, and many men were added to the pay rolls of the arms makers. In order to avoid sabotage and labour trouble, some factories followed the practice of manufacturing only parts of arms, leaving the assembling to be done in the Far East. Now and then socialist and pacifist labour groups delayed shipment of arms by demonstrations or strikes; on the other hand it is reported that a German labour leader in the Ruhr declared: "We would rejoice if war broke out in the Far East. Then our workers would again fill their pocket-books." [16]

Accurate statistics are difficult to secure, but it would seem that Great Britain was the chief source of supply for Japan. This seems only natural, since

Britain had taken the leading rôle in furnishing arms and building up the arms industry there. Chinese financial troubles made the arms merchants a bit wary in selling to her ; hence it is not surprising that exports to Japan from Britain were four times as great as those to China. Official statistics on this traffic, whether derived from the League of Nations or from the British Board of Trade, are very fragmentary, because they do not include aeroplanes, ships of war or transports, chemicals, scrap iron, and all manner of raw materials.[17]

British exports include thousands of machine guns, millions of rounds of ammunition, aircraft and anti-aircraft guns, millions of shells and grenades and bombs, and steamships. Japan purchased 76 British ships, many of them for scrap iron, others, among them one of 45,000 tons, for transporting troops and supplies to the Chinese mainland. Officially, British exports of war materials to the Far East amounted to £5,039,836 in 1929, £3,969,372 in 1930, and £3,281,050 in 1931. But in this case these figures belong in the third category of Mark Twain's list of lies : black lies, white lies, and statistics.

Even more is this so in the case of France. French official figures list no arms exports to Japan.[18] Statistics like these are almost fantastic. Press reports have repeatedly indicated great activity in the French arms industry and they have specified that Japanese orders have caused the " boom." One Paris report has it that the Japanese representative " coolly gave an order for the entire stock of munitions on hand in the factories and warehouses of the Schneider-Creusot Company to be sent immediately to Japan. Now the 12,000 employees in this great armament town are working on a fresh order so large that workshops usually reserved for the manufacture of tractor wheels, locomotive parts and rails, and other instruments of peace, have been converted into munition shops." [19] A *United Press* report of March 11, 1933, declares that French arms plants are working overtime for Japan. There is a " boom " at the aircraft works at Breguet and Potez. " Whippet " tanks ordered from the Renault Motor Works were tested in the Jehol drive. Hotchkiss is filling large orders for machine guns, and the Japanese military attaché in Paris has a permanent room on the Hotchkiss testing range.[20] The New York *Times* reports that the export of arms by France went up 50 per cent. in the first six months of 1933 and that the chief purchasers of these arms are Japan, China, and the South and Central American republics.[21] Artillery exports have gone up from 187 tons to 1,017 tons, in francs, from 13,056,000 to 83,900,000.[22] France has also shipped powder to German factories in order to make cartridges for the Far East.[23] There can hardly be a doubt then that the French arms industry is actively aiding the Far Eastern " war." Schneider's subsidiary, Skoda, is also an active participant in this traffic, as its greatly increased profits clearly indicate.[24]

The rôle of the arms makers of the United States in this Far Eastern imbroglio has not been very prominent. This is probably due to the higher prices of American manufactured arms.[25] The statement frequently made that American armament makers were shipping to Japan nearly $200,000,000 worth of goods appears to be a wild and uncorroborated tale.[26] Trade in chemicals, scrap iron, and other raw materials flourished. Between January 17 and February 23,

1933, a total of 5,000 tons of nitrate of soda, the main ingredient of TNT, was shipped to Japan from Newport News alone.[27] No adequate statistics are available on other items. The steel industry of Japan, for instance, has made great strides forward in the last years until it has come to occupy the ninth place in the world. But there is a dearth of local resources, and iron ore and scrap iron must be bought largely abroad. Imports for finished steel products normally have almost ceased; by contrast, imports for iron ore and scrap iron have steadily increased. The United States has become the chief source of steel scrap for Japan, and Japan is the best customer for this raw material which the United States has. Taking items like these into consideration, the rôle of the American arms makers in the Manchurian expedition of Japan has not been unimportant.[28]

Other countries have not been overlooked in the arms orders from the Far East. Germany is reported by both Japan and China as one of their chief sources of supply.[29] The German Bergius process of deriving oil from coal was sought by Japanese agents from the Royal Dutch Oil Company, because Japan had only eight months' supply of fuel.[30] Switzerland has received large orders from China after a huge bribe was passed between a Swiss military man and the Chinese purchasing agent.[31] Holland, Belgium, and Norway are also active in the traffic.[32]

The League of Nations was concerned with the Sino-Japanese conflict. The Lytton Report found Japan guilty of aggression and there was much talk of a boycott against that country. Meanwhile public opinion in Great Britain was exerting pressure on the government to do something about the British exports in war materials to the Far East. Great Britain has a licensing system for the arms industry, and this could readily be invoked to halt the traffic in arms. Of course, what the League and others had in mind was an embargo on arms exports to Japan alone, but the British government now placed an embargo on exports to Japan and China. This was not the act of a pacifist government but a clever political trick, because it did not antagonise Japan nearly so much as a one-sided embargo would have done. But the British arms merchants were not worried. They went right on with the manufacture of arms and before long they were able to sell again to both belligerents. Since no other nation followed the lead of Great Britain, the embargo was soon revoked and the British government could point to a " noble gesture " which other governments had nullified by their inaction.

The most curious incident of this entire episode happened in a British arms factory. It was told to the House of Commons on February 27, 1933, by Mr. Morgan Jones, M.P.

> " At a certain factory armaments were being prepared in one part of the building for Japan and in another for China. By an unfortunate chance, the representatives of both governments arrived at the factory at the same time and were shown into the same room. There they began to discuss the charges made by the firm for their munitions, with the result that they agreed to a joint ultimatum asking for a reduction in prices." [33]

An octopus never starves, particularly in Japan, where military hegemony is complete. While far-seeing Japanese statesmen and economists wonder where the nation is heading, now that Manchuria and Jehol have been taken, they look out upon an amazing picture, a new visage which the country of the Mikado has acquired. Societies of the Black Dragon—far fiercer than Fascisti or Nazis—assassinations of conciliatory statesmen, the sword-rattlers running the show, a national economic system which clusters around the arms factories like a medieval town encircling a baron's castle. Yet it is only eighty years since the painters of the school of Hokusai were the chief artisans of the islands, since the noble broadsword was the sole accepted implement of honourable combat, and since the Son of Heaven dozed peacefully before a Shinto shrine. The four black ships from the Occident were indeed of "evil mien."

CHAPTER XVII

STATUS QUO

When I rest, I rust.—Motto of Thyssen's shops.

DOZENS of volumes have already appeared describing "the next war." The Inferno depicted by these prophets makes Dante's Hell a rather pleasant place. From the point of view of this study the most significant thing about all of these prognostications is the increasing importance of various kinds of arms and the decreasing need of man-power. "Rationalisation" has overtaken Mars and there will probably never again be the enormous aggregation of armed men as in the World War. Machines are steadily displacing men, also in warfare.

The change which has already taken place in this direction may be seen by a comparison of an average regiment of 1914 and one of 1932. In 1914 the average regiment was made up of 3,300 men and 6 machine guns. In 1932 the same regiment consists of 2,500 men with 108 sub-machine guns, 16 machine guns, 4 bomb throwers, and 2 small cannon. In other words, man-power has decreased 25 per cent., while automatic arms have increased 210 per cent.[1]

Industrial invention has made huge strides ahead in armaments since 1918. Already the death machines of the World War seem curiously out-dated and old-fashioned. The new German "pocket-battleship" of 10,000 tons is as swift as a cruiser and as strong as a dreadnought; the Vickers amphibian tank swims like a water tortoise; the British fighting planes fly more than 230 miles an hour.[2] The new French submarine *Surcouf* is like a small cruiser; it has 18 torpedo tubes, is equipped with wireless and many periscopes, and contains a hangar for a folding aeroplane.[3] Chemical warfare is still in its infancy and 33 nations have ratified a treaty outlawing it. Still all the great powers have a chemical warfare division with large budgets for experimentation and the German chemical trust has already evolved more than a thousand different poison gases for use in war.[4] Modern scientific warfare is thus wholly dependent on the armament industry.

Perhaps the most important and largest arms manufacturing country to-day is France. Owing to the territorial changes due to the war and other causes, the French steel industry now occupies the second place in the world, surpassed only by that of the United States. The powerful Comité des Forges, the French steel trust, is closely allied with the arms industry; likewise with the French government.[5]

Every kind of armament is made in France, from aeroplanes and artillery to submarines and complete battleships. The Schneider group of industrialists dominates the industry, while Hotchkiss is also powerful. Schneider's factories are at Creusot, Chalons-sur-Saône, Londe-les-Maures, and at Havre. This latter factory, which is the most important, was acquired in 1897 and has since been enormously developed. Submarines are made at Creux-Saint-Georges, near Toulon, and artillery parts at Bordeaux.[6]

The export of armaments makes up about 15 to 20 per cent. of the total business of the French arms makers. Various measures have been adopted in order to facilitate this foreign business. Poland and other good customers maintain permanent missions for the purchase of war materials in France. The principal ports have been organised as military and naval bases for French friends and allies. Cherbourg takes care of Polish trade, Lorient of Rumanian, Marseilles of Yugoslav. Similar arrangements are made for other steady buyers.[7]

But foreign trade is less than one-fifth of the French arms business. The best customer of the French arms industry is its own government. Since the close of the war France has been re-arming frantically. All arms have been modernised and kept strictly up-to-date. Huge aeroplane fleets have been assembled, tanks multiplied, and chemical warfare highly developed. Still somehow France did not achieve a sense of security. More must be done, it was felt. There was that long frontier line and every inch of it was a danger point. Belgium was a friend, but in 1914 it had served as the back door into France; Germany could never be trusted; Switzerland was being spoken of as another back door; and Mussolini's Italy was too ambitious and jealous to be a safe neighbour.

France could think of but one thing to do in this situation: fortify the entire frontier. A huge programme of frontier defence was evolved, existing forts were strengthened, others were added, many of them underground. Over a billion francs were spent in drawing a steel and cement chain along the eastern boundaries.

Even that has not brought the feeling of safety. There are 2,700 kilometres of undefended seaboard, not to mention Corsica and the North African colonies.

All of these are danger spots and a few hundred million spent in fortifying them would merely be an " insurance premium " on which the country could collect later. So the campaign is on to " defend " the coasts of France—which incidentally remained unscathed in the World War—and to fortify the colonies.

The work already completed and in prospect is highly gratifying to the French arms industry and its ally, the Comité des Forges. This powerful group of industrialists averages 75 million francs a year in "advertising," which is used chiefly for influencing the press, subsidising journalists, etc. It is said to have a secret fund of 20 to 30 million a year by which it keeps its political fences in repair. Its connection with the government is very close. Tardieu, former premier and powerful politician, and André François Poncet, ambassador to Berlin, are former directors of the Comité.[8] A British journalist who wished to visit the factories at Creusot had to get the permission of the French government to do so.[9]

Finally it may be noted that the League of Nations figures on the French armament industry are curiously unreliable, as they are in most other cases. For 1932, for instance, no exports to Japan are listed, while reports persist that large orders were filled in France for that country.

Schneider's greatest foreign subsidiary is Skoda in Czechoslovakia. This company was formerly the leading armament firm of Austria-Hungary. With the break-up of the Austrian empire, business headquarters were moved from Vienna to Prague, while its chief factories are in Pilsen. The various succession states which supplanted the Dual Monarchy were lately under

French tutelage. What more fitting, then, that, with Skoda in bad financial difficulties in 1920, Schneider should step in and take control. Skoda is the chief source of supply for the Little Entente, notably Yugoslavia and Rumania, which again is an extension of French influence. In the years 1926–31, inclusive, Skoda sold to Yugoslavia 330,000 rifles, 20,000 machine guns, 400,000 hand grenades, 1,040 pieces of artillery, and 20 tanks. In this same period Rumania bought from Skoda 125,000 rifles, 7,000 machine guns, 2,000 cannons, 161 aeroplanes, and 1,000,000 gas masks.[10]

Skoda's home market in Czechoslovakia is comparatively small. More than any other arms-producing country, except Sweden, Czechoslovakia depends on exports. At least 40 per cent. of Skoda's manufactures go to foreign countries, which include, next to the Little Entente and Poland, China and Japan, Spain and Switzerland, the South American republics, and even France, England and Italy. The export of arms constitutes 10 per cent. of the total exports of Czechoslovakia.

Great Britain's armament industry is a close second to that of France. It is centred in the great Vickers-Armstrong firm and in other powerful combines. Vickers-Armstrong is probably the largest single armament company in the world. It produces all manner of arms, but it appears to be taking the lead in the manufacture of certain types of military and naval aircraft, tanks, and machine guns.

One reason for the dominant position of the British arms industry is its virtual monopoly of the colonial and dominion trade. Canada buys largely from the United States, but the other British dominions and colonies secure from 60 to 95 per cent. of their war materials from Great Britain. British arms exports go to about forty other countries, especially Japan and China, the South American republics, and Spain. Yet British exports are but 10 per cent. of total production.[11]

The British arms industry continues to follow its tried and tested policy of maintaining close relations with the government through its directors and its stockholders. High army and navy officials find a cosy chair waiting for them in directors' rooms of armament companies when they are ready to retire from service, and the shareholders, of which Vickers has 80,000, include Cabinet members, leading members of Parliament, clergymen, publicists, and people in every walk of life.[12]

The question of the German armament industry since the close of the World War has been the subject of much acrimonious debate. The Treaty of Versailles compelled the Germans to deliver to the Allies their entire fleet, and most of their arms and arms-production machinery. At Essen alone the Krupp factories destroyed 9,300 machines and 800 utensils for the manufacture of armaments, valued at 104 million marks.[13] Some of the German arms makers shipped their machinery to Holland where it was stored in warehouses until times had changed. In 1933 this machinery was returned to Germany.[14] The treaty further forbade to Germany the import and export of war materials of any kind, and the production of armaments was strictly limited to the requirements of German armed forces. But was Germany really disarmed? Had she ceased being one of the great arms producing and exporting countries?

The French have insisted for years that Germany is arming secretly, and a confidential report on this subject has long been held over Germany's head. Moreover, the League of Nations statistics on the import and export of arms show that Germany is a regular exporter of arms. In 1929 no fewer than thirteen countries—including China, Japan, France, Spain, and Belgium—reported Germany as their chief source of foreign supply for arms and munitions. In 1930, 22 countries cited Germany as their first and second largest source of supply. The explanation sometimes offered for these surprising figures is that German exports in fire-arms are for sporting purposes and that the explosives sold abroad are for ordinary commercial uses. Furthermore, much of this material is said to be in transit and, because it is shipped from a German port, credited to Germany, although its source of origin is really a different country. This seems plausible until one discovers that the League of Nations statistics for 1930 list purchases from Germany amount to over £1,500,000, which is more than double the amount of exports listed in German export figures. Such discrepancies are hardly accidental. It would seem then that, despite the Versailles treaty, Germany is again a manufacturer and exporter of arms.[15]

This inference is confirmed by various incidents from the last ten years. There was the Bullerjahn case of 1925. On December 11, 1925, Walter Bullerjahn was sentenced to 15 years in prison for "treason." The trial was held in secret and the public was excluded. Both the crime with which the condemned was charged and the name of the accuser were kept deep and dark secrets. After years of agitation by Dr. Paul Levi and the League for Human Rights, the facts were finally disclosed. The accuser was Paul von Gontard, general director of the Berlin-Karlsruhe Industriewerke, the same man who had used the French press in 1907 in order to increase his machine-gun business. Gontard had been establishing secret arsenals, contrary to treaty provisions, and this fact was discovered by the Allies. Gontard disliked Bullerjahn and had had serious disagreements with him. In order to get rid of him he charged him with revealing to the Allies the fact that Gontard was secretly arming Germany. This was termed " treason " by the court and Bullerjahn was condemned, although not a shred of evidence was ever produced to show his connection with the Allies. The exposure of the facts in the case finally brought the release of Bullerjahn.[16]

Germany's secret arming was also brought to light by the poison-gas accident near Hamburg on May 20, 1928. The facts in the case were clear. A disastrous explosion of poison gas in a factory killed eleven persons, injured many others, and disabled still others who inhaled the gas. Fortunately, the wind was blowing away from the city of Hamburg or else a gruesome tragedy might have overtaken its inhabitants. The contention was at once advanced that the factory was manufacturing chemicals for ordinary commercial purposes. There is good reason, however, to believe that poison gas was being manufactured for the military preparedness programme of the Soviet government. The Allied commission of investigation accepted the German version of the calamity. But it is a curious coincidence that the French commissioner, Moureau, was closely allied with the French and the German chemical industry. The inference again is that Germany was manufacturing poison gas for export.[17]

A little later Carl von Ossietzky, the courageous editor of the *Weltbuehne*, was convicted by a German court of " treason," because he had revealed military secrets in his journal. The secrets he had published were closely related to the secret rearming of Germany contrary to treaty provisions.[18]

There is also some evidence that Germany is importing arms and munitions from other countries. In a confidential report of the exports of Skoda for 1930 and 1931, classified by countries, Germany appears as importer of comparatively large amounts of rifles, portable firearms, aero engines, nitrocellulose, dynamite, and other explosives.[19]

All of this occurred in pre-Hitler Germany. Nazi control of Germany was bound to bring the demand for more armaments. Every device was tried at Geneva in order to modify the prohibitions of the Versailles treaty. Failing in this, the Nazis announced Germany's withdrawal from the Disarmament Conference and its resignation from the League of Nations. Meanwhile the international press was filled with dispatches on German armaments. Here are the facts as outlined in the *Manchester Guardian*, the London *Times*, *Le Journal*, *Le Temps*, *L'Intransigeant*, and a host of other journals.[20]

The man behind Hitler is Thyssen, the steel magnate of the Ruhr. Thyssen supplied more than 3,000,000 marks in campaign funds to the Nazis in the critical years 1930 to 1933 ; he brought about the shortlived Hitler-Von Papen-Hugenberg alliance and the fall of von Schleicher, and thus paved the way for Hitler's rise to power. For this aid Thyssen demanded and received the control of the German Steel Trust, which is the heart of the arms industry.

Hitler at once set to work to rearm Germany. His first budget contains about 800,000,000 marks, which are not allotted. It is assumed that this sum is to be used chiefly for armaments. As if confirming this assumption, iron imports into Germany are mounting with every month; similarly those of copper and scrap iron. Spanish and Swedish ore used for military purposes are arriving in increasing quantities at Emden and Luebeck. And what is happening to these imports?

> "Tanks are being made at the Linke-Hofmann railroad car factory in Breslau and at the Daimler-Benz automobile factory at Offenbach; small arms at the Mauser sporting-rifle factory in Oberndorf, at the Polte iron foundry in Magdeburg, at the Deutsche Waffen-und-Munitionsfabrik in Berlin and Karlsruhe, and at the Bavarian Motor Works engine plant in Eisenach; cannon at Simson's rifle factory in Suhl; mine-throwers at the vehicle factory in Eisenach and at the steel mills of the Dortmunder Union and of the Deutsche Werke in Spandau and at the Polte iron foundry in Magdeburg." [21]

Krupp is again producing cannon. The artillery range at Meppen is once more alive with the testing of huge new guns. Armour plate of a new and special kind is also being made. The German chemical industry, always a world leader, is ready at a moment's notice to produce deadly poisonous gases. Indications are that they are already being manufactured and stored for immediate use. Commercial aeroplanes, readily converted into military weapons, are at hand in great numbers. Subsidiary or friendly factories in Holland, Switzerland, Sweden, Italy, and Turkey are also ready to furnish arms without the least delay.

The rise of Hitler and the Nazis in Germany was also

the signal for the arms makers in other countries to offer their services and wares to a worthy cause. The British, as noted, received an order for sixty of their superior aircraft and only the intervention of the British government prevented that order from being filled. M. Sennac charged at the Radical Socialist Congress on October 14, 1933, that Schneider had recently furnished 400 of the latest model tanks to Germany, sending them through Holland in order to avoid suspicion.[22] France is also supplying raw materials for explosives to the Germans. The Dura factory at Couze-St. Front, near Bordeaux, is shipping thousands of truck-loads of cellulose to Germany every year. This factory is mainly under British ownership. Its contract with Germany stipulates that the cellulose must be used for the manufacture of peaceful products, but it is hardly a secret that it is utilised for making explosives. The I. G. Farben Industrie in Germany which manufactures explosives from this cellulose is owned, to at least 75 per cent., by French capital. These facts are known in France, but nothing is done about them because the Dura factory is one of France's chief explosive factories in case of war, and because American manufacturers would immediately fill the German orders if the French did not. As for the French control of the German chemical industry, the government does not insist on the withdrawal of French capital for the simple reason that the British would immediately replace the French.[23]

Other countries are also taking advantage of their opportunities. The World War demonstrated the great importance of nickel in German armaments. Germany has no nickel resources. Hence the importance of the reports from Canada that Holland has bought about six times as much Canadian nickel in oxide and three times as much fine nickel in the first six months of 1933 as in the corresponding period of 1932. The only explanation offered for this phenomenon is that the nickel is in transit to Germany.[24]

Germany, then, must again be counted among the great arms producing and exporting countries.[25] To a lesser degree this is also true of Italy. Before 1914 Italy was dependent on imports for her arms. The international arms industry considered Italy a "happy hunting ground." Owing to Mussolini, this situation has changed. The arms industry has made notable advances in the Land of the Black Shirts and considerable exports are reported. Italy's customers are chiefly Turkey, Rumania, the South American states, and Finland. Contrary to treaty provisions Italy has also been rearming Hungary.[26] Finally, the Italian arms industry learned to appreciate a real friend when Mussolini accepted the French challenge in frontier defences and increased the military budget by a further £5,400,000 for defending the Italian boundaries.[27]

Italy's arming of Hungary led to the international incident known as the Hirtenberg affair, which occurred at the end of 1932.[28] Italy could not send arms directly into Hungary by rail, because they would have been discovered, as they were in the St. Gothard incident. It was arranged, therefore, that the arms should be unloaded in Hirtenberg, an Austrian town, and thence taken over the frontier into Hungary by means of motor vans. On December 31, 1932, and January 2 and 3, 1933, forty vans of guns and machine-guns from Italy were received at Hirtenberg ready for shipment into Hungary. But the arms were discovered by the Allies and the French and British governments addressed a note to Austria (not Italy!) on February 11, 1933, demanding the return or destruction of the arms because they were shipped in violation of the Treaty of Trianon.

The note caused a sensation, but Austria finally decided to send back the arms to Italy. Attempts are said to have been made to bribe the Austrian Socialist Railway Union to unload the freight cars secretly in Hungary and to send the empty cars to Italy. The Railway Union was to receive 150,000 schillings for its party funds. A great fuss was made in the Austrian National Assembly over this attempted bribery.

Other attempts of Italy to arm Hungary were apparently more successful. The French Chamber of Deputies listened to a story on March 9, 1933, telling how the Italians had sent 60 aeroplanes and 195,000 kilos of gas by railway direct into Hungary. The shipment crossed Austria without attracting attention. Mussolini's reply to these various charges in regard to Hungary was a counter-charge, supplied with detailed statistics, concerning the war materials which France and Czechoslovakia had sent into Yugoslavia and Rumania, partly by way of Austria.

Belgium has not relinquished her centuries-old arms industry. It continues to specialise in small arms and in machine-guns. The uses to which the Belgian products are sometimes put are illustrated by a curious story from the American " Wild West." During the Urschel kidnapping case, the American Express Company entered the home of one of the kidnappers under a court order to satisfy a claim they had against him. Among his effects they found a machine-gun which they confiscated. When the trial of the kidnappers was over, the machine-gun, which had been loaned to the government for the prosecution, was put up for auction in Denver, Colorado. This action of the American Express Company centred attention on the gun and incidentally on the whole question as to the source of supply of the gangsters. The domestic American manufacture of machine-guns is under strict supervision, so that the gangsters can no longer get their " choppers " or " typewriters " from American firearms manufacturers. The Department of Justice agents believe that most gangster machine-guns now come from Belgium, and there are no legal means by which this traffic can be stopped.[29]

Poland imports most of her arms, but she has several factories for the manufacture of arms and munitions. One machine-gun factory was erected with the aid of the Germans.[30] Curiously enough, the rise of the Hitler government in Germany obscured the fear of the Soviets so much in Poland that Polish factories began to manufacture war materials for the Russians.[31]

The arms industry in other European countries is of minor importance. Japan has been considered. There remains the United States. There is no single armament company in the United States comparable to the Schneider group in France or Vickers-Armstrong in England. Instead there are many companies, hundreds of them, capable of producing war materials. Some of them produce armaments in peace time together with many other commercial products ; others can be quickly remodelled for arms production. During the World War, the War Department signed more than 100,000 contracts with private companies for war supplies, and to-day 15,000 factories have been enlisted in the programme of " industrial mobilisation."[32]

The United States government buys from 95 to 97 per cent. of its war materials from private firms. Outstanding among these are the Du Pont Company and the Bethlehem Steel Corporation with its subsidiaries. The supremacy of Du Pont is unchallenged in the United States. It has always been the mainstay of the government for gunpowder and explosives. Its industries are diversified to such an extent that in the last two years less than 2 per cent. of its total business was in military products.[33]

Du Pont also owns large explosive companies in Mexico and Chile and holds a large interest in a Canadian chemical factory.[34] In the near future it contemplates establishing a branch factory in Czechoslovakia.[35] In 1933 it acquired a majority interest in Remington Arms, at which occasion it declared its approval of "the current public discussion of national armaments and the healthy growth of popular opinion against war."[36]

Bethlehem Steel with its subsidiaries generally receives government contracts for armour plate and for battleships. Its subsidiaries to-day number 50, which manufacture nearly a hundred peace-time products besides arms.

The exports of the American arms industry amount to about $15,000,000 a year, that is, about half those of Czechoslovakia, one-third those of Great Britain, and one-fourth those of France. They are made up chiefly of aeroplanes and aircraft engines, machine-guns, and ammunition. Thomas A. Morgan, president of the American Aeronautical Chamber of Commerce, and his lieutenant, Luther K. Bell, recently told a Congressional committee that American aircraft firms exported about $8,000,000 worth of goods a year. This trade is carried on with 46 countries. Guy Vaughan, before the same committee, estimated that 80 per cent. of all aeroplanes can be diverted with ease for military purposes.[37]

American aeroplanes are making history in various parts of the world, particularly in China. The Chinese were interested in speedy fighting aeroplanes, and in order to translate that interest into orders, Major James H. Doolittle, former army speed flier, demonstrated the Curtiss-Hawk pursuit plane to the Chinese. After this, the Curtiss-Wright factory at Buffalo sold 36 planes in the Far East. At the same time it was arranged that Colonel John B. Jouett, the originator of the so-called attack aviation, should go to China with a dozen crack American pilots and four skilled mechanics. This group is under a three-year contract to train Chinese pilots. Every eight months they are to graduate fifty Chinese pilots with at least 180 hours flying time for each.[38] These American ventures were so successful that Curtiss-Wright decided to build an aircraft factory at Hangchow at a cost of $5,000,000. The Nanking government has agreed to buy at least sixty planes a year.[39]

In training these Chinese fliers, a new invention of the Fairchild Aviation Corporation is being used—aerial camera guns. Camera guns "shoot down" a make-believe enemy photographically and bring back the record to prove it. Incidentally, the Italians have also sold to the Chinese 20 bombing planes and are sending Lieutenant-Colonel Mario de Bernardi, one of Italy's most famous fliers, to supervise the instruction of China's fliers. Naturally, the Japanese are disturbed about these activities.

American ammunition is also generously exported. Mr. F. J. Monahan of the Remington Arms Company told a Congressional committee that the exports of his company amounted to about $1,000,000 a year and constituted 10 to 20 per cent. of the firm's business. He insisted that export trade was necessary to keep the industry in training.[40]

Finally it may be added that since the accession to power of the Hitler government in Germany, the business of the armament industry has increased tremendously. Beginning about April, 1933, every great European company shows a sharp rise in sales, due no doubt to the increased expenditures of governments for arms and for frontier defences.[41]

Summing up the world situation according to the League of Nations statistics, the following results: [42]

Total Value of Arms Exports from All Countries

1921	£8,796,837
1922	8,723,098
1923	8,099,883
1924	9,390,863
1925	9,884,013
1926	10,501,109
1927	9,875,424
1928	12,172,397
1929	13,169,382
1930	11,342,773
Total	£101,955,779

Per cent. of Total Exports by Country (1930)

Country	Per cent.
Great Britain	30.8
France	12.9
United States	11.7
Czechoslovakia	9.6
Sweden	7.8
Italy	6.8
The Netherlands	5.4
Belgium	4.4
Denmark	1.9
Japan	1.9

In 1930, then, 55 per cent. of the world exports in arms came from three countries, Great Britain, France, and the United States, while these same three countries account for about 75 per cent. of world exports—more than £94,315,753—from 1920 to 1932.

As has been pointed out frequently, the League of Nations statistics on arms are not reliable. Even officially there are huge discrepancies between export and import figures. The difference in the ten-year period, 1920–30, amounts to £28,219,177. More important than that is the fact that the really expensive armaments—battleships, aeroplanes, etc.—are not included at all in the League statistics, nor is any account taken of the huge smuggling of contraband arms.

Aware of these shortcomings, an independent attempt was made to obtain a more accurate picture of arms exports for the year 1931. The inadequacy of the League figures proved very disconcerting. The League statistics for 1931 show imports of £7,555,555, while the exporting countries reported foreign sales amounting to £7,188,041. Thus there is a discrepancy in the official figures of about £410,958. But when an attempt is made to include the items not listed by the League, total exports approach the sum of £41,095,890.[43] Of this, £12,329,450 is credited to France, £8,630,137 to Great Britain, £6,164,383 to Czechoslovakia, £3,082,191 to the United States, £2,465,890 to Italy, leaving some £8,219,632 to be divided among Germany, Sweden, The Netherlands, Belgium, Denmark, and Japan. The League of Nations statistics are thus shown to be about 17·5 per cent. correct; that is, a more accurate figure will be arrived at by multiplying the League total by 5·5.

This survey also moves the United States into fourth place as arms-exporting country, while Czechoslovakia takes third place.

Interesting as this is, another conclusion to be drawn from these figures is still more significant. In 1931, the world total for maintaining armies and navies amounted to about £924,657,534. About 15 per cent. of army budgets and 40 to 50 per cent. of naval and air budgets are spent on *material*, that is, find their way into the coffers of the arms industry—which amounts to about £308,219,178 annually.[44] If we accept the League figure of £7,603,081 for arms exports for 1931, or the revised estimate of £41,095,890, the percentage of exports in the total business of the arms industry is ridiculously small, in one case about 2·5 per cent., in the other about 13·3 per cent. Branch factories are a further factor in keeping exports low. It is obvious then that the export trade in arms is a very minor item in the total sales of the industry and that the chief customers of the arms merchants are their own governments. The importance of this foreign trade in international politics is another matter.

To complete the picture of the *status quo*, a word must be added here on chemical warfare. The Hague Convention of 1908 forbade the use of poison gas in war. This prohibition was reaffirmed in the so-called Poison Gas Protocol of 1925, which 33 nations have now ratified.[45] Curiously enough, the various war departments throughout the world seem never to have heard of this international agreement. Certainly none of them believe that poison gas will be absent in the next war. Chemical warfare divisions are to be found in most countries and huge appropriations annually serve for further experimentation and for creating gas-bomb stores and reserves.

Even with the co-operation of all governments, the control or elimination of poison gas preparedness is indeed a knotty problem. A simple gas like chlorine, which has a dozen peace-time industrial uses, was the first poison gas used in the World War. To prohibit the manufacture of chlorine would be absurd. The famous " mustard gas " was merely a combination of three very common and very useful gases. Wherever there is a chemical or dye-stuff industry, the possibilities are given for rapid production of poison gases for war.

It is not surprising, then, that the great chemical factories of the world are to be found within the borders of the great powers. The largest companies or combines are I. G. Farben Industrie in Germany, the Imperial Chemical Industries in England, Kuhlmann in France, Du Pont de Nemours, the Allied Chemical and Dye Corporation, and the Union Carbide and Carbon Corporation in the United States.

The Germans have always been leaders in the chemical industry. In the industrial reorganisation which followed the war, the great chemical trust, I. G. Farben Industrie, was formed in 1925, with headquarters at Frankfurt and factories in a dozen places. The board of directors is made up of various nationalities, all leaders, of the chemical industry in their several countries. The capital of the trust, as noted, is owned, to at least 75 per cent., by the French. The German chemical trust has close connections with other chemical companies in Spain, Italy, France, England, and even in the United States.[46] I. G.

STATUS QUO

Farben Industrie has evolved more than a thousand poison gases for use in the next war.

The French Etablissements Kuhlmann owes its origin to the Germans. Immediately after the war the German industrialists agreed to establish a chemical industry in France. In 1923, during the Ruhr invasion, negotiations were completed and in the next year German experts came to France to train French chemists in the use of German chemical patents. Naturally they were well paid. Kuhlmann maintains close industrial relations with the German chemical trust and with the Spanish dynamite companies. Financially it is tied to Dillon, Read of New York, the Crédit Suisse of Zurich, and Mendelsohn of Berlin.

In England the Imperial Chemical Industries (I.C.I.) monopolises the chemical industry. It, too, owes its real importance to German patents which it secured after the war. It is very closely tied to the government and frankly acknowledges its readiness for war. It was this company in which Sir John Simon held 1,512 shares which he sold during the Far Eastern disturbances. Sir Austen Chamberlain was at the same time shown in possession of 666 shares and Neville Chamberlain the holder of 11,747 shares. In order to guarantee its national character, it is provided that non-Britons may never hold more than 25 per cent. of the total shares.

The United States boasts of a flourishing chemical industry which also owes its present status to German patents. A number of giants with many international ramifications are dominant, above all Du Pont de Nemours and the Allied Chemical and Dye Corporation.

Already the peace-time dangers of this new weapon are apparent. The Hamburg poison gas explosion in

1928 has been noted. A similar incident occurred in the Meuse Valley in Belgium on December 6, 1930. Sixty-four deaths among the inhabitants of this valley were attributed by investigators to the escape of poison gas. While there were a number of factories producing ordinarily harmless chemical products in this locality, the investigations indicated that escape of gases from these customary processes could not have resulted in the calamity. Radical papers asserted that the manner of death resembled that from poison gas during the war and they charged that factories in this section were secretly manufacturing war gas. Circulation of a report that the deaths were caused by a fog lent colour to accusations that the origin of the disaster was being obscured by official pressure.[47]

Poison gas promises to produce a flourishing new industry, gas-masks. Since it is evident that the gas will be released on the helpless civilian population behind the lines, various governments are already taking precautions against this menace. The civilian populations are being fitted out with gas-masks and drills are held at frequent intervals in using them. An organisation known as the Violet Cross is carrying on a systematic campaign for the universal introduction of gas-masks. It is not surprising to learn that it also contains a clause in its constitution which permits it to be interested in the manufacture of them.[48]

Fifteen years have elapsed since the " war to end all wars." Yet the arms industry has moved forward with growing momentum as if the pacific resolutions of the various peoples and governments had never existed. All these technical improvements, all the international mergers, the co-operation between governments and the industry bear an uncomfortable resemblance to the situation during the epoch preceding 1914. Is this present situation necessarily a preparation for another world struggle and what, if any, are the solutions to these problems?

CHAPTER XVIII

THE OUTLOOK

> I join with you most heartily in rejoicing at the return of peace. I hope it will be lasting and that mankind will at length, as they call themselves reasonable creatures, have reason enough to settle their differences without cutting their throats; for in my opinion, there never was a good war or a bad peace.—BENJAMIN FRANKLIN.

THE story of the rise and development of the arms merchants reveals them as a growing menace to world peace. When they began centuries ago to adapt gunpowder for war, their products were primitive and crude; to-day their death machines represent the acme of scientific achievement. For centuries the development of arms and munitions depended on the haphazard and isolated work of the individual inventor; to-day industrial research laboratories have systematised and accelerated invention to an appalling degree. In the early days of the industry the making of arms and munitions was literally manu-facture, that is, hand work, which was naturally slow and inexact; to-day the Industrial Revolution and the Machine Age have brought about mass production with the greatest exactitude.

Wars have undergone a similar fundamental change. Feudal and dynastic conflicts fought with small armies and few casualties have been transformed into national wars with millions of men and millions of victims. Ancient and medieval wars were fought with

Lilliputian arms. The map of the world was changed and the political destinies of nations were decided by 5,000 to 30,000 soldiers. The Greek forces engaged in the battle of Marathon, for instance, so decisive in the history of ancient Greece, amounted to 5,000 to 6,000.[1] Alexander the Great's epoch-making wars were fought with 30,000 to 40,000 Macedonians.[2] The battle of Hastings, which delivered England into the hands of the Normans, found 7,000 Normans arrayed against 4,000 to 7,000 Anglo-Saxons.[3] The Hussite armies of the fifteenth century which held all Europe in nervous terror, never numbered more than 5,000.[4]

The early armies of America were naturally rather small. At Bunker Hill the American army numbered 16,000; Burgoyne's vital campaign was carried on with 6,000 soldiers; Yorktown found 9,000 Americans and 7,000 French opposed to 7,000 British; the first American standing peace-time army consisted of 80 men.[5] But with the French Revolution national wars and national armies appeared on the scene. Immediately the size of armies began to increase. Napoleon's famous battles were fought with hundreds of thousands;[6] by 1870, in the Franco-Prussian War, almost a million Germans were in France;[7] and in the World War the enlisted men exceeded 66,000,000.

A similar significant development took place in armaments. The simple, relatively inexpensive weapons of earlier ages were displaced by highly scientific death machines, and the cost of these, together with the upkeep of the huge armies, brought a rapid increase in national war budgets.

This increase is reflected in the statistics of the expenditure of ammunition since 1859 which follow:

Expenditure of Artillery Ammunition in Recent Wars [8]

Years	War	Country	Ammunition expended
1859	Italian	Austria	15,326 rounds
1861–65	U.S. Civil	Union	5,000,000
1866	Austro-Prussian	Austria	96,472
		Prussia	36,199
1870–71	Franco-Prussian	Germany	817,000
1904–05	Russo-Japanese	Russia	954,000
1912–13	Balkan	Bulgaria	900,000
1918	World War	France and England	12,710,000 (one month)

The development is shown even more pointedly in the following table which covers one year of the U.S. Civil War and one year of the World War:

Year	War	Country	Ammunition expended
1864	Civil War	Union	1,950,000 rounds
1918	World War	U.S.	8,100,000
		Great Britain	71,445,000
		France	81,070,000

The money costs of these arms and armies is stupendous. In order to equip the first 5,000,000 American soldiers in the World War, the cost of ordnance alone was estimated at between $12,000,000,000 and $13,000,000,000.

> "This was equal to about half of all the moneys appropriated by Congresses of the United States from the first Continental Congress down to our declaration of war against Germany ... out of which appropriations have been paid for the cost of every war we ever fought, including the Civil War, and the whole enormous expenses of the Government in every official capacity for 140 years." [9]

Another way to realise what the "new warfare"

costs is to take the military and naval budgets of various countries from 1863 to 1913.[10]

Year	Great Britain (pounds sterling)	France (francs)
1863–1864	25,796,000	540,392,787
1879–1880	25,662,094	764,293,739
1889–1890	31,021,300	759,481,775
1899–1900	47,212,000	978,382,421
1912–1913	71,945,000	1,418,546,120

Year	Russia (roubles)	Germany (marks)
1863–1864	127,165,723	—
1879–1880	207,761,670	410,035,949
1889–1890	261,234,866	415,088,408
1899–1900	410,971,701	588,927,600
1912–1913	775,956,153	870,047,800

The figures for the United States from 1791 down to the present are also illuminating:

Year or Average	Army and Navy Budgets
1791–1800	$2,614,000
1851–1860	27,780,000
1871–1875	63,514,000
1880	51,654,000
1890	66,589,000
1900	190,728,000
1910	312,997,000
1914	348,032,000
1923	678,256,000
1927	684,608,000
1929	792,037,000
1931	838,547,144

No fundamental political attitudes have been changed by the World War. The nations continue their reliance on "mass murder" as a means of settling vexing problems. Armies and navies and air forces have increased, military budgets mount every year, new and more frightful weapons make their appearance every month. None of the basic causes of war have been removed and the League of Nations, the Kellogg Pact, and other agencies and methods designed to bring about a peaceful settlement of international disputes have shown a distressing ineptitude in dealing with pressing world problems.

Every modern war threatens to involve half the world, bring disaster to world economy, and blot out civilisation. The question is urgent then : What will be done about the armament industry ?

The future may very well bring fiercer and more destructive wars and increased business for the arms makers. Certainly one great current of world affairs is flowing strongly in that direction. The business of the arms industry is steadily increasing—it was the only industry which flourished in spite of the world depression—and governments are everywhere drawing closer the ties which bind them in a virtual partnership with the merchants of death.

If wars continue, it is not at all fantastic to predict that the arms merchants will grow increasingly important. Already the stage in national affairs has been reached where the largest item in national budgets is for past and future wars. Already war appears as the greatest and most important activity of government. The economic consequences of this new nationalistic militarism will soon be apparent in the arms industry.

The arms merchants will supply to the government its most vital necessities and inevitably they will grow constantly more important in the councils of state. An example of what the future holds along this line may be seen in Japan. There the arms industry is the very centre of economic life. It was established first, and all other industries were built around it. The manufacture and trade in arms in Japan is a definite index to its entire economic life. The whole economic life of Japan is thus oriented toward war and the arms industry is naturally the heart of this economy.

It is not such a far cry from this Japanese arrangement to the system of "industrial mobilisation" now adopted by most of the great powers. While these nations slur over or extemporise plans for the elimination of unemployment, for wiping out the slums, for establishing social insurance, or any of a dozen constructive measures that might be mentioned, they are preparing the most elaborate blue prints providing for action in case of war. It would almost seem as though governments exist merely to prepare for war.

This "industrial mobilisation" is the education and preparation of industries in peace time for their tasks in war.[11] The World War has taught governments that modern war involves the entire economic life of the nation. What this means may be gauged by a statement of a former United States Secretary of War before a Congressional committee. He declared that the needs of an army in war included a list of 35,000 different items made up of 700,000 component parts. To equip an army of 2,000,000 men with shoes requires the hides of 4,462,500 steers for the soles and 3,750,000 cows for the upper parts of the shoes.[12] Without making undue demands on the imagination, it can readily be seen what a gigantic economic task is involved in modern war. In order to prepare for this "emergency," the U.S. government has already made contracts with 15,000 industrialists, instructing them in detail what will be expected of them in war. The War Department is eager to take another step and give out "educational orders" to these firms, but thus far it has been unable to carry this out.

This system of industrial mobilisation is a long step toward placing war in the centre of economic life, or to put it another way, to make the arms industry the hub of the industrial machine. An alliance of governments with war industries threatens to make the armament manufacturers supreme in economic life and after that in government. A world dominated economically and politically by the armament industry will eventually result, if wars continue unabated.

But other counter-currents are active also. A growing demand is being voiced that the arms merchants must be rigidly controlled. Some call for complete government ownership and operation of the industry; others put their trust in international control and supervision. Both of these expedients have a history.

The advocates of government ownership of the arms industry believe that the *private* arms makers with their unrestricted international sales are one of the chief obstacles to peace. If now the industry were nationalised, international sale would virtually disappear and the world could live in peace. This argument deserves close examination.

It requires great industrial skill and equipment and very considerable natural resources of a specialised kind to produce modern armaments. Only the leading industrial countries of the world command these qualifications. For other less favoured nations it is far cheaper and much more efficient to buy their arms abroad than to make them at home. Only about ten countries in the world to-day manufacture armaments sufficient to sell to other countries, and three of these (Great Britain, France and the United States) account for 75 per cent. of all arms exports. Furthermore, no nation in the world to-day produces *all* of its arms and munitions at home; every nation imports some war materials, because some other country produces some type of armament better or cheaper than it does. Concretely this means that even France, England, and the United States import some armaments.

The non-producing countries saw this situation clearly and nothing recurs more persistently in international conferences and treaties on disarmament than the demand of the non-producing countries that their *right to buy armaments abroad* must not be restricted. The Hague Convention of 1907 declared: "A neutral power is not bound to prevent the export or transit, for the use of either belligerent, of arms, ammunition, or, in general, of anything which could be of use to an army or fleet." The Covenant of the League of Nations is more explicit. After recognising that the private manufacture of arms is "open to grave objections," it continues: "The Council shall advise how the evil effects attendant upon such manufacture can be prevented, *due regard being had to the necessities of those members of the League which are not able to manufacture the munitions and implements of war necessary for their safety.*" The League of Nations Conference for the Supervision of the International Trade in Arms was dominated by the insistence of the non-producing countries that the producing countries *must* sell. Terms like "obligation to sell," "right of sovereignty includes right to buy," etc., were flung about daily.

The international sale of arms, then, has far deeper roots than the "conscienceless greed" of the armament manufacturers. If all private arms makers decided to discontinue their international traffic tomorrow, a world-wide protest of *governments* would not permit them to do it. As long as war is a possibility, nations will demand arms. The world economic situation makes it difficult or impossible for most, if not all, of them to manufacture all types of armaments which they demand. Hence it is laid down and affirmed in solemn international treaties that arms must at all times be sold freely, even in times of war. The rules of contraband may interrupt this traffic in war times, but in times of peace and under normal conditions the " obligation to sell " is clearly established.

Thus the programme for the nationalisation of armament industries clearly involves a major change in international politics, to which, as long as war clouds obscure the horizon, the non-producing countries of the world will never agree. True enough, it might be arranged that over a period of years every nation be given its chance to establish its own national armament industry, and thus international traffic might end. But this expedient is of doubtful value. Even if all nations agreed to this arrangement—which is very questionable—the result would probably be a vast expansion of arms industries, and international trade would continue in raw materials rather than in finished products. Furthermore, has not the Japanese arms industry been government-owned from its earliest beginnings and does it not remain so—with some exceptions—to this day? Has that fact eliminated war from the Japanese horizon?

From another aspect there might be a real gain. It is true that the export trade in arms to-day is only somewhere between 2 and 15 per cent. of the total arms production. But this apparently minor traffic is far more important than it would appear. It frequently brings into play the peculiar business methods of the arms merchants, including bribery of officials, control of the press, war scares, etc. It acts as a lever by which orders can be pried out of other governments. Furthermore, so many of these sales are made at times when international friction has developed, or during war, that they are a distinct contribution to the origin or continuance of wars. British armament manufacturers selling tanks to the Soviets or aeroplanes to Hitler when diplomatic relations were strained are interfering in international politics. Arms merchants selling war materials to South American countries during the recent hostilities are obstructing peace.

Even more important is another aspect of the situation. Peace-time sales of arms to other countries are merely the preliminary to war-time sales. No great war has been fought in modern times without lively international traffic in arms. How long, for instance, would the World War have lasted without international sales of war materials? Or the Japanese expeditions into Manchuria? If now the nationalisation of the arms industry included the complete and absolute prohibition to export arms of all kinds in times of peace, and especially in times of war, it would be a decided gain for world peace.

But viewing the problem as a whole, with its economic and political background, it seems improbable that this step will be taken, or that, if taken, it would include the most important provision of including times of war. The simple fact is that the prohibition of the traffic in arms would be almost a revolution in international politics, and the non-producing countries would look upon it as a hostile act of the producing countries, to whose tender—or otherwise—mercies they would thereby be committed in a warring world.

The other important proposal advanced for the solution of the problem is international control. Several equivocal efforts in this direction have been made. The Brussels Convention of 1890, for instance, prohibited the export of arms to all of Africa. This was said to be in the interest of the suppression of the slave trade. It probably was. At the same time it was obviously a selfish measure of the great imperialist powers to keep modern weapons out of their colonies and to hold them in submission. It is a curious sidelight on this agreement that Abyssinia was so successful in smuggling arms through French Somaliland that it won the historic battle of Adowa in 1896 over the Italians, thus constituting itself the one country in Africa which has maintained its independence against the imperialism of the great powers. Nor was that the only example of smuggling. A lively and very profitable trade in contraband arms has flourished for decades, especially along the Mediterranean coast of Africa, which has led to much unrest among the native tribes.[13]

Not much more can be said for the Convention of Saint-Germain-en-Laye of 1919. This treaty obviously grew out of the fears of the great powers as to the disposal of the enormous stocks of arms and munitions after the war. It laid down as a principle that arms could be sold only to the recognised government of another state—not to revolutionaries or rebels. At the same time it extended the " prohibited zones " of the Brussels treaty to the Asiatic Near East. This convention was signed by 23 states and ratified by 11. It never went into effect, because the great arms-producing countries had all stipulated that they must ratify in a body or not at all. The United States refused to ratify, because it did not wish to refuse arms to revolutionary governments in South and Central America. The barely concealed purpose of the convention was to protect the great powers in the possession of their colonies, protectorates, and mandates.[14]

The next move was made by the League of Nations. After some preliminary work by a sub-committee in 1921, a conference was called "for the supervision of the international trade in arms and ammunition and in implements of war." The conference met from May 14 to June 17, 1925, 44 states being represented. The old provisions as to "prohibited zones" and "legal buyers" were reaffirmed, with modifications, and an attempt was made to secure adequate statistics of the export of arms in place of the utterly unreliable statistics now being gathered by the League. The ratification of all important arms-producing countries was again made a prerequisite for adoption, with the result that the treaty is not yet in force.[15]

The concrete achievements of this conference were negligible, but the problem of international control of the arms industry was clearly revealed. Amid all the polite speeches of the delegates several things were conspicuous. The non-producing countries were almost panic-stricken when they considered the possibility that any restrictions might be placed on their "right to buy," and they insisted that no such action could be taken. Similarly it was clear that no move would be tolerated against the private arms industry. When this was under discussion, the Hon. Theodore Burton, Congressman from Ohio, for years president of the American Peace Society and a leader of the right wing of the American peace movement, leader also of the

United States delegation to the Conference, arose to an impassioned defence of the private manufacturer of armaments: "What of the private manufacturers, many of whom have the most pacific intentions? What have they done that there should be this discrimination against them? What hope have the lovers of peace in prohibiting private manufacture if government manufacture may still go on to an unlimited extent?" [16]

Burton's plea was obviously not personal, but represented the policy of the United States government which depends so largely on private manufacture for its armaments. As such it discloses the basic problem of international control of the arms makers, that is, that *few governments, if any, really want international supervision of the traffic in war materials.* Most governments believe that the unhindered international sale of arms would insure their military preparedness, especially since most of them are entirely dependent on imports for their war materials. The great arms-producing countries, on the other hand, are averse to harming one of their industries on which they themselves so largely rely for their "national defence."

If this conclusion seems unwarranted, a glance at another meeting will perhaps prove convincing. After the Geneva conference Theodore Burton introduced into the United States Congress a bill proposing an embargo in war times on all war materials. The bill was specific and aimed at actual armaments, such as guns, ammunition, cannon, machine-guns, or their parts. It deliberately avoided the problem of so-called secondary war materials, such as soldiers' shoes and uniforms. It was introduced on December 5, 1927, reported out of committee on January 30, 1928, and was ready for House action after that. Suddenly in March, 1928, the House Military Affairs Committee asked the Foreign Affairs Committee for another hearing on the bill, since it " might impair the preparedness programme " or " impinge upon national defence." Accordingly another hearing was held.

There appeared before the committee the Secretary of War, the Secretary of the Navy, military and naval aides, a representative of the Chemical Foundation summoned by the Speaker of the House, and others. All of these opposed the bill for reasons of national defence. They said in effect: The United States depends on the private manufacturer of arms for most of its war materials. If these manufacturers are not permitted to sell freely to all nations, they will not be ready when their own government needs them most in time of war. Furthermore, if foreign nations know that they will not be able to buy from American arms makers in war, they will not buy in peace times. An embargo in war was represented as a very dangerous procedure, because it might lead to war. The significance of all this lies in the fact that government department heads led the defence of the private arms maker and of his right to unrestricted international sale "in the interest of national defence." [17]

The problem of international control is further complicated by the fact that the borderline between war materials and non-war materials is exceedingly tenuous. Before the Committee proceedings just mentioned, for instance, the representative of the Chemical Foundation insisted that chemicals must not be considered war materials. Similarly it has been argued in regard to all metals, cotton, aeroplanes, scientific instruments, and a host of other items. All of these are useful in peace and indispensable in war. The British faced this problem during the World War in their blockade of Germany. Their orders in council finally included virtually everything, since it might prove useful in war. The very character of modern war and armaments makes effective international control difficult, yet something might be achieved if the governments themselves were not so reluctant to submit to any supervision in this matter.

There remains then but one real way out, disarmament. The various futile conferences on disarmament have not been in vain if they have opened the eyes of the peace forces to the real problem which confronts them. Disarmament has not been achieved because of the international political situation. International politics in turn are determined by our whole civilisation. Our civilisation has permitted and even fostered warmaking forces, such as nationalism and chauvinism, economic rivalry and competitive capitalism, imperialism and colonialism, political and territorial disputes, race hatred and pressure of population. The traditional way of establishing an equilibrium between these rival forces has been and is violence, armed warfare.

Disarmament is thus a problem of our civilisation. It will never be achieved unless these war-making forces are crushed or eliminated. The problem of disarmament is therefore the problem of building a new civilisation. All attempts at dealing with disarmament by itself, without consideration of the deeper issues involved, are doomed to failure. Minor agreements may be reached, limited to a short period of time, but the world will never cease being an armed camp until the basic elements of our present civilisation have been changed.

The same holds true of the armament industry. A world which recognises and expects war cannot get along without an enterprising, progressive, and up-to-date arms industry. All attempts to attack the problem of the arms makers in isolation—by nationalisation or by international control—are almost certain to fail.

The arms industry is plainly a perfectly natural product of our present civilisation. More than that, it is an essential element in the chaos and anarchy which characterise our international politics. To eliminate it requires the creation of a world which can get along without war by settling its differences and disputes by peaceful means. And that involves remaking our entire civilisation.

Meanwhile those interested in creating a war-less world need not be idle and await the dawn of a new day. They can support every move made for the peaceful settlement of international disputes; they can help to reduce the exorbitant budgets of war and navy departments; they can work for regional limitation of armaments and back all treaties which tend to avoid competition in arms; they can oppose nationalism and chauvinism wherever they show themselves, in the press, in the schools, on the lecture platform; they can strive to bring order into the chaotic, economic and political conditions of the world.

The skies are again overcast with lowering war clouds and the Four Horsemen are again getting ready to ride, leaving destruction, suffering and death in their path. Wars are man-made, and peace, when it comes, will also be man-made. Surely the challenge of war and of the armament maker is one that no intelligent or civilised being can evade.

NOTES AND REFERENCES

CHAPTER I

[1] Charles A. Beard, *The Navy, Defence or Portent?* pp. 156–184.
[2] Paul Faure, *Les Marchands de Canons contre la Paix.*
[3] *The Secret International*, p. 22.
[4] *Parliamentary Debates*, August 2, 1926.
[5] Lehmann-Russbueldt, *Die Revolution des Friedens*, p. 26.
[6] *New York Times*, July 5, 1933.
[7] Union of Democratic Control, *Patriotism, Ltd.*, pp. 24–30 ; Reber, " Puissance de la Skoda et son Trust," *Le Monde*, No. 255, April 22, 1933.
[8] Francis Delaisi, " Corruption in Armaments," *Living Age*, September, 1931, p. 56.
[9] Lehmann-Russbueldt, *War for Profits*, p. 131.

CHAPTER II

[1] *Revue Economique Internationale*, 3 (3) Sept. 1929, pp. 471–492. Albion : *Introduction to Military History*, pp. 5–44.
[2] Camille Richard, *Le Comité de Salut Public et les Fabrications de Guerre sous la Terreur* ; Charles Poisson, *Les Fournisseurs aux Armées sous la Revolution Française : le Directoire des Achats* (1792–1793).
[3] H. W. Dickinson : *Robert Fulton*, pp. 65–206.
[4] *Dictionary of National Biography*, Vol. 7, p. 471.

CHAPTER III

[1] The Du Pont story is told in B. G. Du Pont, *E. I. Du Pont de Nemours & Company, A History. 1802–1902.* (New York, 1920) ; Anonymous, *The History of the E. I. Du Pont de Nemours Powder Company.* (Business America, 1912.)
[2] Justin Smith, *War with Mexico*, Vol. II, pp. 68–84.
[3] Anonymous, *The History of the E. I. Du Pont de Nemours Powder Company*, p. 76s.
[4] Ph.D. thesis, University of Pennsylvania, 1912. See also *Quarterly Journal of Economics*, 1912, for summary.

⁵ Clifton Johnson, *The Rise of an American Inventor*, p. 185.
⁶ " Du Pont de Nemours Powder Company, E.I." *Encyclopaedia Britannica* (14th ed.).
⁷ " Research," *Encyclopaedia Britannica* (14th ed.).
⁸ *Stockholders' Bulletin*, June 15, 1933.
⁹ Arthur Warner, *Delaware. The Ward of a Feudal Family* [in Gruening (ed.), *These United States*].

CHAPTER IV

¹ *Extra Census Bulletin*, 1882.
² Brooks Darlington, " The Course of Empire," *Du Pont Magazine*, Vol. 26 (6–7), 1932, p. 4.
³ Henry Barnard, *Armsmear*; W. P. Webb, *The Great Plains*.
⁴ Brooks Darlington, " The Course of Empire," *Du Pont Magazine*, Vol. 26 (6–7), 1933, pp. 3–5.
⁵ The Remington story is told in a richly ornamented volume written and published by the Remington Arms-Union Metallic Cartridge Co., entitled *Remington Arms-Union Metallic Cartridge Co., A New Chapter in an Old Story*. (1912.) All quotations are taken from this volume, unless otherwise indicated.
⁶ See Carl Schurz's speech in the U. S. Senate, May 31, 1872, entitled *Sales of Arms to French Agents and How They Are Officially Justified*.
⁷ H. F. J. Porter, " How Bethlehem Became Armament Maker," *Iron Age*, Nov. 23, 1922, pp. 1339–1341; American Iron and Steel Association, *History of the Manufacture of Armour Plate for the United States Navy*; Rear-Admiral Charles O'Neill, " Armour Plate Making in the United States," *Cassier's Magazine*, Vol. 22 (1902), pp. 567–582.
⁸ Bethlehem Steel Company, *Ordnance Material* (1914), p. 85; American Iron and Steel Association, *History of the Manufacture of Armour Plate for the U. S. Navy*, pp. 18–19.
⁹ *Op. cit.*, p. 5.
¹⁰ John K. Winkler, *Incredible Carnegie*, pp. 226–235; Allan Nevins, *Grover Cleveland, A Study in Courage*, pp. 673–674.

CHAPTER V

¹ *Sporting Goods Dealer*, January, 1903.
² Perris, *The War Traders*, pp. 55ss.
³ Gustavus Myers, *The History of the Great American Fortunes*, III, pp. 127–138.
⁴ *Congressional Globe*, 37th Congress, 2d Session (1862–1863), Part II, Appendix, p. 136.

⁵ Myers, *op. cit.*, III, pp. 169-176.
⁶ *Op. cit.*, p. 3.
⁷ These Mausers were sold by German traders to Spain. Apparently Bannerman also shipped many of them to Panama to aid in the revolt against Colombia. See page 64.
⁸ *Op. cit.*, p. 3.
⁹ *Op. cit.*, p. 4.
¹⁰ *Op. cit.*, p. 3.
¹¹ March 26, 1904.
¹² Roosevelt said: " I took the Canal Zone and let Congress debate; while the debate goes on the Canal does also." See Charles A. and Mary Beard, *The Rise of American Civilization*, II, p. 513.
¹³ *Catalogue*, p. 37.
¹⁴ *Op. cit.*, p. 3.
¹⁵ *Op. cit.*, p. 61.
¹⁶ *Op. cit.*, p. 147.
¹⁷ *Op. cit.*, p. 232.
¹⁸ *Op. cit.*, p. 72.
¹⁹ *Op. cit.*, p. 155.
²⁰ *Op. cit.*, p. 143.
²¹ *Op. cit.*, p. 149.
²² *Op. cit.*, p. 137.
²³ *Op. cit.*, p. 135.
²⁴ *Op. cit.*, p. 61.
²⁵ This is a misconception, as the history of the World War clearly demonstrates. International law makes sales of arms to belligerents subject to confiscation if caught.
²⁶ *Op. cit.*, p. 133.

CHAPTER VI

¹ Wilhelm Berdrow, *Alfred Krupp*, 2 vols.; Wilhelm Berdrow, *Krupp. A Great Business Man Seen Through His Letters* (translation from the German); Murray H. Robertson, *Krupp's and the International Armaments Ring*; R. Ehrenberg, *Grosse Vermögen*; Franz Richter, " Alfred Krupp und das Ausland," *Nord und Sued*, 1917, pp. 179-190; Viktor Niemeyer, *Alfred Krupp: A Sketch of His Life and Work* (translation from the German); H. Frobenius, *Alfred Krupp*; L. Katzenstein, " Les deux Krupp et leur oeuvre," *Revue Economique Internationale*, May, 1906, pp. 322-346; John Colton, " The Only Woman the Kaiser is Afraid Of," *Every Week*, July 3, 1916, p. 15; Raphael, *Krupp et Thyssen*; F. C. G. Mueller, *Krupp's Steel Works* (translated from the German); Felix Pinner, *Deutsche Wirtschaftsführer*; Anony-

mous, *A Century's History of the Krupp Works* (1812–1912) (translated from the German); Hermann Hasse, *Krupp in Essen. Die Bedeutung der deutschen Waffenschmiede.*
2. Murray H. Robertson, *op. cit.*, p. 74.
3. Berdrow, *Krupp. A Great Business Man Seen Through His Letters*, p. 174.
4. Berdrow, *op. cit.*, p. 182.
5. Berdrow, *op. cit.*, p. 185.
6. Berdrow, *op. cit.*, p. 226.
7. Frobenius, *op. cit.*, p. 108.
8. Niemeyer, *op. cit.*, p. 26.
9. H. Robertson Murray, *op. cit.*, p. 31.
10. Lehmann-Russbueldt, *Die Revolution des Friedens*, p. 27.

CHAPTER VII

1. Clifton Johnson, *The Rise of an American Inventor*. (New York, 1927.)
2. *My Life*, p. 238.
3. *My Life*, p. 185.
4. *My Life*, pp. 196–198.
5. *My Life*, p. 210.
6. *Op. cit.*, p. 268.
7. The Russo-Japanese War of 1904–1905.
8. *My Life*, p. 258s.
9. *My Life*, p. 265s.

CHAPTER VIII

1. Mennevée, *Sir Basil Zaharoff*; Lewinsohn, *The Mystery Man of Europe: Basil Zaharoff.*
2. Perris, *The War Traders*, p. 81.

CHAPTER IX

1. Lewinsohn, *The Mystery Man of Europe.*
2. F. W. Hirst, *The Political Economy of War*, pp. 98–102.
3. Murray H. Robertson, *op. cit.*, pp. 150ss.
4. Philip Snowden, *Dreadnoughts and Dividends.*
5. Francis McCullagh, *Syndicates for War*, p. 6.
6. McCullagh, *op. cit.*, p. 5.
7. Snowden, *op. cit.*
8. Perris, *The War Traders*, pp. 103–116.
9. *The Secret International*, p. 38.
10. George A. Drew, *The Truth about the War Makers*, p. 9.
11. *The Secret International*, p. 39.

CHAPTER X

1 Jean Poiry-Clement, *Schneider et Le Creusot*.
2 This is very probable, because Krupp guns were being beaten elsewhere before the World War by both the French and British guns.
3 These stories are derived from a source hostile to Krupp and favourable toward Schneider and France. Still there is no reason to doubt the facts. See Maitrot, *La France et les republiques Sud-Americaines*, pp. 14-25.
4 B. de Siebert, *Entente Diplomacy and the World* ; Lewis S. Gannett, *The Nation*, Feb. 6 and 11, 1924 ; G. L. Dickinson, *The International Anarchy*, pp. 44-46 ; Anonymous, *Hinter den Kulissen des Franzoesischen Journalismus*.
5 Perris, *The War Traders*, pp. 76-85.
6 Perris, *ibidem*.
7 Francis Delaisi, " Le Patriotisme des Plaques Blindées," *La Paix par le Droit*, Feb. 10, March 10, May 25, 1914.
8 Perris, *The War Traders*.
9 Francis Delaisi, *op. cit.*
10 Paul Faure, *op. cit.*

CHAPTER XI

1 *New Republic*, April 19, 1933.
2 *New Republic*, June 28, 1933, p. 175.
3 Launay and Sennac, *op. cit.*, pp. 102ss.
4 *Ibid.*, p. 23s.
5 *Ibid.*, p. 114s.
6 *Ibid.*, p. 66s.
7 *Ibid.*, p. 23s.
8 *Stockholders' Bulletin*, June 15, 1933.
9 U. S. (House) Foreign Affairs Committee, 72d Congress, 2d Session, *Exportation of Arms or Munitions of War*. (1933.)
10 William T. Stone, " International Traffic in Arms and Ammunition," *Foreign Policy Reports*, Vol. IX, No. 12, Aug. 16, 1933, p. 137 ; U. S. (House) Foreign Affairs Committee, 72d Congress, 2d Session, *Exportation of Arms or Munitions of War*. (1933.)
11 Francis McCullagh, *Syndicates for War*, p. 8.
12 Murray H. Robertson, *op. cit.*, pp. 201-204.
13 Launay and Sennac, *op. cit.*, p. 239.
14 *The Nation*, June 7, 1933.
15 *Documents Politiques*, June, 1928, p. 34.
16 Fenner Brockway, *The Bloody Traffic*, pp. 165-166.

[17] Anonymous, *Hinter den Kulissen des Franzoesischen Journalismus*, p. 130 ; Lehmann-Russbueldt, *Die Blutige Internationale*, p. 19.
[18] Murray H. Robertson, *op. cit.*, p. 173.
[19] Flynn, *Graft in Business*, pp. 66, 67.
[20] McCullagh, *op. cit.*, p. 9.
[21] *Ibid.*, p. 10.
[22] F. W. Hirst, *The Political Economy of War*, p. 98.
[23] McCullagh, *op. cit.*, p. 11.
[24] Bywater and Ferraby, *Strange Intelligence, passim.*
[25] See, for instance, M. Baclé, "Armour Plates at the Paris Exhibition," *Engineering*, Vol. 71 (1901), pp. 66, 99, 131, 161 ; Anonymous, " The Army and Navy Building at the Paris Exhibition," *Engineering*, Vol. 71 (1901), pp. 325, 360, 397.
[26] Charles B. Norton and W. J. Valentine, *Report to the Government of the United States on the Munitions of War Exhibited at the Paris Universal Exhibition, 1867.*
[27] U. S. (House) 63d Congress, 3d Session, Document No. 1620, *Report of the Committee to Investigate the Cost of an Armour Plant for the United States.* (1915.)
[28] W. H. H. Waters, *Secret and Confidential*, p. 104.

CHAPTER XII

[1] *World Almanac.*
[2] Kirby Page, *National Defence*, pp. 160–161 ; 170–173.
[3] Murray F. Sueter, *Airmen or Noahs.*
[4] Rudolf Fuchs, *Die Kriegsgewinne der verschiedenen Witschaftszweige in den einzelnen Staaten an Hand statistischer Daten dargestellt.*
[5] Tomaschek, *Die Weltkrise, Sir Basileios Zaharoff und die Frage des Weltfriedens.*
[6] *The Diary of Lord Bertie.* June 25, 1917, Vol. II, p. 141.
[7] Launay and Sennac, *op. cit.*, p. 102ss ; Lehmann-Russbueldt, *Die Blutige Internationale*, p. 31s.
[8] *Documents Politiques* (1923), pp. 419ss.
[9] Mathiez, " Robespierre Terreuriste," *Annales Revolutionnaires* (1920), pp. 178–179.
[10] *Documents Politiques* (1923), pp. 380ss.
[11] *Documents Politiques* (1923), pp. 410–415.
[12] Gaudin de Villaine, *Les Briseurs de Blocus*, pp. 1–23 ; J. E. Favre, *L'Internationale Financiere. Les Metaux Sanglants*, pp. 22ss.
[13] Gaudin de Villaine, *op. cit.*, pp. 23–26 ; Favre, *op. cit.*, pp. 7–19.
[14] *Berliner Tageblatt*, Jan. 4, 1925.

NOTES AND REFERENCES 283

¹⁵ Arthur Saternus, *Die Schwerindustrie in und nach dem Kriege*, pp. 14–16.

¹⁶ *Documents Politiques* (1923), pp. 415–418; Launay and Sennac, *op. cit.*, pp. 133ss; Rusch, *Die Blutschuld. Rote Zahlen und Bluttropfenkarte. Von einem alten Schweizer Industriellen.*

¹⁷ Traugott Geering, *Handel und Industrie der Schweiz unter dem Einfluss des Weltkrieges.*

¹⁸ Lehmann-Russbueldt, *Die Blutige Internationale*, p. 27.

¹⁹ Paul Allard, "Les Marchands des Canons ont-ils besoin de la Guerre?" *Les Annales*, April 7, 1933.

²⁰ Allard, *op. cit.*

CHAPTER XIII

¹ Presidential Proclamation, August 14, 1914.

² C. Hartley Grattan, *Why We Fought*, chap. 3; John Kenneth Turner, *Shall It Be Again?* pp. 274ss.

³ Grattan, *op. cit.*, p. 136.

⁴ Turner, *op. cit.*, pp. 275ss.

⁵ Noyes, *The War Period of American Finance, 1908–1925.*

⁶ U. S. (House) Foreign Affairs Committee, 70th Congress, 1st Session, *Exportation of Arms, Munitions, and Implements of War to Belligerent Nations*, p. 97.

⁷ Turner, *op. cit.*, pp. 256ss.

⁸ U. S. Federal Trade Commission, *Profiteering*. Document No. 248. 65th Congress, 2d Session, 1918.

⁹ *Moody's Analysis of Investments. Public Utilities and Industries, 1912–1919.*

¹⁰ "Du Pont de Nemours and Co., E. I.," *Encyclopaedia Britannica*. (14th ed.)

¹¹ Arthur Warner, *Delaware. The Ward of a Feudal Family* (in Gruening, *These United States*), p. 130.

¹² William T. Stone, "International Traffic in Arms and Ammunition," *Foreign Policy Reports*, Vol. IX, No. 12, Aug. 16, 1933, p. 136.

¹³ Clifton Johnson, *The Rise of an American Inventor*, p. 192.

¹⁴ *Op. cit.*, p. 4.

¹⁵ Arthur Ponsonby, *Falsehood in War Time*, p. 147.

¹⁶ See the pamphlet "*Worth Knowing.*" *The Story of an Advertisement, or The Explosion of a Poisonous Shell.*—Vital Issue Booklets No. 7 (1915).

¹⁷ U. S. (House) 63d Congress, 3d Session, Document No. 1620, *Report of the Committee to Investigate the Cost of an Armour Plant for the United States (1915).*

¹⁸ These materials have been collected under the title, *The*

Bethlehem Steel Company appeals to the People against the Proposal to expend $11,000,000 of the People's Money for a Government Armour Plant. The press comments on its advertising campaign were published separately in *What Congress Has Done Concerning a Government Armour Plant and What the People are Thinking about it.* One widely distributed bulletin was entitled, *A Proposed Waste of $11,000,000 to Build a Government Armour Plant.*

[19] William T. Stone, *op. cit.*, p. 135.
[20] Anonymous, "Arms and Two Men," *Du Pont Magazine*, May, 1932, pp. 5–7s.
[21] *Ibid.*, p. 24.
[22] Crowell and Wilson, *The Armies of Industry*, pp. 225–237; U. S. (House) Foreign Affairs Committee, 70th Congress, 1st Session, *Exportation of Arms, Munitions, or Implements of War to Belligerent Nations (March, 1928)*, pp. 79ss.
[23] Brooks Darlington, "The Ketridge Shop," *Du Pont Magazine*, Vol. 26 (8–9) Summer, 1932, pp. 1, 2, 23, 24.
[24] Turner, *Shall It Be Again?* p. 308.
[25] Seymour Waldman, *Death and Profits*, pp. 74–82.

CHAPTER XIV

[1] Francis Delaisi, "Corruption in Armaments," *Living Age*, September, 1931.
[2] Francis Delaisi, *ibid.*
[3] Walter B. Harris, *France, Spain, and the Rif*, pp. 246, 321.
[4] Georges Hoog, "L'Acier contre la Paix," *Living Age*, November, 1932, pp. 198–204.
[5] Charles Reber, "Puissance de la Skoda et son Trust," *Le Monde*, April 22, 1933.
[6] Reber, *ibid.*
[7] Paul Faure, *Les Marchands de Canons contre la Paix.*
[8] Reber, *op. cit.*
[9] *La République*, February 21, 1932.
[10] Georges Hoog, *op. cit.*
[11] *The Secret International*, p. 22.
[12] *The Secret International*, p. 16.
[13] Paul Faure, *op. cit.*; Allard, in *Les Annales*, April 14, 1933.
[14] *The Secret International*, p. 21.
[15] Allard in *Les Annales*, April 14, 1933.
[16] Charles Reber, "Multiple Puissance de Vickers," *Le Monde*, April 29, 1933.
[17] Lewinsohn, *The Mystery Man of Europe*, Chap. 8; Mennevée, *Sir Basil Zaharoff.*
[18] Allard in *Les Annales*, April 14, 1933.

CHAPTER XV

[1] *English Review*, Vol. 45, pp. 256–263.

[2] U. S. (Senate) Naval Affairs Committee Hearings, *Alleged Activities at the Geneva Conference.* 71 : 1–2, pp. 437–438 ; 656–657.

[3] *Ibid.*, p. 400 ; 498–499 ; 529 ; 538.

[4] *Ibid.*, p. 551.

[5] *Ibid.*, p. 540.

[6] *Ibid.*, p. 539.

[7] *Ibid.*, pp. 599–600.

[8] *Ibid.*, pp. 29 f. and p. 149.

[9] *Ibid.*, pp. 90, 94, 111, 473, 652.

[10] *Nation*, September 2, 1931.

CHAPTER XVI

[1] Masuda, *Military Industries of Japan*, pp. 3–26 ; " The Reign Meiji," pp. 30–37 ; 87–97, *Fortune*, July, 1933.

[2] *Fortune, op. cit.*

[3] *Fortune, op. cit.*

[4] Payson J. Treat, *Diplomatic Relations between the United States and Japan, 1853–1895*, Vol. I, p. 59.

[5] Masuda, *op. cit.*, p. 42.

[6] Frederic Manning, *The Life of Sir William White.*

[7] Manning, *op. cit.*, p. 335ss, 345.

[8] Giichi Ono, *War and Armament Expenditure of Japan* ; Ushisaburo Kobayashi, *War and Armament Loans of Japan* ; Giichi Ono, *Expenditures of the Sino-Japanese War* ; Ushisaburo Kobayashi, *War and Armament Taxes of Japan* ; Gotara Ogawa, *Expenditures of the Russo-Japanese War.*

[9] *Fortune, op. cit.*

[10] Manning, *op. cit.*, p. 340ss ; *Fortune, op. cit.*

[11] Masuda, *op. cit.*, pp. 85–160, 183.

[12] Masuda, *op. cit.*, p. 261.

[13] Allard, *op. cit.*

[14] Francis Delaisi, cited in Georges Hoog, *op. cit.*, p. 204.

[15] H. C. Engelbrecht, " The Traffic in Death," *World Tomorrow*, Oct. 5, 1932.

[16] Engelbrecht, *ibid.*

[17] Union of Democratic Control, *Statistics showing the Trade in Arms and Ammunition between the Armament Firms of Great Britain and the Far East, August, 1931 to January, 1933* ; Anonymous, " L'Angleterre principal fournisseur de guerre du Japon," *Front Mondial*, March, 1933, p. 11 ; Anonymous, " How the Arms Traffic is Stimulated by Far Eastern Crisis,"

China Weekly Review, January 7, 1933, pp. 258–260 ; Anonymous, " Exports of War Materials from Britain Decreases," *China Weekly Review*, December 31, 1932, p. 225 ; Fenner Brockway, *The Bloody Traffic*, pp. 107–118.

[18] William T. Stone, " International Traffic in Arms and Ammunition," *Foreign Policy Reports*, Vol. IX, No. 12, August 16, 1933, p. 131.

[19] Fenner Brockway, *op. cit.*, p. 112.

[20] *New York Herald Tribune*, March 12, 1933.

[21] *New York Times*, " Exports of Arms by France up 50 per cent," July 27, 1933.

[22] Anonymous, " Les Exportations d'Armes de la France," *Front Mondial*, March, 1933, p. 11.

[23] National Council for Prevention of War, *Who Wants War ?*

[24] Union of Democratic Control, *Patriotism, Ltd.*, p. 30.

[25] William T. Stone, *op. cit.*, p. 132.

[26] For instance, in George A. Drew, *Enemies of Peace*, p. 11. Official figures of the U. S. Department of Commerce list exports in firearms, ammunition, aircraft and explosives as follows : To Japan, $147,213 in 1931, and $371,635 for 1932 ; to China, $1,115,797 in 1931, and $205,315 in 1932. Most of these exports were aeroplanes and parts.

[27] National Council for Prevention of War, *Who Wants War ?*

[28] George S. Herrick, " Japan's Steel Industry has Become Our Best Scrap Customer Abroad," *Iron Age*, July 10, 1930, pp. 84–86 ; Harold Huggins, " Steel Industry of Japan," *Far Eastern Review*, October, 1931–February, 1932.

[29] William T. Stone, *op. cit.*, p. 132.

[30] *New York Herald Tribune*, March 12, 1933.

[31] Engelbrecht, *op. cit.*, p. 311.

[32] *Front Mondial*, March, 1933, p. 11.

[33] Fenner Brockway, *op. cit.*, p. 114.

CHAPTER XVII

[1] Anonymous, *I Mercanti di Cannoni*, p. 103.

[2] Freda White, *Traffic in Arms*, p. 4.

[3] Anonymous, *I Mercanti di Cannoni*, p. 148.

[4] Freda White, *op. cit.*, p. 22 ; *Living Age*, Oct. 1933, p. 127.

[5] E. Zettem, *Les Maîtres de la France. Le Comité des Forges et la Classe Ouvrière*.

[6] Beverley Nichols, *Cry Havoc !*

[7] C. Lepériscope, " Le Commerce des Armes Echappe á la Crise," *Front Mondial*, March, 1933, pp. 8–9.

[8] Anonymous, *I Mercanti di Cannoni*.

[9] Beverley Nichols, *op. cit.*

NOTES AND REFERENCES 287

[10] John Gunther in *Chicago Daily News*, August 3, 4, 5, 1933; C. Lepériscope, *op. cit.*
[11] William T. Stone, *op. cit.*, p. 131; C. Lepériscope, *op. cit.*
[12] George A. Drew, *Enemies of Peace*, p. 13.
[13] Anonymous, *I Mercanti di Cannoni*, p. 40.
[14] *New York Times*, October 28, 1933.
[15] William T. Stone, *op. cit.*, p. 132.
[16] Josef Bernstein, "Bullerjahn Historie," *Tagebuch*, Vol. 13, No. 50, 1932, pp. 1942–1949.
[17] Lehmann-Russbüldt, *Die Blutige Internationale*, p. 44.
[18] *Tagebuch*, 1931, pp. 1804, 1841, 1843.
[19] John Gunther, *Chicago Daily News*, August 4, 1933.
[20] *Living Age*, October 1933, pp. 117–131.
[21] *Living Age*, October 1933, p. 126.
[22] *New York Herald Tribune*, Oct. 15, 1933.
[23] *New York Sun*, October 13, 1933.
[24] *New York Times*, October 19, 1933.
[25] Further details on the German situation may be found in *Patriotism Ltd. An Exposure of the War Machine*, pp. 6–19.
[26] C. Lepériscope, *op. cit.*
[27] Drew, *Salesmen of Death*, p. 18.
[28] *Patriotism Ltd.*, pp. 20–23.
[29] *Christian Science Monitor*, October 4, 1933.
[30] Lehmann-Russbüldt, *Die Revolution des Friedens*, p. 26.
[31] *New York Times*, October 9, 1933.
[32] William T. Stone, *op. cit.*, p. 134s.
[33] *Stockholders' Bulletin*, June 15, 1933.
[34] William T. Stone, *op. cit.*, p. 135s.
[35] *New York Times*, August 31, 1933.
[36] *Stockholders' Bulletin*, June 15, 1933.
[37] U. S. (House) Foreign Affairs Committee, 72d Congress, 2d Session, *Exportation of Arms or Munitions of War (1933)*, pp. 25ss. 32s, 50ss.
[38] *New York World-Telegram*, August 21, 1933.
[39] *New York Times*, December 8, 1933.
[40] U. S. (House) Foreign Affairs Committee, 72d Congress, 2d Session, *Exportation of Arms or Munitions of War (1933)*, p. 69ss.
[41] *Patriotism Ltd.*, pp. 30, 51, 55.
[42] William T. Stone, *op. cit.*, p. 130.
[43] C. Lepériscope, *op. cit.*
[44] The Japanese spend 40 per cent. of their military budgets for arms. If this proportion applies everywhere, this figure must be raised considerably.

45 Freda White, *op. cit.*, p. 21s.
46 A. H. " L'internationale des Gaz," *Monde*, July 8, 1933, p. 5 ; Lehmann-Russbüldt, *Die Blutige Internationale*, pp. 42–45.
47 *L'Humanité*, December 7–10, 1930.
48 Allard, *Annales*, April 28, 1933.

CHAPTER XVIII

1 Delbrueck, *Geschichte der Kriegskunst im Rahmen der politischen Geschichte*, Vol. I, p. 41.
2 Delbrueck, *op. cit.*, I, p. 149.
3 *Ibid.*, III, p. 153.
4 *Ibid.*, I, p. 9.
5 Albion, *Introduction to Military History*, pp. 147, 195–217.
6 Gottschalk, *The Era of the French Revolution*, pp. 407, 444ss.
7 Dumas and Vedel-Petersen, *Losses of Life Caused by War*, pp. 51, 57.
8 Crowell and Wilson, *op. cit.*, p. 31.
9 Crowell and Wilson, *op. cit.*, p. 32.
10 Kirby Page, *National Defence*, pp. 56, 222s.
11 *War Policies Commission Hearings*, 71st Congress, 2d Session, Parts 1, 2, and 3 ; *Documents by the War Policies Commission*, Nos. 264–271, 72d Congress, 1st Session ; Seymour Waldman, *Death and Profits. A Study of the War Policies Commission* ; Charles Stevenson, " The U. S. is Prepared for Anything," *Liberty*, Aug. 5, 1933, pp. 48–50 ; Anonymous, *Die wirtschaftlichen Vorbereitungen der Auslandsstaaten für den Zukunftskrieg*. (Includes the programme of 13 countries.)
12 U. S. (House) Foreign Affairs Committee, 70th Congress, 1st Session, *Exportation of Arms*, etc., p. 8.
13 Freda White, *Traffic in Arms*, pp. 13–15 ; Walter B. Harris, *France, Spain, and the Rif*, pp. 64, 74, 75, etc.
14 Freda White, *op. cit.*, pp. 18–19 ; for text of this Convention see *International Conciliation*, No. 164, July, 1921.
15 Freda White, *op. cit.*, pp. 19–23 ; League of Nations, *Proceedings of the Conference for the Supervision of the International Trade in Arms and Ammunition and in Implements of War*.
16 League of Nations, *Proceedings*, etc., p. 251.
17 U. S. (House) Foreign Affairs Committee, 70th Congress, 1st Session, *Exportation of Arms, Munitions, or Implements of War to Belligerent Nations (March, 1928)*.

BIBLIOGRAPHY

Abad, C. H., " The Munitions Industry in World Affairs," *Scribner's*, September, 1933, pp. 176–81.

Allard, Paul, " Le Comité des Forges Seul Vainqueur de la Guerre," *Vu*, October 4, 1933, pp. 1525ss.

Allard, Paul, " Les Marchands de Canons ont-ils Besoin de la Guerre ? " *Les Annales*, April 7, 1933.

Anonymous, " Arms and Two Men," *Du Pont Magazine*, Vol. 26, No. 5, May, 1932, pp. 5ss.

Anonymous, *Die wirtschaftlichen Vorbereitungen der Auslandsstaaten für den Zukunftskrieg.* Berlin, Mittler, 1926.

Anonymous, " The Export of War Materials from Britain Decreases," *China Weekly Review*, December 31, 1932, p. 225.

Anonymous, " Germany Mobilises," *Living Age*, October, 1933, pp. 123–31. (Article from *Die Neue Weltbühne*.)

Anonymous, *Hinter den Kulissen des französischen Journalismus.* Berlin, Deutsche Rundschau, 1925.

Anonymous, *History of the Manufacture of Armour Plate for the United States Navy.* Philadelphia, American Iron and Steel Association, 1899.

Anonymous, " How the Arms Traffic is Stimulated by Far Eastern Crisis," *China Weekly Review*, January 7, 1933, pp. 258–60.

Anonymous, *I Mercanti di Cannoni.* Milan, Corbaccio, 1932.

Anonymous, " L'Oligarchie devant les Patries et les Peuples," *Documents Politiques*, May, June, August, October, November, 1923.

Anonymous, *Remington Arms-Union Metallic Cartridge Co. A New Chapter in an Old Story.* 1912.

Anonymous, *Report of the Committee of the Massachusetts Reform Club Appointed to Collect Testimony in Relation to the Spanish-American War, 1898–1899.*

Anonymous, "The Army and Navy Building at the Paris Exhibition," *Engineering*, Vol. 71, 1901, pp. 325, 360, 397.

Anonymous, *The History of the E. I. Du Pont de Nemours Powder Company*. New York, Business America, 1912.

Anonymous, "Worth Knowing." *The Story of an Advertisement or The Explosion of a Poisonous Shell*. Vital Issue Booklets No. 7. New York, 1915.

Baclé, M., "Armour Plates at the Paris Exhibition," *Engineering*, Vol. 71, 1901, pp. 66, 99, 131, 397.

Bannerman & Sons, Francis, *War Weapons, Antique and Modern—Cannon, Pistols, Muskets, Rifles, Saddles, Uniforms, Cartridges*. New York, 1933.

Barnard, Henry, *Armsmear. The Home, the Arm, and the Armoury of Samuel Colt*. New York, 1866.

Bauer, Lothar, "Die Rüstungsindustrie der Welt," *Wirtschaftskurve*.—I. Der Konzern Schneider-Creusot, Vol. 11, No. 2, 1932; II. Der Konzern Vickers, Vol. 11, No. 3, 1932.

Baxter, James Phinney, *The Introduction of the Ironclad Warship*. Cambridge, Harvard University Press, 1933.

Beard, Charles A., *The Navy—Defence or Portent?* New York, Harper's, 1932.

Berdrow, Wilhelm, *Alfred Krupp*. 2 vols. Berlin, Reimar Hobbing, 1927.

Berdrow, Wilhelm, *Krupp. A Great Business Man Seen through his Letters*. New York, Lincoln MacVeagh, 1930. (Translated from the German.)

Bethlehem Steel Co., *Mobile Artillery Material*. 1916. (English and Spanish text.)

Bethlehem Steel Co., *A Proposed Waste of $11,000,000 to Build a Government Armour Plant*. 1916.

Bethlehem Steel Co., *Ordnance Material*. 1904. (English, French, and Spanish text.)

Bethlehem Steel Co., *Ordnance Material*. 1914. (English, French, and Spanish text.)

Bethlehem Steel Co., *The Bethlehem Steel Company Appeals to the People against the Proposal to Expend $11,000,000 of the People's Money for a Government Armour Plant*. 1916.

Bethlehem Steel Co., *What Congress has Done Concerning a Government Armour Plant and What the People Are Thinking about It.* 1916.

Bogart, Ernest L., *Direct Costs of the Present War.* New York, Carnegie Endowment for International Peace, 1918.

Brockway, A. Fenner, "Munitions Morality," *Maclean's*, August 10, 1933.

Brockway, A. Fenner, *The Bloody Traffic.* London, Gollancz, 1933.

Bywater, Hector C., and Ferraby, H. C., *Strange Intelligence. Memoirs of Naval Secret Service.* London, Constable, 1931.

Cadoux, Gaston, "Les Magnats de la Ruhr," *Revue Politique et Parlementaire*, Vol. 115, 1923, pp. 491–500 ; Vol. 116, 1923, pp. 82–94.

Colton, John, "The Only Woman the Kaiser is Afraid of," *Every Week*, July 3, 1916, p. 15.

Consett, M. W. W. P., *The Triumph of Unarmed Forces (1914–1918).* London, Williams and Norgate, 1923.

Convention for the Control of the Trade in Arms and Ammunition and Protocol Signed at Saint-Germain-en-Laye, September 10, 1919.—International Conciliation, No. 164, July, 1921.

Crowell, Benedict, and Wilson, Robert Forrest, *The Armies of Industry. Our Nation's Manufacture of Munitions for a World in Arms, 1917–1918.* 2 vols. New Haven, Yale University Press, 1921.

Crowell, J. Franklin, *Government War Contracts.* New York, Oxford University Press, 1923.

Darlington, Brooks, "The Course of Empire," *Du Pont Magazine*, Vol. 26 (6–7), 1932, pp. 3ss.

Darlington, Brooks, "The 'Ketridge Shop' and how it Grew," *Du Pont Magazine*, Vol. 26 (8–9), Summer, 1932, pp. 1ss.

Delaisi, Francis, "Corruption in Armaments," *Living Age*, September, 1931. (Article from *Crapouillot*.)

Delaisi, Francis, "Le Patriotise des Plaques Blindées," *La Paix par le Droit*, 24 (3) February 10, 1914, pp. 65–74 ; March 10, 1914, pp. 129–38 ; May 25, 1914, pp. 286–96.

Delbrueck, Hans, *Geschichte der Kriegskunst im Rahmen der politischen Geschichte*. 3 vols. Berlin, Stilke, 1900–1907.

Delbrueck, Hans, " Heeresstärken," *Preussische Jahrbücher*, 70 (1) 1892, pp. 133–35.

Drew, George A., *Enemies of Peace. An Exposé of Armament Manufacturers*. Toronto, Women's League of Nations Association, 1933.

Drew, George A., *Salesmen of Death. The Truth about War Makers*. Toronto, Women's League of Nations Association, 1933.

Dumas, Samuel, and Vedel-Petersen, K. O., *Losses of Life Caused by War*. Oxford, Clarendon Press, 1923.

Du Pont, Bessie G., *E. I. Du Pont de Nemours and Company. A History, 1802–1902*. New York, Houghton Mifflin, 1920.

Du Pont, Bessie G., *The Life of Eleuthère Irénée Du Pont from Contemporary Correspondence. Translated from the French*. 12 vols. Newark, Del., University of Delaware Press, 1923–1927.

Du Pont de Nemours and Co., *A History of the Du Pont Company's Relations with the United States Government, 1802–1927*. Wilmington, Del., 1928.

Ehrenberg, R., *Grosse Vermögen*. Jena, Fischer, 1902.

Encyclopædia Britannica (14th edition), Articles " Armour Plates," " Bow and Arrow," " Du Pont de Nemours and Company, E.I.," " Research."

Engelbrecht, H. C., " The Bloody International," *World To-morrow*, October, 1931.

Engelbrecht, H. C., " The Traffic in Death," *World Tomorrow*, October 5, 1932.

Faure, Paul, *Les Marchands de Canons contre la Paix*. Paris, Librairie Populaire, 1932.

Favre, J. E., *L'Internationale Financière. Les Métaux Sanglants*. Paris, Bibliothèque Financière, 1919.

Fitch, Charles H., *Report on the Manufacture of Fire-arms and Ammunition*. Extra Census Bulletin, 1882.

Fraikin, J., " L'Industrie des Armes a Feu de Liége," *Revue Economique Internationale*, 3 (3) September, 1929, pp. 471–92.

Friend, Vita and Joseph, "How the Arms Makers Work," *Forum*, November, 1933, pp. 278–84.
Frobenius, *Alfried Krupp*. Dresden and Leipzig, Reissner, 1898.
Fuchs, Rudolf, *Die Kriegsgewinne der verschiedenen Wirtschaftszweige in den einzelnen Staaten an der Hand statistischer Daten dargestellt*. Zurich, 1918.
Gaudin de Villaine, *Les Briseurs de Blocus. La Haute Banque et la Guerre*. Paris, Pierre Tequi, 1917.
Geering, Traugott, *Handel und Industrie der Schweiz unter dem Einfluss des Weltkrieges*. Basel, B. Schwabe, 1928.
Grattan, C. Hartley, *Why We Fought*. New York, Vanguard, 1929.
Gunther, John, "Big Profits in Arms Making," *Chicago Daily News*, August 3, 4, 5, 1933.
Habaru, A., "La Conférence du Désarmement Ajournée," *Le Monde*, No. 265, June 30, 1933.
Habaru, A., "L'Internationale des Gaz," *Le Monde*, No. 266, July 8, 1933.
Hasse, Hermann, *Krupp in Essen. Die Bedeutung der deutschen Waffenschmiede*. Series: *Deutsche Kraft*, No. 2, Berlin, 1915.
Hauteclocque, Xavier de, "Zaharoff, Merchant of Death," *Living Age*, May, 1932.
Henri, Ernst, "The Man behind Hitler," *Living Age*, October, 1933, pp. 117–23.
Hoog, Georges, "Steel against Peace," *Living Age*, November, 1932, pp. 198–204. (From pamphlet of *Jeune République* group entitled *L'Acier contre la Paix*.)
Hotchkiss Ordnance Company, Ltd., *Descriptive Catalogue of War Material*. 1893.
Johnson, Clifton, *The Rise of an American Inventor. Hudson Maxim's Story*. New York, Doubleday Page, 1927.
Katzenstein, L., "Les deux Krupp et leur Oeuvre," *Revue Economique Internationale*, May, 1906, pp. 322–46.
Kobayashi, Ushisaburo, *War and Armament Loans of Japan*. New York, Oxford University Press, 1922.
Kobayashi, Ushisaburo, *War and Armament Taxes of Japan*. New York, Oxford University Press, 1923.

Krupp Co., *A Century's History of the Krupp Works, 1812-1912*. (Translated from the German. No date or place of publication.)

Launay, Louis, and Sennac, Jean, *Les Relations Internationales des Industries de Guerre*. Paris, Editions Républicaines, 1932.

League of Nations, *Armament Year Book*. (Annual publication.)

League of Nations, *Proceedings of the Conference for the Supervision of the International Trade in Arms and Ammunition and in Implements of War*. (Geneva, May 4 to June 17, 1925.)

Legórburu, Justo de, *Un Problema Nacional. La Industria y la Guerra*. Bilbao, Editorial Vizcaina, 1924.

Lehmann-Russbueldt, Otto, *Die Blutige Internationale der Rüstungsindustrie*. Hamburg-Bergedorf, Fackelreiter Verlag, 1929. (English Translation : *War for Profits*.)

Lehmann-Russbueldt, Otto, *Die Revolution des Friedens*. Berlin, E. Laubsche Verlagsbuchhandlung, 1932.

Lewinsohn, Richard, *Die Umschichtung der europäischen Vermögen*. Berlin, S. Fischer, 1925.

Lewinsohn, Richard, *The Mystery Man of Europe : Sir Basil Zaharoff*. Philadelphia, Lippincott, 1929. (Translation from the German : *Der Mann im Dunkel*.)

McCullagh, Francis, *Syndicates for War. World Peace Foundation Pamphlets*, Series No. 2, Part III, July, 1911.

Maitrot, *La France et les Républiques Sud-Américaines*. Nancy, Berger-Levrault, 1920.

Manning, Frederic, *The Life of Sir William White*. New York, Dutton, 1923.

Masuda, Norimoto, *Military Industries of Japan*. New York, Oxford University Press, 1922.

Maxim, Hiram S., *My Life*. London, Methuen, 1915.

Mennevée, R., *Sir Basil Zaharoff*. Paris, Documents Politiques, 1928.

Millis, Walter, *The Martial Spirit*. Cambridge, Riverside Press, 1931.

Morvau, Jean, *Le Soldat Impérial*. 2 vols. Paris, 1904.

Mottelay, P. Fleury, *The Life and Work of Sir Hiram*

Maxim, Knight, Chevalier de la Légion d'Honneur, etc.
London, John Lane, 1920.
Mueller, Friedrich C. G., *Krupp's Steel Works*. London, Heinemann, 1898. (Translation from the German.)
Myers, Gustavus, *The History of the Great American Fortunes*. 3 vols. Chicago, Kerr, 1908–10.
Newbold, J. T. Walton, *How Europe Armed for War*. London, 1916.
Newbold, J. T. Walton, *The War Trusts Exposed*, London, 1916.
Nichols, Alan, *Neutralität und amerikanische Waffenausfuhr*. Berlin, Ebering, 1932.
Nichols, Beverley, *Cry Havoc!* London, Jonathan Cape, 1933.
Niemeyer, Victor, *Alfred Krupp : A Sketch of His Life and Work*. New York, Prosser and Son, 1888. (Translation from the German.)
Norton, Charles B. and Valentine, W. J., *Report to the Government of the United States on the Munitions of War Exhibited at the Paris Universal Exhibition, 1867.* New York, Army and Navy Journal, 1868.
Noyes, Alexander D., *The War Period of American Finance, 1908–1925*. New York, Putnam, 1926.
Ogawa, Gotara, *Expenditures of the Russo-Japanese War*. New York, Oxford University Press, 1923.
Oman, Charles, *A History of the Art of War in the Middle Ages*. London, Methuen, 1900.
O'Neill, Charles, " Armour Plate Making in the United States," *Cassier's Magazine*, Vol. 22, 1902, pp. 567–82.
Ono, Giichi, *Expenditures of the Sino-Japanese War (1894–1895)*. New York, Oxford University Press, 1922.
Ono, Giichi, *War and Armament Expenditures of Japan*. New York, Oxford University Press, 1922.
Perris, George Herbert, *The War Traders*. London, National Peace Council, 1914.
Pinner, Felix, *Deutsche Wirtschaftsführer*. Charlottenburg, Verlag der Weltbühne, 1924.
Poeschl, Viktor, *Stoff und Kraft im Kriege*. Mannheim, J. Bensheimer, 1916.
Pohl, *Amerikas Waffenausfuhr und Neutralität*. Berlin, 1917.

Poiry-Clement, Jean, *Schneider et le Creusot*. Paris, Conflans, 1924.
Poisson, Charles, *Les Fournisseurs aux Armées sous la Révolution Française: le Directoire des Achats (1792–1793)*. Paris, Librairie Margroff, 1932.
Ponsonby, Arthur, *Falsehood in War Time*. London, Allen and Unwin, 1928.
Porter, H. F. J., "How Bethlehem became Armament Maker," *Iron Age*, November 23, 1922, pp. 1339–41.
Raphael, Gaston, *Krupp et Thyssen*. Paris, Société d'Editions "Les Belles Lettres," 1925.
Reber, Charles, "L'Affaire de la Skoda ou la Puissance des Tenebres," *Le Monde*, 1933.
Reber, Charles, "Multiple Puissance de la Vickers," *Le Monde* No. 256, April 29, 1933.
Reber, Charles, "Puissance de la Skoda et son Trust," *Le Monde*, No. 255, April 22, 1933.
R., F., "La Technique Moderne des Armements S'Améliore," *Le Monde*, 1933.
Richard, Camille, *Le Comité de Salut Public et les Fabrications de Guerre sous la Terreur*. Paris, F. Rieder, 1921.
Richter, Franz, "Alfried Krupp und das Ausland," *Nord und Sued*, 1917, pp. 179–90.
Robertson, H. Murray, *Krupp's and the International Armaments Ring. The Scandal of Modern Civilization*. London, Holden and Hardingham, 1915.
Rusch, Johann Baptist, *Die Blutschuld. Rote Zahlen und Bluttropfenkarte. Von einem alten Schweitzer Industriellen*. Zurich, Gruetliverein, 1918.
Schurz, Carl, *Sale of Arms to French Agents and How They Are Officially Justified*. U.S. Senate Speech, May 31, 1872.
Shaw, Albert, "Founder of an American Family," *Review of Reviews*, April, 1928, pp. 379–82.
Simpson, V. L., "Youthful and Progressive," *Du Pont Magazine*, Vol. 27 (7–8) July-August, 1933, pp. 4ss. (Story of Western Cartridge Company.)
Simpson, V. L., "The Youngest Ammunition Company," *Du Pont Magazine*, Vol. 27 (3) March, 1933, pp. 3ss. (Story of the Federal Cartridge Corporation.)

Snowden, Philip, *Dreadnoughts and Dividends*. World Peace Foundation Pamphlets, Vol. I.

Stevens, William S., *The Powder Trust, 1872–1912*. Philadelphia, University of Pennsylvania, 1912. (See also *Quarterly Journal of Economics*, 1912, for summary.)

Stevenson, Charles, " The U.S. is Prepared for Anything," *Liberty*, August 5, 1933.

Stimson, R. H., *The Control of the Manufacture of Armaments*. Urbana, 1930.

Stone, William T., " International Traffic in Arms and Ammunition," *Foreign Policy Reports*, Vol. 9, No. 12, August 16, 1933.

Streit, C. K., *Where Iron Is, There Is no Fatherland*. New York, Huebsch, 1920.

Sueter, Murray F., *Airmen or Noahs?* London, Pitman and Sons, 1928.

Sueter, Murray F., *The Evolution of the Submarine Boat, Mine and Torpedo from the Sixteenth Century to the Present Time*. Portsmouth, J. Griffin and Co., 1907.

Thompson, Ralph, " Who is Sir Basil Zaharoff? " *Current History*, November, 1932, pp. 173–78.

Troimaux, *L'Affaire des Carbures*. Paris, Bibliothèque Financière, 1918.

Turner, John Kenneth, *Shall It Be Again?* New York, Huebsch, 1922.

Tuttle, F. C., " Ammunition by Peters. A story of Progress," *Du Pont Magazine*, Vol. 26 (10–11), Fall, 1932, pp. 3ss.

Union of Democratic Control, *Patriotism, Ltd. An Exposure of the War Machine*. London, 1933.

Union of Democratic Control, *Statistics Showing the Trade in Arms and Ammunition between the Armament Firms of Great Britain and the Far East, August, 1931 to January, 1933*. London, 1933. (Mimeographed.)

Union of Democratic Control, *The Secret International. Armament Firms at Work*. London, 1932.

Union of Democratic Control, *The International Industry of War*. London, 1915.

United States, Federal Trade Commission, Document No. 248, 65th Congress, 2d Session, 1918, *Profiteering*.

United States, House Document No. 1620, 63d Congress, 3d Session, *Report of the Committee to Investigate the Costs of an Armour Plant for the United States.* 1915.

United States, House, Foreign Affair Committee, 70th Congress, 1st Session, *Exportation of Arms, Munitions, or Implements of War to Belligerent Nations (March, 1928).* 1929.

United States, House, Foreign Affairs Committee, 72d Congress, 2d Session, *Exportation of Arms or Munitions of War.* 1933.

United States, House, Foreign Affairs Committee, 73d Congress, 1st Session, *Exportation of Arms or Munitions of War (March 28, 1933).*

United States, Senate, Naval Affairs Committee, 71st Congress, 1st Session, *Alleged Activities at the Geneva Conference.*

United States, *War Expenditure, Hearings.* (Graham Committee Reports.) Many volumes.

United States, 71st Congress, 2d Session, *War Policies Commission Hearings.* 1932.

United States, 72d Congress, 1st Session, *War Policies Commission Documents.* No. 264 and 271.

Van Gelder, Arthur P., and Schlatter, Hugo, *History of the Explosives Industry in America.* New York, Columbia University Press, 1927.

Waldman, Seymour, *Death and Profits.* New York, Brewer, Warren and Putnam, 1932.

Warner, Arthur, *Delaware. The Ward of a Feudal Family.* (In Gruening, E., ed., *These United States.* New York, Boni and Liveright, 1923.)

Washburn, Mabel T. R., " In the Service of the Republic," *Journal of American History,* Vol. 9, 1915, pp. 593–7.

Washburn, Mabel T. R., " The Du Pont Powder Wagon and how it Helped Win Perry's Victory," *Journal of American History,* Vol. 9, 1915, pp. 598–621.

Waters, W. H. H., *Secret and Confidential.* New York, Stokes, 1926.

Webb, Walter Prescott, *The Great Plains.* Boston, Ginn and Co. 1931.

Wells, H. G., *The Work, Wealth and Happiness of Mankind.* Chapter 12.

White, Freda, *Traffic in Arms*. London, League of Nations Union, 3d edition, 1932.

Zettem, E., *Les Maîtres de la France. Le Comité des Forges et la Classe Ouvrière*. Paris, Bureau d'Editions, 1932.

INDEX

A

Abdel Krim, rebellion and arms supply, 192, 193
Abyssinia, and arms smuggling, 270
Addis, Tom, Winchester salesman, 43, 44
Aerial camera gun, in China, 252
Aeroplanes: failures, U. S., in World War, 188–89; order in Great Britain by Hitler, 4; U. S. exports, 251, 252
Affaire des carbures, World War scandal, 170, 171
Aluminium, use in World War, 171
Alva, Duke of, purchase of arms from Liége, 14
American Legion, and Shearer, 211
American Machinist, advertisement of shrapnel shell machine in World War, 182, 183
Andorra, and Krupp guns, 79
Arabs: and Maxim Gun, 91; use of second-hand guns, 57; and Winchester rifle, 42
Argentina, Krupp - Schneider competition, 124, 125
Armaments (*see also* Armour Plate, Artillery, Guns, Machine Guns): development, early, 12–21; and raw materials, 271
Armaments, Export of: control, 267–72; Du Pont, 251; France, 239; Germany, 248; Great Britain, 241, 242; Remington Arms, [252;

Armaments, Export of (*contd.*)
Skoda, 240, 241; U. S. arms industry, 251; various countries, 253–54
Armament Industry
and bankers, 131–39, 144–45
Belgium, present status, 249
branch factories: 153; contract, 103; Du Pont, 251; U. S. in China, 252
bribery (*see also* Bribery), 150, 151
directors (*see also* Directorates), choice of, 140–42
and disarmament, 271–74
in engineering journals, 152
France, present status, 238–40
in French Revolution, 17
Germany, present status, 242–48
and governments, 143
Great Britain, present status, 239–40
history, early, 12–21
Italy, present status, 248–49
license fee and royalty for new inventions, 152
and military conservatism (*see also* Military Conservatism), 15–16
and military missions, 149
and military secrets, 135, 137, 151–53
motion pictures, use of, 147
nationalisation: analysis, 266–69; Japan, 224, 227
peace forces' view, 6–8
and peace treaties (1919), 190, 191
Poland, present status, 250
as political figure, 8–9

302 INDEX

Armament Industry (*continued*)
  and the press (*see also* The Press), 146–47
  problem, 84
  profits in World War: Europe, 159; U. S., 178–79
  public testing of new inventions, 152
  as result of our civilisation, 6–9
  sabotage, 150–51
  shareholders (*see also* Shareholders), 149, 150
  Skoda, present status, 238–39
  U. S., present status, 250–52
  and war scares (*see also* War Scares), 147–48
  at world's fairs and industrial exhibitions, 152

Armaments, Second-Hand: Bannerman and Sons, 61–68; in U. S. Civil War, 57–61; use, 56–69; Winchester rifle and Arabs, 42

Armies, size, ancient and modern, 261

Armour Plate: defective, of Carnegie, Phipps Co., 53–55; development, 53; Krupp's, 80–81; plans for government factory, U. S., 183–85; U. S. manufacturers and "trade secrets," 153

Armstrong, reorganisation after World War, 200

Armstrong, Whitworth and Co.: directors (1911), 114; and Putiloff affair, 130; R. L. Thompson, salesman, 110–11

Von Arthaber, financial backer of Hitler, 3

Artillery (*see also* Guns): ammunition expenditure, various wars, 262; failure of U. S. arms industry in World War, 188; Krupp and crucible steel, 71

Austria, and Maxim Gun, 93–94, 98–99

Austro-Prussian War (1866), and Krupp, 76, 78

B

Banks, and the arms industry, 131–39, 144–45

Bannerman and Sons, Francis, second-hand arms merchant, 61–68

Barbed wire, German sale in World War, 172

Bardo, C. L., and Shearer, 208, 213–17

Bauxite, use in World War, 170–71

Bedford Park cannon, story, 4

Belgium
  arms industry: early, 13–15; present status, 249
  Meuse valley poison gas deaths, 258
  sale of arms: to Japan, Manchurian expedition, 234; second-hand arms, 57

Berdrow, Wilhelm, Krupp historian, 70

Bethlehem Steel Co.: as armour plate maker, 53; blocking U. S. government armour plant in World War, 183–85; foreign catalogues and sales, 53; present status, 251; and Shearer, 208

Blaine, James G., stockholder in Spencer Arms Co., 67

Boer War, Maxim Gun use by Boers, 88

Bofors, Swedish arms maker, 204

Bolo Pasha, trial and execution, 6

Branch Factories, 153; contract, 103; Du Pont, 251; U. S. in China, 252

Brandt, bribery of German War Office, 83

Brazil, Krupp-Schneider competition, 124

Bribery: by arms industry, 150–51; of French press, 126–28; German arms makers, South America, 150; Japanese officials by Vickers, 118–19; by Krupp

INDEX 303

Bribery (*continued*)
agents, 83; refusal, Remington Arms Co., 45–46; Seletzki case, Rumania, 5; Young Turk government, 150

Britten, Fred A., and Montauk Point Development Corporation, 217

John Brown and Co.: directors (1911), 113; and Sir John Fisher, 114; and Putiloff affair, 130

Brown Boveri Co., and Shearer, 210

Brussels Convention for arms control, 270

Bulgaria, purchase of arms from Schneider, 138

Bullerjahn case, 243–44

Burton, Theodore, and arms control, 271–72

Butler, Nicholas Murray, attacked by Shearer, 210

C

Canada: nickel in World War, 166; sale of nickel to Germany (1933), 247; and Vickers, 118

Cannon, *see* Artillery

Carnegie, Andrew, founder of peace foundation, 10

Carnegie, Phipps Co., fine for defective armour plate, 53–55

Carnegie Steel Co., as armour plate maker, 53

Chamberlain, Sir Austen, I.C.I. shareholder, 257

Chamberlain, Neville, I.C.I. shareholder, 257

Charles the Bold (Burgundy), and Liége arms makers, 14

Chemicals, sale in World War, 169

Chemical Warfare: cellulose sale to Germany by France, 247; gas production in World War, 181; Hamburg

Chemical Warfare (*continued*)
poison gas accident, 244; Meuse valley poison gas deaths, 258; preparedness, various countries, 255–58

Chile, Krupp-Schneider competition, 125–26

China: and international arms industry, 229–30; and Krupp guns, 79; loans and armament sales, 145; and Maxim Gun, 90; purchase of arms from Japan, 229; Remington rifles, 46; U. S. aeroplanes, 252

Civil War (U. S., 1861–1865): artillery ammunition expenditure, 262; and Du Pont, 31; J. P. Morgan, Sr., sale of Hall's carbines, 59–61; second-hand arms, use, 57–61; Spencer Carbine, 67

Cleveland, President Grover, and Carnegie defective armour plate, 54–55

Cleveland Automatic Machine Co., advertisement in *American Machinist*, World War, 181–83

Colombia, Remington rifles, purchase, 49

Colt revolver, history, 39–42

Comité des Forges: as armament maker, 238; control of press, 3

Consett, M. W. W. P., and trade with Germany in World War, 164–65

Copper, in World War, 165

Cordite, invention and spread, 154

Crimean War: and arms makers, 11; and Du Pont, 30

Crowell Publishing Co., Morgan connections, 146

Cuba: purchase of munitions from Bannerman and Sons, 63; revolt, and Remington rifles and ammunition, 48

Curtiss-Wright, aeroplane sales to China, 252

D

Danubian Confederation, and arms makers, 195
Dawney, Col. F. G. C., and disarmament conference, 197
Denmark : and Maxim Gun, 90 ; war trade, World War, 165
Deutschland (submarine) cargo of nickel in World War, 167
Dillingen Co., directors, 142
Directorates : of arms industry, 140–42 ; British arms companies, analysed, 114 ; former government officials, 112 ; of Zaharoff, 104
Disarmament : and arms industry, 274–76 ; opposed by French arms makers, 196–97 ; and Shearer, 206–18
Druses, rebellion and arms supply, 192
Dumont, Charles, and disarmament conference, 197
Du Pont de Nemours and Co., E. I. : control of press, 146 ; history, 22–37 ; peace gesture, 9 ; present status, 251 ; in World War, 179–80
Von Duschnitz, financial backer of Hitler, 3

E

Egypt, purchase of cannon from Krupp, 71
Electrical Power, Swiss sales, World War, 171
Elibank, Master of, 104, 105
Embargo on Arms : Goss, E. W., opposition, 144 ; Great Britain, in Manchurian war, 235 ; U. S. government opposition, 271–73
Enfield rifles, in World War, 186–87
Engineering journals, and arms industry, 151

F

Fairchild Aviation Corporation, aerial camera gun in China, 252
I. G. *Farbenindustrie*, and German chemical warfare industry, 256
Faure, Paul : exposé of Schneider's work, 194
Feisal, Emir, rebellion and arms supply, 192
Fisher, Sir John, and arms industry, 113
Forsyth, Alexander, invention of percussion cap, 19–21
France (*see also* Schneider-Creusot)
armaments : exports, 238 ; industry, present status, 238–40
Bolo Pasha trial, 6
Briey iron mines in World War, 160–62
chemical warfare industries, 257
frontier defences, 239–40
honour to Zaharoff, 104–05
and Krupp, 76, 77–78
and Maxim Gun, 88
nickel policy, World War, 166
press : corruption, 127–28, 148 ; and Japan, 195–96 ; World War, 162–63
Remington as agent in Prussian War, 49–52
Rif rebellion, arms supply, 192–93
sale : of arms to Japan, Manchurian war, 232–33 ; of cellulose to Hitler Germany, 247 ; of second-hand arms, 57
Turpin affair, and Zaharoff, 101
World War : press, 162–63 ; scandal, 6 ; Swiss trade, 169–71
Franco–Prussian War (1870–1871) : and Krupp, 78–79 ; Remington rôle, 49–52 ; and Schneider, 123

Frémont, General John C., purchase of Hall's carbines, Civil War, 60–61
French Revolution: arms industry, 17; and Fulton's submarine, 18–19
Frontier Defences: France, 239–40; Italy, 248
Fujii, Rear Admiral, bribery by Vickers, 118–19
Fulton, Robert, and submarine, 18–19

G

Gangsters, and Belgian machine guns, 249
Gardner gun, 86
Gas Mask Industry, 258–59
Gatling gun, 50, 86
Germany (*see also* Hitler, Krupp) arms industry, present status, 242–47
Bullerjahn case, 243
chemical warfare industries, 256
Gontard war scare, 147–48
Hamburg poison gas accident, 244
and Maxim Gun, 89
military mission, Turkey, 149
Ossietzky trial, 245
purchase of Canadian nickel (1933), 247
sale of arms to Japan, Manchurian war, 243
World War: *American Machinist* advertisement, 182–83; Briey iron mines, 160–62; Possehl, trading with enemy, 168–69; press, 162–63; Swiss trade, 169–71
Glycerine, in World War, 164–65
Gontard: and Bullerjahn case, 243–44; war-scare, 147–48
Goss, E. W., opposition to arms embargo, 144
Government Loans: and arms sales, 145; France to Hungary, 194

Grace, Eugene, and Shearer, 213, 216
Graham Committee, reports on U. S. World War expenditures, 189
Great Britain (*see also* Vickers, Ltd.)
arms industry: history, 108–20; present status, 241–42
Bedford Park cannon, 4
British in Japan (1808), 224
chemical warfare industries, 257
and Colt revolver, 41–42
cordite, invention, 154
embargo on arms, Manchurian war, 235
and Fulton's submarine, 18–19
mines sold to Turkey, 4
Mulliner war-scare (1909) 116–17
naval missions, Turkey and Japan, 149
order of 60 aeroplanes by Hitler government, 4
percussion cap, invention, 19–21
sale of arms: to Japan, Manchurian war, 231–32; second-hand arms, 57
World War, trade with enemy, 164–65
Greece: purchase of submarine, 98; and Zaharoff, 98
Gunpowder: cocoa powder, Maxim's work, 88; cordite, history, 154; Du Pont, history, 22–37; powder trust, history, 33–35
Guns (*see also* Small Arms), percusion cap, invention, 19–21

H

Hague Convention, 267
Hamburg poison gas accident, 244
Harding, President Warren G., on failures of arms industry in World War, 188

x

Harris, Townsend, and Japan, 219, 222
Harvey United Steel Co. : directors, 142 ; organisation, 111
Harveyised steel, for armour plate, 53
Havas Agency, bribery by Russians, 127
Hearst, W. R., and Shearer, 213
Hirtenberg affair, 248
Hitler, Adolf (*see also* Germany) and German re-armament, 245–47
  order of 60 British aeroplanes, 4
  purchase of 400 French tanks, 247
  stimulus to arms industry, 253
  support by : Pintsch Co., 201 ; Skoda directors, 2–3 ; Thyssen, 245
Hugenberg, Alfred, Krupp director, 146
Hungary : arming by Schneider, 194 ; purchase of arms from Italy, 248–49

I

Imperial Chemical Industries, and gas warfare, Great Britain, 257
India, second-hand arms, northwest frontier, 57
Industrial mobilisation, meaning, 265–66
Iron and Steel, in World War, 169–70
Italy : arms industry, post-war ; 248–49 ; and French '75's, 138 ; and Maxim Gun, 89

J

Japan : arms industry, rise and present status, 219–36 ; bribery of officials by Vickers, 118–19 ; British naval mission, 149 ; early gun-

Japan (*continued*)
  powder, 15 ; Manchurian expedition, arms source, 229–34 ; military budget, 229 ; military government, 227 ; sale of arms to China, 229 ; and Schneider-Creusot, 195–96 ; westernisation, 221–25 ; in World War, 229
Jefferson, Thomas, and Du Pont, 24
Juarez, Benito, and Winchester rifles, 42–44
Justice, Philip S., second-hand arms merchant, Civil War, 58

K

Krupp (*see also* Germany, Hitler)
  armament work after World War, 204–05, 246
  armour plate, development, 53, 80–81
  and Austro-Prussian War, 75–76
  company historian, 71
  competition with Schneider : in Serbia, 145 ; in South America, 124–26
  and Franco-Prussian War, 78–79
  hand grenade fuse suit against Vickers, 6
  history, 70–84
  Meppen, artillery testing ground, 81
  and Napoleon III, 77–78
  and patriotism, 74–77
  press, control, 82–83, 146
  and Putiloff affair, 132–39
  Russian work, 74, 82
  sale of arms to Turkey, 139
  shipbuilding, 82
  statistics of plant, workers and sales, 72, 83
  submarine building, 81
Kuhlmann, French chemical warfare industry, 257

INDEX

L

Lead, in World War, 167
League of Nations : arms statistics analysed and criticised, 231–32, 253–55 ; conference on international sale of arms, 267, 271–74
Libby, F. J., and Britten, 216
Liége, arms industry, 13–15
Li Hung Chang : and Maxim Gun, 90 ; and Remington rifles, 47
Little Entente, and Schneider, 195
Lloyd George : end of career, 203 ; and Zaharoff, 104
Lonza Co. : directors, 142 ; in World War, 170
Lyautey, Marshal, in Rif rebellion, 192

M

Machine Gun : history, 86 ; Maxim Gun, 85–94
Manchurian Expedition, Japan, arms source, 229–34
Maxim, Hiram : life and work, 85–94 ; and Zaharoff contest, 93–94, 98–99
Maxim Gun, invention and sale, 85–94
Maximilian of Mexico, and Winchester rifles, 42–44
Mechanisation of war, 235–36
Meppen, Krupp's artillery testing ground, 81, 151
Mexican War (1846) : Colt's revolver, 41 ; and Du Pont, 28–30
Mexico, Winchester rifle in Maximilian episode, 42–44
Midvale Steel Co. : armour plate maker, 53 ; founder of Navy League, 2
Military Budgets : Japan, 227 ; various countries (1863–1913), 263

Military Conservatism : and arms industry, 15–16 ; and Du Pont, 31 ; Prussia, 71 ; and Whitney, 39
Military Missions, and sale of armaments, 149
Military Secrets, and arms industry, 135, 137, 151–53
Montauk Point Development Corporation, and U. S. navy, 217
Monte Carlo, and Zaharoff, 203
Morgan, J. P., Sr., sale of Hall's carbines, Civil War, 59–61
Morgan, J. P., Jr., founder of Navy League, 2
J. P. Morgan Co., and American arms industry, 141–42
Motion Pictures, use by arms industry, 147
Mulliner, H. H., war-scare of 1909, 116–17
Murata, Japanese rifle, 224

N

Napoleon I : aid to Du Pont, 23 ; bid for Forsyth's percussion cap, 19–21 ; and Liége arms makers, 14
Napoleon III, and Krupp, 77–78
Nationalisation of Arms Industry : analysis, 266–69 ; Japan, 224, 227
Navy League, promoter of armaments, 1–2
Netherlands : Dutch in Japan, sixteenth century, 219
New Caledonia, nickel in World War, 166, 167
New York Shipbuilding Co., and Shearer, 208, 210
Newport News Shipbuilding Co., and Shearer, 208
Newspapers (see The Press)
Neutrality, U. S. breach in Franco-Prussian War, 49
Nickel : Canadian exports to Germany (1933), 247 ; in World War, 165–67

Nobel, Alfred: dynamite companies, 142 ; peace prize, 9
Nobel Dynamite Trust, dissolution in World War, 160
Nordenfeldt, Tosten Vilhelm, arms maker, 97
Nordenfeldt gun, 86
Norway: sale of arms to Japan, Manchurian war, 234 ; trade with Germany, World War, 165

O

Omdurman, battle, Maxim Gun, 92
Ossietzky, Carl von, and German rearmament, 245

P

Palen, F. P., and Shearer, 208, 215
Panama, revolution, source of arms, 64
Paris World's Fair, armament exhibits, U. S. report, 152
Penarroya lead mines, in World War, 167
Perry, Commodore M. C., in Japan, 221
Persia, and Maxim Gun, 91
Pintsch Co., arms maker and supporter of Hitler, 201
Poison Gas (*see* Chemical Warfare)
Poland: arms industry, present status, 250 ; purchase of French arms, 239
Portugal, and Maxim Gun, 91
Possehl, Senator (Luebeck), trading with the enemy, World War, 168–69
The Press
and arms industry, 146–47
Bethlehem Steel Co., use, World War, 183–85
Du Pont control in Delaware, 36

The Press (*continued*)
France: control by arms makers, 3 ; corruption, 126–28 ; and disarmament, 196–97 ; and Japan, 195–96 ; in World War, 162–63
in Gontard affair, 148
Krupp's, 82
Schneider, use, 136
and Shearer, 207, 211
in World War: France and Germany, 162–63 ; in U. S., 177
and Zaharoff, 106
Prix Balzac, endowed by Zaharoff, 105
Profiteering, in U. S., World War, 178
Prussia: and Krupp, 72–76 ; and Remington rifles, 45
Putiloff affair, 128–39

R

Raffalovich, Arthur, and corruption of French press, 126–27
Raw Materials, and armaments, 273
Redfield, Secretary of Commerce, and *American Machinist* advertisement, 183
Remington Arms Co.: Chinese catalogue, 47 ; Enfield rifles, World War, 186–87 ; foreign sales, 45–46 ; history, 44–52 ; in World War, 186–87
Reynolds, W. W., Remington agent in Paris, 51–52
Rif, rebellion and arms supply, 192–93
Von Roon, Albrecht, and Krupp, 75–76
Rothschild Bank, and nickel and lead in World War, 166–68
Rumania, Seletzki scandal, 5
Russia: charge of sabotage against German arms makers, 151 ; cordite, use, 154 ; and Maxim Gun, 89 ; military rehabilitation after

INDEX

Russia (*continued*)
1905, 82, 128–39; Russians in Japan (1807), 221; Schneider's work, 126–39; Zaharoff's work, 102
Russo-Japanese War (1904–1905), purchase of arms from Bannerman and Sons, 64
Russo-Turkish War (1879), Remington orders, 47

S

Sabotage, by arms industry, 151
Saint-Germain-en-Laye, Convention, and arms control, 270
Saltpetre, in World War, 170–71
Schneider-Creusot (*see also* France)
 arming of Hungary, 194
 competition with Krupp: in Serbia, 145; in South America, 124–26
 control of Skoda, 3, 193
 and disarmament, 196–97
 expansion after World War, 193–95
 Faure, Paul, defeat in elections, 197–98
 history, 121–39
 and Japan, 195–96
 and Little Entente, 195
 present status, 238–41
 press: and Japan, 195–96; use of, 136
 sale of arms: to Bulgaria, 138; to Japan, Manchurian war, 232–33; to Turkey, 138–39; 400 tanks to Hitler, 247
 and Turko-Greek War (1919), 191, 201–02
Schurz, Carl, and French purchase of munitions (1870–1871), 51
Schwab, Charles H.: and defective armour plate, 54; founder of Navy League, 2; peace gesture, 9; and Shearer, 214, 216

Scovill Manufacturing Co., and E. W. Goss, 144
Seletzki, Bruno, Rumanian arms scandals, 5
Serbia, Krupp-Schneider competition, 145
Shareholders in Arms Industry: 149; chemical warfare industries, 247; Great Britain, 115; Vickers, 242; William II, Germany, 166
Shearer, William B., and disarmament, 207–18
Shipbuilding: Krupp work, 81; U. S. in World War, 188
Simon, Sir John, I.C.I. shareholder, 257
Sino-Japanese War, Vickers sales, 110
Skoda: controlled by Schneider, 3, 193–94; financial backer of Hitler, 2–3; present status, 240–41; and Putiloff affair, 132; sale of arms to Turkey, 139; Seletzki scandal, 5
Skuludis, Etienne, and Zaharoff, 96
Small Arms: Colt revolver, history, 38–42; machinery, U. S. sale, 38; Murata, Japanese rifle, 224; Remington rifle, history, 44; Winchester rifle, history, 42–44; U. S. manufacturers, 38–52
Smuggling of Arms: and Abyssinia, 270; in Rif rebellion, 192–93
Snowden, Philip, attack on arms industry, 112, 114–15
Société Générale, and Putiloff affair, 131–39
South America (*see also* names of countries): German arms makers, bribery, 150; purchase from Bannerman, 63–64; Schneider-Krupp competition, 124–26; U. S. military missions, 149
South Carolina, secession movement (1833) and Du Pont, 26

Sopwith Co., and Spanish lead, World War, 168
Spain: and Krupp guns, 79; lead mines in World War, 167; and Maxim Gun, 91; Remington rifles, purchase, 47–48; Rif rebellion, arms supply, 192–93; Vickers purchases, 110
Spanish-American War (1898): and Maxim, 92–93; sale of arms to U. S., 68; Záharoff's sales to Spain, 100
Spencer Arms Co., in Civil War, 67
Springfield rifle, in World War, 186–87
St. Gothard incident, 248
Stinnes, Hugo, control of press, 146
Submarines: French *Surcouf*, 238; and Fulton, 18–19; Krupp work, 81; Zaharoff sale to Greece and Turkey, 98
Sweden: Bofors, armament-work, 204–05; trade with Germany, World War, 165
Switzerland: arms traffic, French Revolution, 17–18; commerce, World War, 169–71; sale of arms to China, Manchurian war, 234
Syria, rebellion and arms supply, 192

T

Tanks: amphibian, 238; origin, 156; Vickers sale to USSR, 4
Tavenner, Claude H., disclosures on Navy League, 2
Texas Rangers, and Colt revolver, 40
Thompson, R. L., salesman for Armstrong-Whitworth, 110
Thompson, Col. R. M., founder of Navy League, 2

Thyssen, supporter of Hitler, 245
Tracy, B. F., founder of Navy League, 2
Trusts: Harvey United Steel Co., 111; powder, 33–35
Turkey
bribery in arms contracts, 150
British: mines in Dardanelles campaign, 4; naval mission, 149
German military mission, 149
and Maxim Gun, 91
purchase of arms: from Schneider, 139; from Skoda and Krupp, 139
purchase of submarine, 98
and Remington rifles, 45
Zaharoff's sales, 102
Turko-Greek War (1919), arms supply, 191, 201–02
Turpin affair, and Zaharoff, 101

U

Union Metallic Cartridge Co., amalgamation with Remington Arms, 46
Union Parisienne, Schneider's bank, 131–39
USSR, purchase of 60 tanks from Vickers, 4
United States (*see also* names of companies)
armour plate industry: history, 53–54; and "trade secrets," 153
arms industry, present status, 250–52
Census Bureau report on small arms manufacture, 39
chemical warfare industries, 257
Du Pont co-operation with government, 32
foreign powder companies, plan for factory, 34
military budgets (1791–1931), 263

INDEX 311

United States (*continued*)
  military missions, South America, 149
  navy and Montauk Point Development Corporation, 217
  opposition to arms embargo, 271–73
  plans for government armour plant, 183–85
  press and Shearer, 207–10
  report on arms exhibit at Paris World's Fair (1867), 152
  sale of arms to Japan, Manchurian war, 233
  small arms makers, 38–52
  World War: failures of arms industry, 188–89; Graham Committee reports, 189; rôle, 173–89
United States Cartridge Co., in World War, 187
Urschel kidnapping, and Belgian machine gun, 249

V

Venezuela, Remington munitions, purchase, 49
Vickers, Ltd.: arms supply of Emir Feisal, 192; bribery of Japanese, 118–19; and Canadian officials, 118; history, 108–10; in Japan, 228; Krupp hand grenade fuse suit, 6; and Maxim, 87; and Putiloff affair, 130–39; reorganisation after World War, 198–201; sale of tanks to USSR, 4; shareholders, 242; and Turko-Greek War (1919), 191, 201–02
Vickers-Armstrong: expansion after World War, 200; use of motion pictures, 147
Vickers's Sons and Maxims, directors (1911), 113
Violet Cross, and gas mask industry, 258

W

Wakeman, Samuel W., and Shearer, 208, 216
War of 1812: and Du Pont, 25; Whitney's muskets, 39
War Scares: by arms makers, 147–48; Mulliner's (1909), 116–17; plans for U. S., World War, 176; Russian-Rumanian (1930), basis, 5
Welby, Lord, attack on arms makers, 114
White, Sir William, naval work in Japan, 224–27
Whitehead Torpedo Co., directors and organisation, 106, 142
Whitney, Eli, and interchangeable parts in guns, 39
Wilder, L. R., and Montauk Point Development Corporation, 217
Winchester Repeating Arms Co.: Enfield rifle, World War, 186–87; World War work, 180–81
Winchester rifle, history, 42–44
World War (*see also* names of countries)
  Allied purchases in U. S., 174
  American Machinist advertisement, 181–83
  armament press, France and Germany, 162–63
  arming of enemy through prewar sales, 156–58
  artillery ammunition expenditure, 262
  Bedford Park cannon, 4
  Bolo Pasha, trial and execution, 6
  Briey iron mines, 160–62
  copper, use, 165
  Dardanelles mines, origin, 4
  Du Pont's work, 35–36, 179–80
  Enfield rifle, 186–87
  in Europe, 155–72
  failures, U. S. arms industry, 188–89

World War (*continued*)
  financial costs, 155, 177, 262
  glycerine, use, 164–65
  government armour plate plans, U. S., 183–85
  Graham Committee reports, U. S., 189
  Japanese work, 229
  Krupp hand grenade fuse suit v. Vickers, 6
  net profits of arms industry: Europe, 159; U. S., 178–79
  new implements of war, 156
  nickel, use, 165–67
  Nobel Dynamite Trust, dissolution, 160
  poison gas production, 181
  Remington Arms, work, 186–87
  statistics, 155
  Swiss trade, 169–71
  traffic in war materials, 163–72
  United States Cartridge Co., work, 187

World War (*continued*)
  U. S., role, 173–89
  Winchester Arms, work, 180–81
  Zaharoff's work, 160

Z

Zaharoff, Sir Basil: international connections, 104; life and work, 95–107; and Maxim, at Vienna, 93–94, 98–99; in Monte Carlo, 203; and the press, 106; in reorganisation of Vickers and Armstrong, 199–200; and Turko-Greek War (1919), 191, 202–203; and Vickers, 108–10; during World War, 160
Zeiss instruments, sale to British during World War, 172